ations of Computing

l Garey and Albert Meyer, editors

xity Issues in VLSI: Optimal Layouts for the Shuffle-Exchange Graph and Other *ks,* Frank Thomson Leighton, 1983

nal Logic as a Programming Language, Michael J. O'Donnell, 1985

l Theory of Deductive Systems and Its Applications, S. Yu Maslov, 1987

ce Allocation Problems: Algorithmic Approaches, Toshihide Ibaraki and Naoki Ka-88

ic Theory of Processes, Matthew Hennessy, 1988

Computational Logic, Susumu Hayashi and Hiroshi Nakano, 1989

able Marriage Problem: Structure and Algorithms, Dan Gusfield and Robert Irving,

ic Compiler Generation, Peter Lee, 1989

Layer Wire Routing and Compaction, F. Miller Maley, 1990

Category Theory for Computer Scientists, Benjamin C. Pierce, 1991

ries, Types, and Structures: An Introduction to Category Theory for the Working *uter Scientist,* Andrea Asperti and Giuseppe Longo, 1991

tics of Programming Languages: Structures and Techniques, Carl A. Gunter, 1992

ormal Semantics of Programming Languages: An Introduction, Glynn Winskel, 1993

t's Tenth Problem, Yuri V. Matiyasevich, 1993

ring Interior-Point Linear Programming: Algorithms and Software, Ami Arbel, 1993

etical Aspects of Object-Oriented Programming: Types, Semantics, and Language *n,* edited by Carl A. Gunter and John C. Mitchell, 1994

Logic to Logic Programming, Kees Doets, 1994

tructure of Typed Programming Languages, David A. Schmidt, 1994

and Information Flow, edited by Jan van Eijck and Albert Visser, 1994

it Complexity and Neural Networks, Ian Parberry, 1994

rol Flow Semantics, Jaco de Bakker and Erik de Vink, 1996

raic Semantics of Imperative Programs, Joseph A. Goguen and Grant Malcolm, 1996

Algebraic Semantics of Imperative P

Foun
Micha

Compl
Netwo

Equat

Gener

Resou
toh, 1

Algeb

PX: A

The S
1989

Reali

Singl

Basic

Categ
Comp

Sema

The

Hilbe

Expl

Theo
Desi

Fron

The

Logi

Circ

Con

Alg

Algebraic Semantics of Imperative Programs

Joseph A. Goguen and Grant Malcolm

The MIT Press
Cambridge, Massachusetts
London, England

This book was set in LaTeX by the authors and was printed and bound in the United States of America.

Library of Congress Cataloging-in-Publication Data

Goguen, Joseph A.
Algebraic semantics of imperative programs / Joseph A. Goguen and Grant Malcolm.
p. cm.—(Foundations of computing)
Includes bibliographical references and index.
ISBN 0-262-07172-X (hc: alk. paper)
1. Programming languages (Electronic computers)—Semantics. I. Malcolm, Grant. II. Title. III. Series.
QA76.7.G62 1996
005.13′1-dc20 95-47440
CIP

Contents

Series Foreword

Theoretical computer science has now undergone several decades of development. The "classical" topics of automata theory, formal languages, and computational complexity have become firmly established, and their importance to other theoretical work and to practice is widely recognized. Stimulated by technological advances, theoreticians have been rapidly expanding the areas under study, and the time delay between theoretical progress and its practical impact has been decreasing dramatically. Much publicity has been given recently to breakthroughs in cryptography and linear programming, and steady progress is being made on programming language semantics, computational geometry, and efficient data structures. Newer, more speculative, areas of study include relational databases, VLSI theory, and parallel and distributed computation. As this list of topics continues expanding, it is becoming more and more difficult to stay abreast of the progress that is being made and increasingly important that the most significant work be distilled and communicated in a manner that will facilitate further research and application of this work. By publishing comprehensive books and specialized monographs on the theoretical aspects of computer science, the series on Foundations of Computing provides a forum in which important research topics can be presented in their entirety and placed in perspective for researchers, students, and practitioners alike.

Michael R. Garey
Albert R. Meyer

Algebraic Semantics of Imperative Programs

0 Introduction

This book is intended to introduce undergraduate Computing Science students to formal reasoning about imperative programs. Our specific goals include the following:

1. improve intuition and ability in imperative programming, through understanding the semantics of programs and seeing numerous examples;
2. teach how to prove properties of programs;
3. develop the relevant mathematical background;
4. present the OBJ3 system and use it for all proofs; and
5. show that this can be done in a way that is completely rigorous, yet not too difficult or too abstract, by using equational logic, which is simply the logic of substituting equals for equals.

The algebraic semantics of imperative programs is described by specifying a class of abstract machines and giving equational axioms which specify the effect of programs on such machines. The programming language features treated in the book are: assignment, sequential composition, conditional, while-loop, procedure definition and procedure call. The equational axioms which describe the semantics of these features are used to prove the correctness of programs. This work shows that imperative programs can be seen as fully *formalised* mathematical entities, about which theorems can be proved, just as in any other branch of mathematics.

The fundamental idea of program correctness proofs goes back to work of von Neumann and Turing in the 1940s [27, 56]: an *invariant* for an iteration is a property that remains true of the state each time the loop code is executed. Our approach differs from other developments of this idea in our choice of first order equational logic as a foundation and in our systematic use of an implemented formal notation to provide computer support for proofs. It also differs in that we define the semantics of programs using an equational specification for a *class* of abstract machines for storage, by specifying the effects of programs on the states of these machines. An advantage of this approach is that it admits as models any desired organisation of memory, for example, involving caches and/or discs. This is achieved by axiomatising the properties that any suitable storage must have.

Equational logic has some advantages over other, more complex logics:

1. it is very simple — the logic of substituting equals for equals;
2. many problems associated with equational logic are decidable that are not decidable in more complex logics;

3. there are efficient algorithms for deciding many of these problems; and
4. there are mature tools that embody many of these algorithms.

Of course, equational logic cannot be used for every possible application, but because of the above considerations, when equational logic can be used, it may be preferable to do so. In particular, it can be very difficult to reason about specifications that are given in set theory or in denotational semantics.

This book assumes familiarity with some imperative programming language, such as C, Pascal, Basic, or MODULA2, as well as some knowledge of basic mathematics, including mathematical induction and basic first order logic. However, most concepts are explained as they arise. The formal part of the exposition proves the validity of our program correctness rules; these rules are formulated to be compatible with the books by Backhouse [1] and Gries [30], and this text may be used in conjunction with either or both of those books or others of a similar character.

0.1 OBJ

We use the implementation OBJ3 [26] of OBJ[1] as a vehicle for expressing semantics. OBJ is not just another functional programming language, although it does have an executable functional sublanguage. OBJ was designed for algebraic semantics; its declarations introduce symbols for sorts and functions, its statements are equations, and its computations are equational proofs. Thus, an OBJ "program" (if we can use that word) actually *is* an equational theory, and every OBJ computation actually *proves* some theorem about such a theory. This means that an OBJ program used for defining the semantics of a program already has a precise mathematical meaning. Moreover, the standard techniques for mechanising equational reasoning can be used for verifying programs. Indeed, every program correctness proof given in this book has been verified using OBJ3. Its powerful definition and abstraction facilities also allow natural treatments of both refinement and abstract data types. Appendix D gives the complete syntax of OBJ3 and describes how to get the implementation. Note that various completeness results allow us to use full first order logic in our meta-language for specifying and proving properties of programs, and reduce it to equational calculations.

[1] "OBJ" refers to the general design, while "OBJ3" refers to the specific implementation used.

0.2 Related Work

This section briefly surveys some of the most popular alternative approaches to the semantics of imperative programming, and tries to place our approach in that context. It may be of more interest to instructors than to most students.

Roughly speaking, the most popular approaches to the semantics of imperative languages can be divided into three groups: operational, axiomatic, and denotational. An *operational semantics* describes the meaning of a programming language by describing a way of executing its programs. Often, this is done by giving an interpreter or compiler for the language. So-called *structured operational semantics* (also called *natural semantics*) [50] describes computations by giving formal rules of deduction for steps of computation; this may be considered an abstract interpreter.

In *axiomatic* approaches, programming language features are defined by writing axioms in some logical system. First order logic, or some variant of it, is the most popular, since it is the logical system most widely used in mathematics and its foundations. An axiomatic approach using assertions and invariants was pioneered by Alan Turing [56] and John von Neumann [27] and later made more formal by Robert Floyd [11] and Tony Hoare [35].

By contrast, *denotational* approaches build models of programming language features; these models are called *denotations*. For example, the denotation of a program might be a partial function from inputs to outputs. Usually set theory is used in constructing these denotations, perhaps with some technical constraints, such as continuity. In this approach, the denotation of a program is constructed by composing the denotations of its parts. Denotational semantics was pioneered by John McCarthy [44] and greatly extended by Christopher Strachey and Dana Scott [54].

Our approach might be called *algebraic denotational semantics*, which we hereafter abbreviate as *ADS*. The chapters that follow give a formal account of ADS, but here we discuss briefly how it differs from some of the more traditional approaches.

In classical denotational semantics (which is often called *Scott-Strachey semantics*; see [55, 28]), the model of storage can be criticised as being too concrete. However, ADS axiomatises the notion of storage, so that any model satisfying the axioms can be used, thus avoiding the need to select one particular model;[2] that is,

---

[2] As a historical sidelight, it is interesting to notice that lists of publications of the Programming Research Group round 1971 listed "An Abstract Model of Storage" by Christopher Strachey as being "in preparation." Later, this paper was listed as "cancelled." Although we have not been able to obtain a copy of a draft of this paper, it is interesting to speculate that Strachey recognised that in classical denotational semantics, it is necessary to construct a particular model for storage, and that this is necessarily too concrete. Perhaps he had in mind some clever way to get around

ADS uses so-called "loose" algebraic semantics to specify a *class* (i.e., "variety") of models for storage. For example, the algebra modeling storage may involve cache and/or disc memories.[3] Another criticism of classical denotational semantics is that it can be very difficult to prove properties of programs in this framework. We will see that proofs in the ADS framework can be surprisingly easy.

So-called *weakest precondition semantics* (hereafter abbreviated *WP*) is a well-known variety of axiomatic semantics developed by Edsger Dijkstra [8, 9]. Standard textbooks using this approach have been written by David Gries [30] and Roland Backhouse [1]. These works contain some wonderful examples and are warmly recommended. In this approach, the semantics of programming language constructs is given by axioms which prescribe how those constructs transform predicates on states; thus, this semantics also has a denotational aspect, in that programs denote functions from sets of states to sets of states. A difficulty with WP is that the semantics of iteration is rather complicated: in fact, Dijkstra, Gries, and others assume that first order logic is adequate for WP, but it seems that *infinitary logic* (i.e., the logic of infinitely long sentences!) is needed for the weakest preconditions of general iterations (see Engeler [10]); alternatively, one might use second order logic or abandon predicates in favour of sets defined by infinite least upper bounds. In contrast, first order equational logic is sufficient for ADS.

Iteration also raises the issues of termination and well-defined values. In Gries's [30] approach to WP, a 3-valued logic is used to handle non-termination (VDM [39] also uses a 3-valued logic); however, ADS uses only ordinary 2-valued logic. We believe that ADS gives a simpler treatment of iteration because it distinguishes between the semantics of programs and other properties of programs, such as termination and correctness. The semantics of iteration is given by two very simple OBJ equations that describe the effects on states in possible models of storage; moreover, because OBJ itself has a precise and concise semantics in equational logic, we can use the semantics of OBJ to reason about properties of such models, and hence about properties of programs. The result is that ADS provides a simple semantics, unclouded by issues of correctness or termination of programs, and in addition, we are able to use equational logic (as a meta-metalanguage!) to give a separate, and also very simple treatment of correctness and termination. The use of order sorted algebra, as described in Appendix C, plays a key rôle in our treatment of non-termination.

Another issue raised by WP and other axiomatic approaches to semantics (e.g.,

---

this limitation.

[3] Meseguer's so-called "logical semantics" for the λ-calculus [46] is abstract in a similar way.

Hoare et al.'s "Laws of Programming" [38]) is non-determinism. Although programming languages are necessarily deterministic, a "non-deterministic" algorithm can be viewed as an equivalence class of procedures, where each procedure is a refinement, or possible implementation, of the algorithm. This is what we call *loose* semantics. Alternatively, non-determinism can be seen as a property of specifications in a specification language having a formal notion of one specification being more deterministic than another, as in the semantics underlying the Laws of Programming approach. For simplicity, this book avoids both of these senses of non-determinism: as presented in this book, ADS gives a deterministic treatment of deterministic languages. However, ADS could be enriched with additional operations to support a loose semantics of non-determinism, as described in [43]. Other elegant algebraic treatments of specification languages with non-determinism are given in recent research of Backhouse et al. [2] and de Moor [48].

The main motivations for non-deterministic specification are that it allows postponing design decisions, and that it leads to simple proofs of program correctness; there are even claims that, with the right semantics, algorithm development becomes an easy, near-mechanical process of looking for simple proofs. In this book, we concentrate on the semantics of programming languages, and while we agree that a clear and simple formalism should lead to clarity of proof, we steer clear of any claims about the easy automatic development of algorithms. Actually, there seem to be good reasons to believe the contrary. However, in simpler cases, one can use proof construction as an aid to program construction (we give an example in Section 5.1.1), and it seems to us that it may be easier to do this in ADS than in more complex settings.

Most approaches to the semantics of imperative languages do not treat data types rigorously and do not treat abstract data types at all (these are data types defined in a way that is independent of how they happen to be implemented). Also, most approaches to the semantics of imperative languages do not treat the refinement of data structures, and most of those that do treat it in a way that is neither rigorous nor simple. Because abstract data types are in some sense actually the *basis* of ADS, this approach can give a relatively simple yet completely rigorous approach to refinement, including the refinement of data structures.

One particular pitfall for those who wish to develop a formal semantics for imperative programming lies in the surprising variety of different kinds of variable that are involved. In fact, one must distinguish among at least the following:

1. variables that occur *in* programs (such as `X` in `X := X + 1`);

2. variables that range over data types used in programs (such as integers and Booleans); and
3. variables that range *over* programs and program parts (such as expressions);
4. variables that range over meta-logical entities used in reasoning about programs (such as computation sequences).

Furthermore, each kind of variable may have many different types. In general, textbooks on program semantics have not been very rigorous about all this. An exemplary exception is the book by John Reynolds [52]. However, such rigour is necessary for our use of OBJ as a meta-language and also for any discussion of the semantics of procedures with parameters. The formal parameters to a procedure are variables which range over program variables; if this point is not clearly made in the semantics of procedure calls, much confusion can arise.

In summary, our Algebraic Denotational Semantics combines aspects of denotational, axiomatic, and operational semantics. The denotational aspect arises because everything we specify has a denotation in an algebra; the axiomatic aspect arises from the fact that we specify these algebras using equations; and the operational aspect arises from the fact that we can symbolically execute programs using the term rewriting facility of OBJ. The success of this enterprise seems to arise in large measure from the simplicity and efficiency of equational logic, with its armoury of powerful theorems and algorithms.

A so-called metalogical framework has been developed using OBJ3 [23], to support theorem proving in any desired logical system, including first order logic. Perhaps surprisingly, we have not needed this extra power for the semantics of imperative programs; OBJ3 seems to be sufficient for the purposes of this book. It is also worth noting that the approach taken in this book can be extended without great difficulty to the object paradigm [14].

0.3 Some Caveats

Contrary to claims in many books on semantics, we believe that programming is not purely formal. Programming is a skill, and to be really good at it can take years of hard work. One must learn how to use tools like configuration managers and debuggers. For large programs, one must learn how to work in a team; and for really large projects, management and other social issues are often dominant [19]. One must learn discipline and organisation and how to read and write documentation. One must keep learning new languages, tools, concepts, algorithms, and skills;

sometimes one must even invent these things. Software Engineering is a difficult area requiring diverse skills and knowledge, and the material taught in this book provides little help with those aspects that are not formal and cannot be formalised.

It is not healthy to confuse a formal notation with a formal method. A *method* should say how to do something, whereas a notation allows one to express something [19]. Thus, OBJ is only a notation, but using it as described in this book gives an effective method for proving properties of imperative programs.

The problems that arise for large programs are qualitatively very different from those that arise for small programs. The reader should not assume that it is just as easy to find specifications and invariants for the flight control software of a real aircraft as it is for a sorting algorithm, or indeed that finding specifications and invariants will be a major activity in real industrial work. On the contrary, it turns out that finding requirements (i.e., determining what kind of system to build), structuring the system (modular design), understanding what has already been done (reading documentation and talking to others), and organising the efforts of a large team, are all much more important for a large system development effort.

Nevertheless, we hope that having a precise understanding of programming constructs and of what programs mean will be a good basis for further professional development. In particular, we hope that the way we use OBJ for specification can be an inspiration for documentation, and that the way we use OBJ modules can be an inspiration for structuring large programs. We also hope that the material in this book will be useful to those who wish to design new languages, new computers, new operating systems, etc., or to develop new theories that support such endeavours. We believe that algebra is particularly promising for such efforts, and we hope that this book can provide a foundation for approaching the large literature that applies algebraic techniques in Computing Science in general and to formal methods in particular.

0.4 Order of Presentation

This book is structured as follows: Chapter 1 gives a tutorial introduction to both OBJ3 and the algebra necessary to understand its semantics. Chapter 2 discusses the semantics of assignment, which is the central concept of our algebraic denotational semantics. Chapter 3 discusses conditionals and the sequential composition of programs. Chapter 4 discusses correctness, Chapter 5 iteration, Chapter 6 arrays, and Chapter 7 procedures, including recursively defined procedures.

Each chapter contains a number of exercises of varying difficulty, designed to test the student's comprehension of the material presented. Many of these exercises require proving a property of a given program, and all such proofs can be mechanically verified (i.e., the student can structure the proof and then let OBJ3 verify the subgoals). It would be best if students had access to an implementation of OBJ3, but because the semantics is presented equationally, the proofs are usually easy enough to construct entirely by hand.

Appendix E gives an outline showing how a course based on this book has been taught at Oxford; in particular, it addresses the undesirability of giving too large a dose of theory before any program semantics and verification is encountered. Someone reading this book without the benefit of a course may still want to organise their reading as suggested there.

0.5 Summary

Among the features that distinguish this book from others with which we are familiar are the following:

- *equational logic* is used as a foundation;
- a *rigorous implemented notation* is used to define languages and programs; and
- the *mechanical verification* of programs is supported, and students are encouraged to do the exercises using that implementation.

In fact, this book is "executable," in the sense that the definitions are given in an executable notation, and the proof of program properties can all be carried out by executing that notation.

Acknowledgements

Successive classes of students who took our course at Oxford have helped improve the presentation of this material; we are grateful for their encouragement, suggestions, and diligence in finding typographical mistakes. We also thank Frances Page for help with the preparation of the manuscript, and Francisco Pinheiro for designing the figures used in this book.

During the period in which this book was written, our work has been supported in part by the Science and Engineering Research Council, the CEC under ESPRIT-2 BRA Working Groups 6071, IS-CORE (Information Systems COrrectness and

REusability) and 6112, COMPASS (COMPrehensive Algebraic Approach to System Specification and development), Fujitsu Laboratories Limited, and a contract under the management of the Information Technology Promotion Agency (IPA), Japan, as part of the Industrial Science and Technology Frontier Program "New Models for Software Architectures," sponsored by NEDO (New Energy and Industrial Technology Development Organization).

Grant Malcolm also thanks his parents, Reynold and Morag Malcolm, and his wife, Julie, for their support and love.

1 Background in General Algebra and OBJ

This chapter gives a rather informal, intuitive introduction to some basic concepts from general algebra that are important for our exposition. These include signature, algebra, term, substitution, equation, and equational deduction. Use of the OBJ3 system makes the discussion more concrete, and also prepares for the mechanical specifications and verifications that come later in the book. A more formal exposition of the same material is given in [15].

1.1 Signatures

Our approach to the description of programming languages involves declaring a number of different *sorts* of entity, such as integers, variables, arrays, boolean expressions, integer expressions, and programs. Our approach also involves declaring a number of different operations among items of these various sorts, such as the usual arithmetic operations on integers, and various operations for forming programs out of their parts. For example, the assignment operation takes a variable and an expression as its "inputs" and produces a program as its "output". In OBJ3, this operation is declared as follows,

```
op _:=_ : Var Exp -> Pgm .
```

where the OBJ keyword "`op`" indicates that (the syntax of) an operation is being declared, while `Var`, `Exp` and `Pgm` are sort names, with the output sort after the "`->`" and the input sorts listed between the "`:`" and the "`->`". The *form* of this operation is "`_:=_`" where the underbars are place holders that indicate where entities of sort `Var` and `Exp` go, respectively. For example,

```
'X := 'X + 1
```

is of sort `Pgm`, assuming that `'X` is of sort `Var` and that the entities of sort `Exp` include expressions like `'X + 1`.

Of course, `Var` and `Exp` must have been previously declared, or the above operation declaration will be invalid. An entirely new sort is introduced using a declaration of the form

```
sort Exp .
```

(We will later introduce the sort `Var` as a renaming of the built in sort of identifiers, rather than as an entirely new sort.)

Given a declaration of an operation, say σ, the sort after the "->" in its declaration is called its *value sort*, the list of sorts between the ":" and the "->" is called its *arity*, and sometimes the pair (arity, value) is called its *rank*. In order to distinguish σ from the functions that it denotes in models (that is, in algebras, as discussed in the next section), we may call it a *function symbol* or an *operation symbol*. For example, the value sort of the assignment operation name "_:=_" above is `Pgm`, while its arity is `Var Exp` and its rank is (`Var Exp`, `Pgm`).

A collection of sort and operation declarations is called a *signature*. Following [24], it is traditional to denote a signature by a capital Greek letter, such as Σ, to let S denote its set of sorts, and to let $\Sigma_{w,s}$ denote the set of all operation symbols in Σ having arity $w \in S^*$ and value sort $s \in S$, where S^* denotes the set of all finite strings of elements from S, including the empty string, which is denoted [].

It is interesting to notice how *constants* appear in this framework. Intuitively, a constant can be seen as a function with *no* inputs, i.e., as something whose value depends on nothing. Thus, a constant of sort $s \in S$ has arity [] and value sort s, and is therefore an element of $\Sigma_{[],s}$. These considerations are enough to motivate the following formal definition of signature:

Definition 1 A **signature** Σ consists of a set S of **sorts** and a family $\{\Sigma_{w,s} \mid w \in S^*, s \in S\}$ of sets, indexed by their rank and value sort. □

In OBJ3, signatures appear as parts of either *objects* or *theories*. The distinction between these two is important, although it may seem subtle at first: an *object* is used to define a fixed standard structure containing certain abstract entities, usually data items such as the integers, Booleans, or programs; whereas a *theory* is used to define a *class* of similar structures, such as graphs, automata, or groups. We use the term **initial semantics** to refer to the intended meaning of object modules (this is further explained in Section 1.6.2 below), and we use the term **loose semantics** to refer to the denotation of classes of models by theories.

For example, a simple object for the natural numbers looks as follows,

```
obj NAT is
   sort Nat .
   op 0  : -> Nat .
   op s_ : Nat -> Nat .
endo
```

whereas a theory for automata is

```
th AUTOM is
   sorts Input State Output .
   op i : -> State .
   op f : Input State -> State .
   op g : State -> Output .
endth
```

Notice the keyword **sorts** in the above theory. It is actually a synonym for the keyword **sort**, and either keyword can be used to introduce any number of new sorts.

It can be suggestive to draw so-called *ADJ diagrams*[1] for signatures, in which the circles indicate sorts, and the edges indicate operations. Figure 1.1 presents the signature of **AUTOM** in this notation.

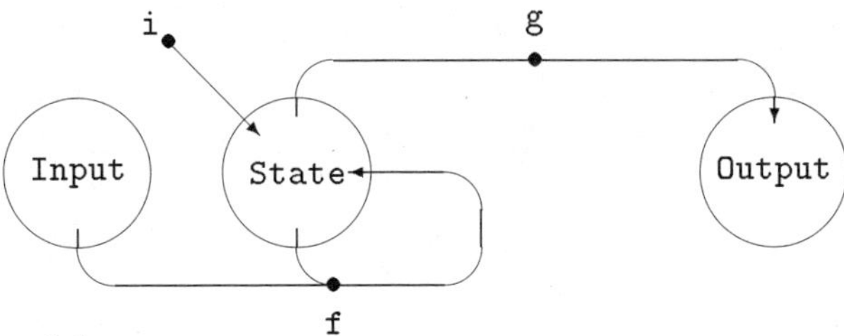

Figure 1.1
Signature for Automata

Similarly, an object for natural number expressions (only their syntax) is

```
obj NATEXP is
   sort Exp .
   op 0   : -> Exp .
   op s_  : Exp -> Exp .
   op _+_ : Exp Exp -> Exp .
   op _*_ : Exp Exp -> Exp .
endo
```

whereas the following is a theory for (directed, unordered) graphs, which are represented as a set of edges, a set of nodes, and two functions which give the *source* and the *target* node of each edge:

[1] This name was suggested by Cliff Jones for a kind of diagram introduced by Goguen, Thatcher and Wagner [24] in their study of abstract data types. (The reason for the name "ADJ" is that the set {Goguen, Thatcher, Wagner, Wright} called itself ADJ at that time.)

```
th GRAPH is
   sorts Edge Node .
   ops (s_)(t_) : Edge -> Node .
endth
```

Note that not only are two sorts declared together here, but so also are two operations that happen to have the same input and output sorts, using the keyword "**ops**" and using parentheses to separate the two forms. Figures 1.2 and 1.3 present the signatures for **NATEXP** and **GRAPH**, respectively.

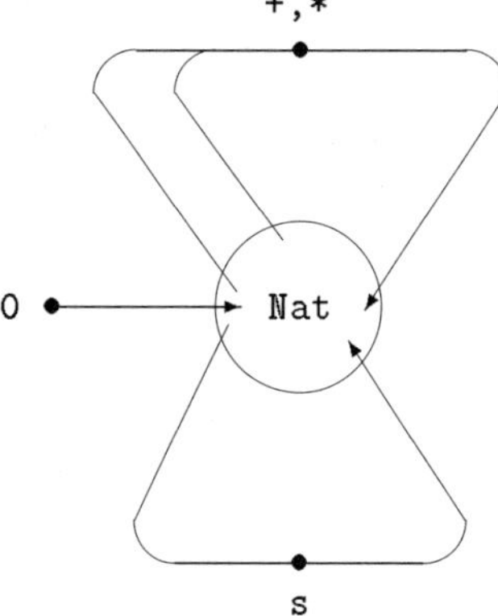

Figure 1.2
Signature for Numerical Expressions

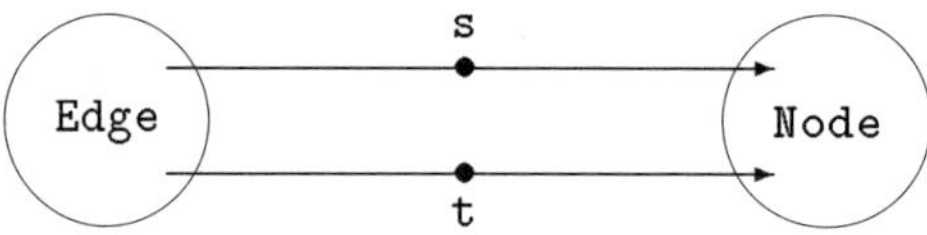

Figure 1.3
Signature for Graphs

There is an especially trivial signature that is sometimes useful: let us call a signature Σ **empty** iff $\Sigma_{w,s} = \emptyset$ for all w, s; we may denote this signature by $\emptyset$.

It is worth mentioning that operation symbols can be *overloaded* in OBJ3, in the sense of having more than one distinct rank. For example, the declarations

```
op _+_ : Nat Nat -> Nat .
op _+_ : Int Int -> Int .
```

indicate that the sum of two naturals is a natural, and the sum of two integers is an integer; Section 1.3 discusses overloading further.

The kind of signature that we have discussed so far is called a **many sorted signature**. However, OBJ3 signatures have the further feature of **subsorts**, which leads to **order sorted signatures**.[2] The intuitive idea is that some sorts may be "contained in" other sorts. For example, the natural numbers are a subsort of the integers. In OBJ3, this is written

```
subsort Nat < Int .
```

which means that every natural number is also an integer (the denotation of subsorts is discussed in the next section).

Subsort declarations can also involve more than two sorts. For example, we can write

```
subsort Nat < Int < Rat < Real .
```

and we can also write

```
subsort Real Im < Cpx .
```

to indicate that

```
subsort Real < Cpx .
subsort Im < Cpx .
```

The keyword `subsorts` is actually a synonym for `subsort`, and sometimes looks better, as in

```
subsorts Zero < Real Im < Cpx .
```

which is equivalent to

```
subsort Zero < Real < Cpx .
subsort Zero < Im < Cpx .
```

The subsort declarations given as part of a signature determine a partial ordering on the set of sorts: let $\leq$ denote the least transitive and reflexive relation on S containing the relation defined by those declarations. (Appendix C gives a formal definition of this "subsort ordering".)

More elaborate structures, such as the object of integers, or the theory of groups, require equations, which are discussed in Section 1.5 below. But before that, in order to better understand the distinction between objects and theories in OBJ, we now turn to *algebras*, which provide denotations, or models, for the syntax that is given by signatures.

---

[2] More information on order sorted algebra is given in Appendix C.

1.2 Algebras

The basic idea is that a sort denotes a set of *data items* of that sort, and an operation denotes a function from input data items (of the appropriate sorts) to output data items. For example, the assignment operation discussed above denotes a function

$$A_{\texttt{Var}} \times A_{\texttt{Exp}} \rightarrow A_{\texttt{Pgm}}$$

where $A_{\texttt{Var}}$ is the set of items of sort `Var` (i.e., the "variables") in some algebra A, where $A_{\texttt{Exp}}$ is its set of items of sort `Exp` (i.e., the "expressions"), and where $A_{\texttt{Pgm}}$ is its set of items of sort `Pgm` (i.e., the "programs"). We can make this precise as follows:

Definition 2 Given a signature Σ with sort set S, a **Σ-algebra** A consists of a **carrier set** A_s for each sort $s \in S$, plus a function $A_\sigma : A_{s_1} \times ... \times A_{s_n} \rightarrow A_s$ for each operation symbol $\sigma \in \Sigma_{w,s}$ where $w = s_1...s_n \neq []$, and a constant $A_\sigma \in A_s$ for each $\sigma \in \Sigma_{[],s}$. □

Here A_s contains the data items of sort s in A, and A_σ is the operation (or constant) in A denoted by the symbol σ. Thus, an algebra is an *interpretation* or *model* of a signature in which sorts are interpreted as sets, and operation (or constant) symbols are interpreted as actual operations (or constants) with inputs and outputs of the appropriate sorts.

Example 3 If we let $\Sigma^{\texttt{NAT}}$ be the signature of the object `NAT` of the previous section, then the natural numbers are a $\Sigma^{\texttt{NAT}}$-algebra in the obvious way: $A_{\texttt{Nat}} = \omega = \{0, 1, 2, ...\}$, $A_{\texttt{0}} = 0$, and $A_{\texttt{s}}(n) = n + 1$. It is usual to denote this algebra ω. □

Although this is the algebra that we have in mind for the signature $\Sigma^{\texttt{NAT}}$, i.e., it is the *standard interpretation* or *model* for that signature, it is far from being the *only* model. Two other models are given in the following:

Example 4 Define B by $B_{\texttt{Nat}} = \{0, 1\}$, $B_{\texttt{0}} = 0$, and $B_{\texttt{s}}(n) = 1 - n$. Define C by $C_{\texttt{Nat}} = \{0\}$, $C_{\texttt{0}} = 0$, and $C_{\texttt{s}}(0) = 0$. □

In a similar way, we can define some models of the theory `AUTOM` of the previous section. Let $\Sigma^{\texttt{AUTOM}}$ denote the signature of `AUTOM`.

Example 5 Define a $\Sigma^{\texttt{AUTOM}}$-algebra E as follows:

$$E_{\texttt{Input}} = E_{\texttt{State}} = E_{\texttt{Output}} = \omega \ ;$$

$E_{\texttt{i}} = 0$; $E_{\texttt{f}}(m,n) = m+n$; and $E_{\texttt{g}}(n) = n$. This automaton has initial state 0, its next state is the sum of its inputs, and its output is its current state. □

Example 6 A rather different $\Sigma^{\texttt{AUTOM}}$-algebra F may be defined as follows:

$$F_{\texttt{Input}} = F_{\texttt{State}} = \omega \ ;$$

$F_{\texttt{Output}} = \{0,1\}$; $F_{\texttt{i}} = 0$; $F_{\texttt{f}}(m,n) = m+n$; and $F_{\texttt{g}}(n) = n \ (mod\ 2)$. This automaton returns output 0 if the sum of its inputs is even, and 1 if it is odd. □

Because the automaton theorist studies all automata, there is no single "standard" model or interpretation for $\Sigma^{\texttt{AUTOM}}$. Rather, any $\Sigma^{\texttt{AUTOM}}$-algebra is assumed to be as good as any other to the specifier who wrote the theory **AUTOM**.

To summarise, the meaning or denotation of a theory is the collection of all algebras that satisfy it, whereas the denotation of an object is a single "standard" algebra that satisfies it. Once equations have been introduced in Section 1.5, the meaning of the word "satisfies" will become clearer.

For the order sorted case, we simply add the requirement that the subsort relation should be interpreted as the subset relation on the carriers: that is, if $s \leq s'$ for $s, s' \in S$ then we require of a Σ-algebra A that $A_s \subseteq A_{s'}$. Some further conditions that relate to the overloading of operations are mentioned in Section 1.3, and order sorted algebra is treated in detail in Appendix C.

1.3 Terms

One of the first things that one wants to do with a collection of operations is to combine them into expressions called *terms*. Such terms are essential for describing programs and their properties. One complication with which we must deal is that some combinations of operation symbols may be *ill formed*, in the sense that the number or the sorts of the inputs may fail to match the required arity. Another complication is the different *forms* that different operations may have, such as prefix, postfix, infix, and most generally "*mixfix*".

In OBJ, as in mathematics, the standard default syntactic form for an operation is prefix with parentheses and commas. Thus, the operation declaration

```
op F : Int Int -> Int .
```

allows one to form expressions such as `F(1,2)`, `F(X,Y)`, and `F(X + 1,3)`, whereas the declaration

```
op _+_ : Int Int -> Int .
```

indicates that `+` is infix, allowing expressions like `1 + 2`, and `X + Y`, and `X +(Y + 1)`. In both cases, there must be two arguments of sort `Int`. Thus, `F(3)`, `F(2/3, false)`, `2/3 + false`, and `+(3)` are all ill formed. Also, in order for OBJ to parse a term involving `+`, it is essential that the next character on each side of the `+` should be either a space or a parenthesis (or another "special symbol," which means "`[`" or "`]`" or "`{`" or "`}`").

If Σ is a signature with sort set S where all operation symbols have the default (prefix with parentheses) syntactic form, then it is easy to give a (recursive) definition of the (well formed) terms. Intuitively, we just say that all the constants are terms, and that applying any operation symbol to terms of the appropriate sorts always yields a term. More formally, well formed terms are strings whose symbols are the operation symbols in Σ together with parentheses and commas:

Definition 7 The set of **Σ-terms** of sort s, denoted $T_{\Sigma,s}$ for $s \in S$, is defined by the following two conditions:

(0) if $\sigma \in \Sigma_{[],s}$ then $\sigma \in T_{\Sigma,s}$

(1) if $\sigma \in \Sigma_{w,s}$ where $w = s_1...s_n \neq []$ and if $t_i \in T_{\Sigma,s_i}$ for $i = 1, ..., n$, then $\sigma(t_1, ..., t_n) \in T_{\Sigma,s}$.

(To be very precise, we should add that the family $T_{\Sigma,s}$ of sets is the *least* family of sets of strings of symbols that satisfies these two conditions.) □

The case where operation symbols have mixfix forms is very similar, but requires more complex notation to express; we omit it here. See [15] for details.

For example, using the signature $\Sigma^{\texttt{NATEXP}}$, the following are well formed terms of sort `Exp`:

```
(s s 0) * (s s s 0)
(s s 0) + ((s 0)*(s s s 0))
(s s((s s 0)*(s s s s 0))) + ((s s s 0)*(s s s 0))
```

Note that parentheses can always be added to expressions. Parentheses are actually needed in order to *disambiguate* the above expressions. For example, the expression

```
s s 0 * s s s 0
```

could be parsed in any of the following three ways:

```
(s s 0) * (s s s 0)
s ((s 0) * (s s s 0))
s s(0 * s s s 0)
```

However, the situation is better than this in OBJ3, because of its *precedence* values. The **precedence** of an operation symbol is a natural number that tells how tightly binding it is; the lower the number, the more tightly binding. A unary prefix operation has default precedence 15, while a binary infix operation has a default precedence 41. By using these defaults, the expression `s s 0 * s s s 0` will in fact be parsed as we expect, that is, as `(s s 0)*(s s s 0)`.

Users can also give their own precedence declarations if they wish. This is done by postfixing an "attribute" of the form "`[prec` *n*`]`" to the operation declaration (but before the period), where *n* is a natural number less than 128. For example, the object `NATEXP` is equivalent to the following:

```
obj NATEXP is
   sort Exp .
   op 0   : -> Exp .
   op s_  : Exp -> Exp [prec 15] .
   op _+_ : Exp Exp -> Exp [prec 41] .
   op _*_ : Exp Exp -> Exp [prec 41] .
endo
```

It is usually possible to get the OBJ3 parser to do what you want with a judicious use of precedence and parentheses. However, sometimes it does jump to an incorrect conclusion and then fail. Thus, it is often the case that an ambiguous expression will actually be parsed as you wish, but it is sometimes the case that an unambiguous expression will fail to parse. Also, OBJ3 may sometimes inform you that there are multiple parses, and print them for you. To see what OBJ3 makes of a given expression *e*, you can give the command

```
parse e .
```

and to see all the details of all parses, you can first give the command

```
set print with parens on .
```

For more details, see [26].

Note that ambiguities can arise through overloading and shared keywords in mixfix syntax, as well as through the phenomena discussed above. Ambiguities due to overloading are generally harmless. For example, in case of the declarations

```
op _+_ : Nat Nat -> Nat .
op _+_ : Int Int -> Int .
```

where `Nat < Int`, the expression `3 + 5` is ambiguous (because 3 and 5 are both naturals and integers), but this doesn't matter, because the result is 8 in either case. In fact, OBJ3 assumes conditions which ensure that expressions like `3 + 5` always have a unique parse of *least sort* (in the above example, `Nat`) and a well defined value. These conditions tend to be satisfied by naturally arising signatures, and users do not need to pay them too much attention unless things go wrong. See Appendix C and [22, 26] for more detail.

The set of all Σ-terms (as in Definition 7) gives rise to a Σ-algebra, called the **term algebra** and denoted T_Σ, where for each sort $s \in S$, the carrier set $(T_\Sigma)_s$ is the set $T_{\Sigma,s}$ of terms of sort s, where each constant $\sigma \in \Sigma_{[],s}$ is interpreted as the term $\sigma \in T_{\Sigma,s}$ and each function symbol $\sigma \in \Sigma_{w,s}$ with $w = s_1 ... s_n$ is interpreted as the operation that sends the inputs $t_1, ..., t_n$ to the string $\sigma(t_1, ..., t_n)$, where $t_i \in T_{\Sigma,s_i}$ for $i = 1, ..., n$ (see (1) of Definition 7).

Basic results (which are discussed in Section 1.6.2) imply that the Σ-term algebra provides a "standard interpretation" for a signature Σ. For example, the carrier of the algebra $T_{\Sigma\texttt{NAT}}$ is the following set of terms:

$$\{\texttt{0, s 0, s s 0, s s s 0, } ...\}.$$

These elements are representations for the natural numbers in so-called "Peano notation." The basic results imply that anything that can be done with the natural numbers can be done using this representation. In fact, the natural numbers are an *abstract data type* in the sense of [24] (see also [15]), for which Peano notation provides one representation among many.

When we write an OBJ module having the keywords "`obj`" and "`endo`", we indicate that the standard interpretation is intended. When there are no equations, one such algebra is the term algebra. For theories, however, the term algebra is not usually very interesting. For example, the term algebra for the theory `AUTOM` has:

$$T_{\Sigma\texttt{AUTOM},\texttt{Input}} = \emptyset$$
$$T_{\Sigma\texttt{AUTOM},\texttt{State}} = \{\texttt{i}\}$$
$$T_{\Sigma\texttt{AUTOM},\texttt{Output}} = \{\texttt{g(i)}\}.$$

There could hardly be a less interesting automaton. Graphs provide an even clearer illustration that the term algebra is not what we want for theories: all of the carriers of the term algebra for `GRAPH` are empty!

Given a signature Σ and a Σ-algebra A, there is a well defined way to interpret any Σ-term t as a value in A, by first evaluating the constants from t in A, and then recursively applying the operations in A that are denoted by the operation symbols that occur in t. Let us denote the result of this by $\overline{\varphi}(t)$ (the reason for the overbar is explained in the next section).

For example, if we let Σ be the signature of **NATEXP** and let A be the Σ-algebra of natural numbers with operations interpreted in the usual way, then we have

$$\overline{\varphi}(s\ 0) = 1$$
$$\overline{\varphi}((s\ s\ 0) + (s\ s\ s\ 0)) = 5$$
$$\overline{\varphi}((s\ s\ 0) * (s\ s\ s\ 0)) = 6$$

just as one would expect.

We can give a precise definition of $\overline{\varphi}$ as follows:

(0) $\overline{\varphi}_s(c) = A_c$ for any constant c in $\Sigma_{[],s}$; and

(1) given σ in $\Sigma_{s1...sn,s}$ and t_i in T_{Σ,s_i} with $\overline{\varphi}(t_i) = a_i$ in A_{s_i} for $i = 1, ..., n$, then $\overline{\varphi}(\sigma(t_1, ..., t_n)) = A_\sigma(a_1, ..., a_n)$.

We may write

$$\overline{\varphi}\colon T_\Sigma \to A$$

as a schematic representation of this situation.

1.4 Variables

Variables are very important in algebra: they allow us to write equations that apply to many instances at once. Variables appear in terms, where they play exactly the same syntactic rôle as constants. In OBJ3, we can declare variables using syntax like the following:

```
vars X Y Z : Exp .
```

(Note that `var` and `vars` are synonyms in this context.) Then we can use these variables to form terms over the signature $\Sigma^{\mathtt{NATEXP}}$ like the following:

```
X + Y
X + (Y + 1)
(X * Y) + (X * Z)
```

These could be checked by executing **parse** on them.

Of course, we can have any number of variables of any number of sorts. For example, we could also declare

```
vars U V : Var .
var P : Pgm .
```

Note the difference between "var" and "Var": the latter has been declared as a sort name (it is used below to denote the sort of integer variables in a programming language), while the former is an OBJ keyword.

After this, assuming the previously declared variables of sort Exp, plus the declarations

```
op _:=_ : Var Exp -> Pgm .
op _;_ : Pgm Pgm -> Pgm .
subsort Var Nat < Exp .
```

the following should work:

```
parse P ; U := X + V .
```

Formally, we can represent all the variable declarations that are in effect at some given moment by a signature that consists entirely of constants. Thus, for the current example, if we denote that signature by Ξ, then

$$\begin{aligned}\Xi_{[],\mathtt{Exp}} &= \{\mathtt{X},\mathtt{Y},\mathtt{Z}\}\\ \Xi_{[],\mathtt{Var}} &= \{\mathtt{U},\mathtt{V}\}\\ \Xi_{[],\mathtt{Pgm}} &= \{\mathtt{P}\}\end{aligned}$$

with

$$\Xi_{w,s} = \emptyset$$

otherwise. Let us call a signature that consists only of constants a **ground signature**.

Given a signature Σ of operations symbols and a ground signature Ξ, then the well formed terms, called **Σ-terms with variables from** Ξ, are just the elements of $T_{\Sigma\cup\Xi}$ where the union of the two signatures is defined by

$$(\Sigma \cup \Xi)_{w,s} = \Sigma_{w,s} \cup \Xi_{w,s}.$$

We will always assume that Σ and Ξ are *disjoint*, in the sense that $\Sigma_{[],s} \cap \Xi_{[],s} = \emptyset$ for all sorts s.

In our example,

$$(\Sigma \cup \Xi)_{[],\mathtt{Pgm}} = \{\mathtt{P}\}$$

and $(T_{\Sigma\cup\Xi})_{\mathtt{Pgm}}$ contains expressions like

```
P ; U := X + U .
```

Now suppose we are given a signature Σ, a ground signature Ξ of variables, and a Σ-algebra A. We already know how to interpret Σ-terms as elements of A (from the end of the previous section), but we can only interpret $(\Sigma \cup \Xi)$-terms if we have some way to interpret the variables in Ξ as elements of A. An *interpretation* of the variable symbols of Ξ in A is an assignment θ of elements of A to elements of Ξ; if X is a variable in Ξ, then $\theta(X)$ is the element of A that we intend to substitute for X in t. Let $\overline{\theta}(t)$ denote that result of doing such a substitution for each X in Ξ. This will give rise to a family of functions

$$\overline{\theta}_s : (T_{\Sigma\cup\Xi})_s \rightarrow A_s$$

one for the terms of each sort s in S. The following may make this clearer:

Example 8 Let Σ be the signature of the object `NATEXP` given before, and let Ξ contain the variables X, Y, Z of sort `Exp`. Also, let the Σ-algebra A be the natural numbers with the operations in Σ interpreted in the familiar way. If we now define $\theta : \Xi \rightarrow A$ by $\theta(X) = 1$, $\theta(Y) = 2$, and $\theta(Z) = 3$, then we have

$$\overline{\theta}(X + (Y + Z)) = 6$$
$$\overline{\theta}(X * Y) = 2$$
$$\overline{\theta}(X + (s\ s\ 0) * Z) = 7.$$

□

We can make the above precise as follows:

Definition 9 Given a signature Σ, a ground signature Ξ disjoint from Σ, and a Σ-algebra A, then an **assignment** of values in A to "variables" in Ξ is a family of functions

$$\theta_s : \Xi_{[],s} \rightarrow A_s$$

one for each $s \in S$. Sometimes, we may call such a θ an **interpretation**, and we may also use the shorter notation

$$\theta : \Xi \to A$$

Given such an interpretation $\theta : \Xi \to A$ of Ξ in A, then we define the functions $\overline{\theta}_s : (T_{\Sigma \cup \Xi})_s \to A_s$ as follows:

(0) $\overline{\theta}_s(X) = \theta(X)$ for X in $\Xi_{[],s}$ and $\overline{\theta}_s(c) = A_c$ for c in $\Sigma_{[],s}$;
(1) given σ in $\Sigma_{s_1 \ldots s_n,s}$ and t_i in T_{Σ,s_i} with $\overline{\theta}(t_i) = a_i$ for $i = 1, ..., n$, then

$$\overline{\theta}(\sigma(t_1, ..., t_n)) = A_\sigma(a_1, ..., a_n) \ .$$

We may use the following short notation for this:

$$\overline{\theta} : T_{\Sigma \cup \Xi} \to A.$$

□

There is a notation for the results of applying a substitution to a term that is sometimes very convenient because it defines the substitution "on the fly" rather than requiring that it be defined before it is used. Thus, if $\theta : \Xi \to A$, if Ξ contains variables $X_1, ..., X_n$, and if $\theta(X_i) = a_i \in A$, then instead of $\overline{\theta}(t)$ we can write $t(X_1 \leftarrow a_1, ..., X_n \leftarrow a_n)$, which should be read "the result of substituting a_1 for X_1, ..., and a_n for X_n in t".

> Those who are interested in such things may wish to note that $\overline{\theta}$ is a Σ-*homomorphism*, that $T_{\Sigma \cup \Xi}$ is the *free* Σ-algebra generated by Ξ, and that $\overline{\theta}$ is the unique Σ-homomorphism from $T_{\Sigma \cup \Xi}$ that extends the mapping θ. Details of this rather elegant algebraic view of substitution are explained in [15], among other places.

To sum up, variables are just new constant symbols that do not have a fixed interpretation in algebras.

1.5 Equations

Equations are the essence of algebra. Anyone who has worked with polynomials in school has a pretty good intuition for equations. But there are some subtle points about equations, especially in a many sorted context. We will define an equation to be a pair of terms with some variables, and then explore what it means for them to be equal.

A typical equation in OBJ3 syntax is

```
eq X + Y = Y + X .
```

where the keyword "eq" indicates that an equation is coming, the "=" sign separates the two terms, and the "." concludes the equation. All of the variable and operation symbols used in the two terms must have been previously declared. In the above example, this would mean the variables X and Y and the operation _+_. Formally, we can give the following:

Definition 10 A Σ-**equation** consists of a ground signature Ξ (disjoint from Σ) and two $(\Sigma \cup \Xi)$-terms of the same sort, called the **left** and **right sides** of the equation. In theoretical discussions, the notation "$(\forall\Xi)\ t_1 = t_2$" will be used, with $t_1, t_2 \in (T_{\Sigma\cup\Xi})_s$ for some sort s in S. An equation of the form $(\forall\Xi)\ t_1 = t_2$ is a **ground** equation iff Ξ is the empty signature; then both terms are necessarily ground terms. □

But what does it mean that the two sides of an equations are "equal?" Actually, they are *not necessarily equal*: it depends on the algebra that is chosen. For example, assuming that $+$ is in Σ, not every Σ-algebra will have $+$ commutative. To be specific, consider the following:

Example 11 Let A_s be the set $\{a, b\}^*$ of all lists of elements from the set $\{a, b\}$, and let $+$ be concatenation for lists. Then the commutative law for $+$ is not satisfied by this A. In particular, if $X = ab$ and $Y = ba$, then $X + Y = abba$, whereas $Y + X = baab$. □

This suggests that we need a precise definition of what it means for an algebra to satisfy an equation. Using our previous discussion of how to interpret variables and terms in algebras, the result is actually rather simple, but also rather abstract:

Definition 12 Given a Σ-equation e of the form $(\forall\Xi)\ t = t'$ and a Σ-algebra A, then A **satisfies** e iff $\overline{\theta}(t) = \overline{\theta}(t')$ for every interpretation $\theta : \Xi \to A$. □

Intuitively, this just means that the values of the two sides are equal in A, no matter what values are substituted for their variables.

In specifications, we use equations to describe the intended models. That is, we write down equations that are satisfied by the models that we have in mind. So if we write down the commutative law, we are (presumably) not thinking about the concatenation of strings.

It is often helpful to use equations that are only satisfied under certain conditions. These are called *conditional equations*. Some typical conditional equations in OBJ3 syntax are the following:

```
cq X = Y if X * Z == Y * Z and Z =/= 0 .
cq N ! = N *(N - 1)! if N > 0 .
```

Notice that the syntactic form of these equations is

```
cq _ = _ if _ .
```

where all three underbars should be filled with terms, the first two of which must have the same sort, and the third of which must have the sort `Bool`, which is automatically imported into every OBJ3 object and theory. The following is a more formal statement of this:

Definition 13 A **conditional** Σ**-equation** consists of three Σ-terms, say t_1, t_2, t_3, over variables from some given ground signature Ξ, such that t_1 and t_2 are of the same sort, and t_3 is of sort `Bool`. In formal discussions, the notation "$(\forall\Xi)\ t_1 = t_2$ `if` t_3" will be used. This conditional Σ-equation is **satisfied** by a Σ-algebra A iff for every substitution $\theta\colon \Xi \to A$, we have $\overline{\theta}(t_1) = \overline{\theta}(t_2)$ whenever $\overline{\theta}(t_3) =$ `true`. □

It is worth noting that there are certain built in Boolean operations, some of which have been used above. One of the simplest of these is conjunction, which has the declaration

```
op _and_ : Bool Bool -> Bool .
```

The OBJ3 "standard prelude" defines all of the built in operations; it is listed in [26].

We conclude this section with some examples that illustrate the use of equations in connection with other features previously described. The first is a theory of groups:

```
th GROUP is
  sort Elt .
  op e   : -> Elt .
```

```
    op _-1 : Elt -> Elt .
    op _*_ : Elt Elt -> Elt .
    vars X Y Z : Elt .
    eq X * e = X .
    eq X *(X -1) = e .
    eq (X * Y)* Z = X *(Y * Z).
  endth
```

The models of the theory `GROUP` are exactly the groups; in this sense, `GROUP` really is a theory of groups.

Our next object uses subsorts in an interesting way; indeed, this kind of example *cannot* be done adequately with just many sorted algebra (this is proved in [21]). The constructors `0` and `s` build natural numbers, while **`nil`** and `*` build lists. The subsort declaration **`Nat < NeList`** says that every number is a (singleton) list. Then **`nil`** is just a list, and `*` builds non-empty lists (of sort **`NeList`**, with of course **`NeList < List`**). A key point is that the selectors **`head`** and **`tail`** are defined only on the non-empty lists. In this approach, **`head(nil)`** is not "undefined" or some such (potentially) vague thing, but is simply an ill formed term. Restricting the domains of operations to subsorts can be a much simpler way to to handle errors than many others that are common in functional languages, such as raising exceptions.

```
  obj NATLIST is
    sorts Nat NeList List .
    subsorts Nat < NeList < List .
    op 0 : -> Nat .
    op s_ : Nat -> Nat .
    op nil : -> List .
    op _*_ : List List -> List .
    op _*_ : NeList List -> NeList .
    op _*_ : List NeList -> NeList .
    op head_ : NeList -> Nat .
    op tail_ : NeList -> List .
    vars X Y Z : List .
    var N : Nat .
    eq X * nil = X .
    eq nil * X = X .
    eq (X * Y)* Z = X *(Y * Z).
    eq head(N * X) = N .
```

```
    eq tail(N * X) = X .
    eq head N = N .
    eq tail N = nil .
  endo
```

Thus, two typical lists are the following:

```
  (0 * 0)* s 0
  ((s 0)*(s s 0))* s s 0
```

Note the need for parentheses in these expressions, despite the presence of the associative law as an equation. We can avoid this awkwardness with suitable precedence declarations.

Let us now consider lists of natural numbers using so-called *error supersorts*:

```
  obj NATLISTE is
    sorts Nat List EList .
    subsorts Nat < List < EList .
    op 0 : -> Nat .
    op s_ : Nat -> Nat .
    op nil : -> List .
    op _*_ : List List -> List .
    op _*_ : EList EList -> EList .
    op head_ : EList -> Nat .
    op tail_ : EList -> EList .
    op errorList : -> EList .
    vars X Y Z : List .
    var N : Nat .
    eq X * nil = X .
    eq nil * X = X .
    eq (X * Y)* Z = X *(Y * Z).
    eq head(N * X) = N .
    eq tail(N * X) = X .
    eq head N = N .
    eq tail N = nil .
    eq head nil = 0 .
    eq tail nil = errorList .
    eq head errorList = 0 .
  endo
```

Although somewhat more complex, the way that the expression `tail nil` is treated here is more flexible than in the object `NATLIST`, because now we get an error message, and we can use it in equations to "trap" and "handle" many cases of exceptional behaviour. See [21] and [22] for more detailed discussion of this topic, including further examples.

By contrast, the way that `head nil` is treated is less satisfactory than in the previous object; we simply deny that it is an error, and assign it an ordinary (but rather arbitrary) value, namely `0`. This means that it will be impossible to trap or handle this condition. But we could easily have treated `head nil` the same way that we treated `tail nil`, by adding an error supersort to the corresponding value sort, say `Nat < ENat`, with a corresponding error message, say `errorNat`.

Notice that there are some strange values of sort `EList`, such as `(nil * s 0)* errorList`. However, these values can be very useful; for example, they can tell us the precise context within which the error occurred. Also, we will find this kind of error value very useful in our discussions of programming language semantics to follow.

A more detailed discussion of error handling in OBJ would have to consider *retracts*; these are also needed for a complete understanding of parsing when there are subsorts. Appendix C discusses retracts briefly, and more detail can be found in [22] and [26].

1.6 Rewriting and Equational Deduction

Equational deduction and rewriting are based on the substitution of equals for equals. We will use a "calculational" notation that is popular in current Computing Science literature, although the idea is actually much older. One starts with a term, say t_0 (over some fixed signature Σ), and then applies equations; each such step yields new terms, say $t_1, t_2, ..., t_k$, each of which is equal to all the previous terms. If the equations applied are $e_1, ..., e_k$ then we may write this in the form

$$
\begin{array}{lll}
 & t_0 & \\
= & & \{ e_1 \} \\
 & t_1 & \\
= & & \{ e_2 \} \\
 & \cdots\cdots & \\
= & & \{ e_k \} \\
 & t_k &
\end{array}
$$

In order to explain what it means to "apply" an equation to a term, let's begin with a simple example, taking Σ to be the object `NATEXP` given earlier, taking t_0 to be the term $s\ 0 + (s\ 0 * s\ 0)$, and taking e_1 to be the equation $(\forall X)\ s\ 0 * X = X$. Then e_1 applies at the subterm $(s\ 0 * s\ 0)$, by matching the variable X in the left side of the equation to the constant $s\ 0$ in the subterm, yielding $s\ 0$ for the corresponding value of the right side. This must now be placed in the context of the original term $s\ 0 + (s\ 0 * s\ 0)$, yielding $s\ 0 + s\ 0$ as the final result. Thus, the general procedure is to match the left side of the equation to a subterm of the given term, and then replace that subterm by the corresponding substitution instance of the right side; the process of matching yields a substitution, i.e., a value for each variable, which is then applied to the right side to get the replacement term. Notice that in order for this to work, all the variables that occur in the right side of the equation must also occur in the left side.

Although this is familiar from experience in school with manipulating polynomials, in fact it is difficult to give a complete formal definition. Fortunately, much of the work has already been done in the previous section, allowing us to define a **term substitution** to be an assignment θ of *terms* to variables,

$$\theta : \Xi \rightarrow T_{\Sigma \cup \Xi'}$$

where Ξ and Ξ' are both ground signatures disjoint from Σ. If X is a variable in Ξ, then $\theta(X)$ is the Σ-term using variables from Ξ' that we intend to substitute for X, where X occurs in Σ-terms having variables from Ξ.

Definition 14 An equation of the form $(\forall \Xi)\ t = t'$ (with $t, t' \in (T_\Sigma \cup \Xi)_s$ for some sort s) is called a **rewrite rule** iff the set of variables that occur in t' is a subset of those that occur in t. In the order sorted case, we also require that the least sort of the left side of the rule is greater than or equal to the least sort of its right side; i.e., we require that rewrite rules are **sort decreasing**. A finite set of rewrite rules over a signature Σ is called a (Σ-)**term rewriting system**, sometimes abbreviated **TRS**. □

By the way, we can define the set of variables that occur in t to be those in the *least* signature Ψ such that $t \in T_{\Sigma \cup \Psi}$.

Definition 15 Given a rewrite rule e of the form $(\forall \Xi)\ t = t'$ with $t, t' \in (T_{\Sigma \cup \Xi})_s$ and a term $t_0 \in (T_\Sigma)_s$, then a substitution $\theta : \Xi \rightarrow T_\Sigma$ is said to be a **direct match** for e iff $\overline{\theta}(t) = t_0$. In this case, the term $t_1 = \overline{\theta}(t')$ is called the **corresponding substitution instance** for the match, and is also called the **result** of **applying** e to t_0. □

But we have seen that direct matches are not enough; we must make a substitution for a match of a *subterm* in a *context*. The following may seem surprisingly technical for such a simple idea:

Definition 16 Given a rewrite rule of the form $(\forall\Xi)\ t = t'$ with $t, t' \in (T_{\Sigma\cup\Xi})_s$ and a term $t_0 \in (T_\Sigma)_s$ let z be a "fresh variable", i.e., a symbol such that $z \notin \Sigma\cup\Xi$. Then we say that a term $t'_0 \in T_\Sigma$ is a **subterm** of t_0 iff $t_0 = c(z \leftarrow t'_0)$ for some term $c \in T_{\Sigma\cup\{z\}}$ called the **context**, and we say that a **match** of e to t_0 consists of a subterm t'_0 of t_0 which is a direct match of e, i.e., such that $t'_0 = \overline{\theta}(t)$ for some substitution $\theta\colon \Xi \to T_\Sigma$. In this case, we say that the term $t_1 = c(z \leftarrow \overline{\theta}(t'))$ is the **result of applying** e to t_0 at the subterm t'_0 using the substitution θ, and we may write $t_0 \Rightarrow t_1$, which is the **one step rewriting** relation. It is extended to **multi-step rewriting** by defining $t_0 \overset{*}{\Rightarrow} t_*$ iff $t_0 = t_*$ or $t_0 \Rightarrow t_1 \overset{*}{\Rightarrow} t_*$. In contexts where it is helpful to indicate the particular signature Σ that is involved, we may write $\Rightarrow_\Sigma$ or $\overset{*}{\Rightarrow}_\Sigma$. □

Example 17 Let Σ be $\Sigma^{\mathtt{NATEXP}}$, let c be the term $s\ 0 + z$, let $\Xi_{[],\mathtt{Nat}} = \{X\}$, and define θ by $\theta(X) = s\ 0$. Then $s\ 0 + (s\ 0 * s\ 0)$ rewrites to $s\ 0 + s\ 0$ as a result of applying the rule $(\forall X)\ s\ 0 * X = X$ at the subterm $(s\ 0 * s\ 0)$ with the substitution θ.

If we now assume the following equations,

$$
\begin{array}{ll}
[ZP] & (\forall X)\ 0 + X = X \\
[SP] & (\forall X, Y)\ (s\ X) + Y = s(X + Y) \\
[ZM] & (\forall X)\ 0 * X = 0 \\
[SM] & (\forall X, Y)\ (s\ X) * Y = (X * Y) + X
\end{array}
$$

then we can do the following calculation,

$$
\begin{array}{ll}
 & 0 + (s\ 0 * 0) \\
\Rightarrow & \qquad \{\ \mathrm{ZP}\ \} \\
 & s\ 0 * 0 \\
\Rightarrow & \qquad \{\ \mathrm{SM}\ \} \\
 & (0 * 0) + 0 \\
\Rightarrow & \qquad \{\ \mathrm{ZM}\ \} \\
 & 0 + 0 \\
\Rightarrow & \qquad \{\ \mathrm{ZP}\ \} \\
 & 0
\end{array}
$$

where each step is an application of the rule indicated to the right of the corresponding $\Rightarrow$ sign; of course, all these terms are actually equal, so we could replace "$\Rightarrow$" by "$=$" if we wanted. □

This process of applying equations in the forward (i.e., left-to-right) direction is called **term rewriting**, and it is quite typical to keep applying equations in this way until a term is reached to which no equation can be applied. This process is called **reduction**, and the resulting term is said to be a **normal form**, or a **reduced term**. In OBJ, reduction is accomplished with the command "`red`" or "`reduce`", as in

```
red 0 + (s 0 * 0).
```

which will return `0` as its result.

However, term rewriting does not give the whole story. In the general case, called **equational deduction**, equations that are not necessarily rewrite rules may be applied either forwards or "backwards", that is, in a right-to-left manner. Although backwards applications cannot in general be done automatically, they can be done "by hand" if the user supplies the necessary values for the variables. For example, using the equation ZM above, we can replace the term `0` by the term `0 * (s s 0)` by supplying the value `(s s 0)` for the variable X. OBJ3 does this using the `apply` command, but because it is not used in this book, it will not be described in detail (see [15] or [26] for a description). However, we do wish to point out that this form of equational deduction is *complete*, in the sense that given a set E of equations, *every* equation that is true of all models of E can be deduced using it. Pure rewriting is only rarely complete in this sense.

Although the above discussion has focussed on reasoning with ground terms, in fact OBJ will do rewriting with non-ground terms, that is, with terms that contain variables. For example, we can write

```
red  X + (- X) .
```

and if `X` has been declared a variable of the sort `Int` in an appropriate module for the integers, then this reduction will return the result `0`. The same can be done with `apply`. However, for reductions, OBJ3 will warn that variables are present.

1.6.1 Attributes of operations

It is natural and convenient to consider certain properties of an operation as *attributes* that are declared at the same time as its syntax. These properties include axioms like associativity, commutativity, and identity that have both syntactic and semantic consequences, as well as others that affect order of evaluation, parsing, etc. In OBJ3, such attributes are given in square brackets after the syntax declaration. Recall that we have already discussed the precedence attribute in Section 1.3. You can see what attributes an operation actually has by using the `show` command. For example,

```
op _or_ : Bool Bool -> Bool [assoc] .
```

indicates that `or` is an associative binary infix operation on Boolean values. This implies that the parser does not require full parenthesisation. For example, we can write `(true or false or true)` instead of `(true or (false or true))`; moreover, the printer will omit all unnecessary parentheses. The `assoc` attribute also gives the semantic effect of an associativity axiom, but this is implemented in a more sophisticated way, with associative matching and the automatic addition of new some equations.

Binary infix operations can be declared commutative with the attribute `comm`, which is semantically a commutativity axiom, but is implemented by rewriting modulo commutativity. Notice that a commutative *equation* would give rise to non-terminating computations, such as

$$a + b \Rightarrow b + a \Rightarrow a + b \Rightarrow \ldots$$

An operation can have both of the attributes `assoc` and `comm`, but associative/commutative matching is an NP-complete problem, so that a really efficient implementation is impossible. The present implementation, which is based on work of Lincoln [42], extended to OSA along the lines of [18], is reasonably efficient, but cannot be expected to be fast for really large problems. However, matching modulo commutativity and/or associativity can really be an enormous convenience for applications to theorem proving, potentially reducing the human effort required by factors from 2 to 10, or even more.

An identity attribute can be declared for a binary operation. For example, in

```
op _or_ : Bool Bool -> Bool [assoc id: false] .
```

the attribute `id: false` gives the effects of the two identity equations `(B or false = B)` and `(false or B = B)`. Identity attributes can be ground terms, and not just constants. OBJ3 implements rewriting modulo identity by a completion process that may generate further equations, which may in turn lead to problems with termination and efficiency. These can be avoided by using the attribute `idr:`, which introduces only the identity equations themselves, without invoking a completion process.

Operations can also be declared idempotent, by using the attribute **idem**; this is implemented simply by adding the idempotent equation to those available in the relevant module. There is no completion.

The following is an integer list object with associative and identity attributes:

```
obj NATLIST1 is
  sorts Nat List NeList .
  subsorts Nat < NeList < List .
  op 0 : -> Nat .
  op s_ : Nat -> Nat [prec 5] .
  op nil : -> List .
  op __ : List List -> List [assoc id: nil] .
  op __ : NeList List -> NeList [assoc] .
  op head_ : NeList -> Nat .
  op tail_ : NeList -> List .
  var N : Nat .   var L : List .
  eq head(N L) = N .
  eq tail(N L) = L .
endo
```

The reduction

```
red 0 nil s 0 nil s s s 0 .
```

is carried out in LIST-OF-INT1 by applications of the identity equation modulo associativity, as follows,

```
   0 nil s 0 nil s s s 0
⇒
   0 s 0 nil s s s 0
⇒
   0 s 0 s s s 0
```

so that OBJ3 prints

```
result NeList: 0 s 0 s s s 0
```

Similarly, we may consider things like

```
red head(0 s 0 s s s 0) .          ***> should be: 0
red tail(0 s 0 s s s 0) .          ***> should be: s 0 s s s 0
red tail(nil 0 s 0 nil s s s 0) . ***> should be: s 0 s s s 0
```

Notice that **NATLIST1** does not include the equations

```
eq head(N) = N .
eq tail(N) = nil .
```

from the module **NATLIST**, because they are not needed! By matching modulo identity, they are actually special cases of the equations

```
eq head(N L) = I .
eq tail(N L) = L .
```

in the module **NATLIST1**. The following test cases illustrate this:

```
red head(s 0) .           ***> should be: s 0
red tail(s 0) .           ***> should be: nil
```

In the first of these, the match θ has $\theta(N) = s\ 0$ and $\theta(L) = nil$.

Comments in OBJ are preceded by `***`, and the OBJ interpreter will ignore all text following `***` until the end of the line. Although it is not necessary, in this book we also use `***` to indicate the end of a comment, thus:

```
*** this is a comment ***
```

Comments preceded by `***>` are treated in a special way by the OBJ interpreter; it will print such a comment onto the screen when it reads it. This is particularly useful when you want OBJ to process a file. Suppose you have a file called `natlist.obj` containing the module **NATLIST1** above and the command

```
red head(s 0) .           ***> should be: s 0
```

This file can be read in to OBJ by typing the command

```
in natlist
```

The following is what appears on the screen as OBJ reads the file:

```
OBJ> in natlist
==========================================
obj NATLIST1
```

```
==========================================
reduce in NATLIST1 : head s 0
rewrites: 1
result Nat: s 0
==========================================
***> should be: s 0
OBJ>
```

1.6.2 Denotational semantics for objects

Because we are representing programs as terms, term rewriting gives an *operational semantics* for programs, by providing an algorithm that computes the result of running a program. In contrast, a *denotational* semantics should give a precise mathematical meaning to a program in a way that is as conceptually clear and simple as possible, and that supports proving properties of programs. Because OBJ is rigorously based upon equational logic, we can directly use the model theory of this logic to get a denotational semantics, so that complex formalisms like Scott-Strachey semantics and Hoare logics are not needed. Because the models of equational logic are algebras, we get an algebraic semantics, in the same sense as the algebraic theory of abstract data types [24, 25].

We will use so-called *initial algebra semantics* to give a denotation for OBJ objects [12, 15, 24]. The basic concept can be explained as follows (after [6]):

Definition 18 Given a signature Σ and a set E of Σ-equations, a Σ-algebra A is **initial** iff it satisfies the following properties:

1. **no junk:** every element of A can be represented by some Σ-term; and
2. **no confusion:** every ground Σ-equation true of A can be proved from the equations in E.

To make the context explicit, we may call such an algebra an **initial** (Σ, E)-**algebra**. □

In order to use initial algebras for denotations, we need existence and uniqueness theorems. The following gives an exact statement of these; the intuitive meaning of two algebras being "isomorphic" is that they are "essentially the same," except that perhaps their elements may have different names (we do not give the precise definition here, but it may be found in many places, e.g., [15]).

Theorem 19 Given any signature Σ and set E of Σ-equations, there is an initial (Σ, E)-algebra. Furthermore, any two initial (Σ, E)-algebras are isomorphic. □

The second assertion allows us to speak of "the" initial algebra. The initial algebra is the "standard" or "most representative" denotation for a set of Σ-equations; i.e., it serves as a representation independent standard of comparison for correctness. Thus, it makes sense to let the denotation of a given OBJ object with signature Σ and equations E be the class of all initial (Σ, E)-algebras.

Under certain conditions on E, the operational rewriting semantics agrees with the denotational initial algebra semantics, in the sense that the reduced terms form an initial algebra (this result was shown in [13], and is explained in detail in [15]). To make this remark precise, we first define some of the most fundamental concepts in term rewriting:

Definition 20 A term rewriting system is **Church-Rosser** iff whenever $t \stackrel{*}{\Rightarrow} t_1$ and $t \stackrel{*}{\Rightarrow} t_2$, there is some term t_0 such that $t_1 \stackrel{*}{\Rightarrow} t_0$ and $t_2 \stackrel{*}{\Rightarrow} t_0$. A term rewriting system is **terminating** iff there are no infinite sequences of proper rewrites,

$$t_0 \Rightarrow t_1 \Rightarrow \ldots \Rightarrow t_n \Rightarrow \ldots$$

A term rewriting system is **canonical** iff it is Church-Rosser and terminating. □

The result is now the following:

Theorem 21 If a given set E of Σ-equations is canonical as a term rewriting system, then every Σ-term has a unique reduced form, and the reduced Σ-terms constitute an initial (Σ, E)-algebra. These terms are also called **canonical** terms. We let $[\![t]\!]$ denote the reduced form of t, or $[\![t]\!]_\Sigma$ if we need to make the signature involved explicit. □

Because OBJ is based on order sorted algebra, it is important to note that the above result extends to that case. Note that there is no reason why theories should be canonical as term rewriting systems; even in the case of objects, non-canonicity does not mean that everything fails; for example, every reduction is still a correct equational proof. However, experience shows that objects are almost always canonical.

A closely related concern is the equality of terms. OBJ3's *polymorphic equality* and *polymorphic inequality* operations have the syntactic forms

```
op _==_  : S S -> Bool .
op _=/=_ : S S -> Bool .
```

for each currently available sort `S`. The operation `==` is implemented as follows: the two terms are each reduced to a normal form; if the two normal forms are identical, then the value `true` is returned; and otherwise, the value `false` is returned. The operation `=/=` is the negation of `==`. The following result says that this implementation is correct:

Theorem 22 If the equations currently available are canonical as a term rewriting system, then `_==_` returns `true` iff the two arguments represent the same value in an initial algebra, and returns `false` otherwise. □

Thus, OBJ checks whether the two terms have the same denotation. OBJ3 also provides operations `===` and `==/=` that test terms for purely *syntactic* identity and non-identity, respectively.

It is worth pointing out that order sorted algebra, and thus OBJ, is a completely general programming formalism, in the sense that any partial computable function can be defined[3], in the sense that given any computable sets and any computable functions among them, if we collect these into a Σ-algebra A, then there is a signature Ω that contains Σ and a set E of Ω-equations such that the (Ω, E)-initial algebra is Σ-isomorphic to A.

1.6.3 The Theorem of Constants

In using OBJ to prove theorems, it is often convenient to introduce constants to stand in place of variables. This is because some theoretical results that support the use of OBJ's term rewriting capability call for using ground terms, whereas the results that we want to prove frequently involve variables. The definition of variables that we have given says that they are actually constants in a supersignature; hence, there is a close mathematical connection between variables and constants that we can exploit. The following result[4] justifies the technique that we will use; although it is well known in logic, it is rarely mentioned in the context of theorem proving.

Theorem 23 (Theorem of Constants) Suppose we are given a signature Σ, a set E of Σ-equations that is canonical as a term rewriting system, and a Σ-equation e of the form $(\forall \Xi)\ t_1 = t_2$. Then e is satisfied by all Σ-models that satisfy E iff $[\![t_1]\!]_{\Sigma\cup\Xi} = [\![t_2]\!]_{\Sigma\cup\Xi}$. Furthermore, even if E is not canonical, e is satisfied by all Σ-models that satisfy E if $[\![t_1]\!]_{\Sigma\cup\Xi} = [\![t_2]\!]_{\Sigma\cup\Xi}$. □

[3] This is an as yet unpublished theorem of Dr. José Meseguer; this result requires order sorted algebra, because the corresponding result for many sorted algebra only gives the total computable functions [3].

[4] The result stated here is actually only a special case, but it is sufficient for the purposes of this book, and the more general result would require us to develop rather a lot of additional machinery.

Here the subscript $\Sigma \cup \Xi$ on $[\![\_]\!]$ indicates that rewriting regards the symbols in Ξ as new constants. But to avoid confusion, we may want to avoid using exactly the same symbols that are in Ξ, and instead use some different constant symbols. For example, if Ξ contains X, Y, Z, then we might declare new constant symbols x, y, z and then replace the old (upper case) variable symbols in our equations by these new (lower case) constants.

Example 24 Suppose we are given the signature $\Sigma^{\texttt{NATEXP}}$ and the equation set E of Example 17, and that we want to prove the following equation e,

$$(\forall X)\ 0 + (0 * X) = 0\ .$$

Then by the Theorem of Constants, if we let Ξ be the signature with just the constant x, and if we show that $[\![0 + (0 * x)]\!]_{\Sigma\cup\Xi} = [\![0]\!]_{\Sigma\cup\Xi}$ then we have shown that any Σ-algebra that satisfied E also satisfies e.

In OBJ3, this proof could be done by executing the following "proof score":

```
obj NATEXPEQ is
  sort Exp .
  op 0   : -> Exp .
  op s_  : Exp -> Exp .
  op _+_ : Exp Exp -> Exp .
  op _*_ : Exp Exp -> Exp .

  vars X Y Z : Exp .
  eq 0 + X = X .
  eq s X + Y = s(X + Y).
  eq 0 * X = 0 .
  eq (s X)* Y = (X * Y)+ X .
endo

open .
op x : -> Exp .
red 0 +(0 * x) == 0 .
close
```

Here "`open`" indicates that any declarations that follow will be added (temporarily) to the previous module; we can also specify the name of the module to be opened by writing, for example,

```
open NATEXPEQ .
```

In this case, we add the new constant `x`. By Theorem 22, the reduction above serves to check that the equation

$$0 + (0 * x) = 0$$

is satisfied by all models of `NATEXPEQ`. After the line "`close`," the module `NATEXPEQ` is returned to its original state. OBJ also allows declarations to be added permanently to a module. This is achieved by the command `openr`, which stands for `open` and `r`emember. All of the declarations made between `openr` and `close` are permanently added to the module, and so will be available the next time the module is opened.

Because OBJ3's reduction mechanism already regards variables in the preceding module as constants, instead of the last four lines above, we could have just written

```
red 0 +(0 * X) == 0 .
```

(However, this simplification is not always available, as we will see later on.) □

1.7 Importing Modules

OBJ allows *importing* previously defined modules, so that their code can be reused. For example, if `FLOAT` is the name of a module defining floating point numbers, then we can write

```
pr FLOAT .
```

to avoid having to redefine floating point numbers every time we want to use them. Placing this statement inside a module `M` imports the module `FLOAT`, so that `M` will have the same meaning as if floating point numbers were defined in it. Furthermore, `FLOAT` will be "shared" among all the modules that import it, as opposed to being regarded as a different copy each time it is imported.

If a module `M` imports a module `M'` that imports a module `M''`, then `M''` is also imported into `M`; that is, "imports" is a *transitive* relation. A given module `M'` can only be imported once into `M`; modules that are multiply imported due to transitivity are considered to be shared.

OBJ3 actually has four different ways to import modules. These are the `protecting`, `extending`, `including`, and `using` modes; the abbreviations `pr`, `ex`, `inc`, and `us` are synonyms for these keywords. The meaning of these four import modes is related to initial algebra semantics, in that an importation of a module `M'` into `M` is:

1. **protecting** iff `M` adds no new data items of sorts from `M'`, and also identifies no old data items of sorts from `M'` (no junk and no confusion);
2. **extending** iff the equations in `M` identify no old data items of sorts from `M'` (no confusion);
3. **including** or **using** if there are no guarantees at all.

OBJ3 exploits these declarations during compilation to implement objects more efficiently; for example, a `protecting` importation allows OBJ to avoid having to recompute whether any new rules must be added to correctly implement rewriting modulo associativity. OBJ3 does not check whether a user's import declarations are correct, because this could require arbitrarily difficult theorem proving. However, the consequences of an incorrect import mode declaration can be serious: there may be incomplete reductions in some cases, and inefficient reductions in others. Also, if an object `A` has a sort `S`, and an object `B` imports `A` and introduces a new subsort `S'` of `S`, then things may not work as you expect, even if mathematically `A` is protected in `B`.

OBJ3 implements an `including` import by incorporation without copying, and in this respect it is similar to `protecting`; if a module is included twice in a given module, only one version is created (if it doesn't already exist) and all references are to the same shared instance. On the other hand, OBJ3 implements a `using` import by copying the imported module's text, and sharing all of the submodules that it imports. If some copied sorts do not have distinct names, or if some copied operations are not uniquely identified by their name and rank, then parsing problems may arise. (For more details on these modes, see [26].)

The import declaration "`including BOOL`" is not meaningful, because a `using` importation that is not an `extending` importation will identify `true` with `false`, which is not only not useful, but also will interfere with the built-in operations `_==_` and `if_then_else_fi`.

For example, the module `NATEXPEQ` of Example 24 is equivalent to the following,

```
obj NATEXPEQ is
  inc NATEXP .

  vars X Y Z : Exp .
  eq 0 + X = X .
```

```
    eq s X + Y = s(X + Y).
    eq 0 * X = 0 .
    eq (s X)* Y = (X * Y)+ X .
  endo
```

which imports the signature defined in the module `NATEXP`; this cannot be a protecting or extending importation, because some terms are identified by the equations that are given.

The module that introduces a given sort often establishes a convention for naming variables of that sort, along with a number of variables for it. The `vars-of` command allows reusing these variables, thus maintaining the conventions. For example,

```
vars-of NATEXPEQ .
```

imports the variable declarations for `X`, `Y`, and `Z` in `NATEXPEQ`.

The first sort mentioned in a module is called its **principal sort**. For example, the principal sort of `NATEXPEQ` is `Exp`, and the principal sort of `BOOL` is `Bool`.

OBJ3 permits redefining any module, just by introducing a new module with the old name; then all future mentions of this name refer to the new definition. This can be very useful in theorem proving; thus, for many theorem proving applications, you may want to replace a built-in module for numbers that is efficient, by another that is less efficient but more logically complete. A warning is issued whenever a module is redefined. Note that redefining a module does not cause the redefinition of modules that have been previously built from it. For example, if we define `A` to be an enrichment of `INT`, then redefine `INT`, and then look at `A`, it will still involve the old definition of `INT`.

`BOOL` is implicitly `protecting` imported into every module, unless an explicit `extending BOOL` declaration is given instead. Usually, it is convenient that `BOOL` has been imported, because conditional equations often make use of the operations that are provided in `BOOL`, such as `==`, `and`, or `not`. But sometimes, especially in applications to theorem proving, it can be inconvenient, because as a theory, `BOOL` is not logically complete. The command

```
set include BOOL off .
```

will cause not importing `BOOL` to become the default. The original default can be restored with the command

```
set include BOOL on .
```

Sometimes we may want to import a copy of a module and at the same time rename its principal sort to something more convenient. For example, the module `QID` of quoted identifiers has principal sort `Id`, and some typical elements are `'A`, `'AA` and `'Z`. Later on we will want to use the quoted identifiers for variables in a programming language, but we want the principal sort to be called `Var` rather than `Id`. The syntax for doing this in OBJ3 is as follows:

```
dfn Var is QID .
```

It should be noted that this is a "protecting" importation.

1.8 Literature

There seems to be no elementary introduction to many sorted general algebra currently in print. A somewhat pedantic but fairly elementary treatment of the unsorted case is given by Henkin [32]. A rather comprehensive treatment at an advanced level is given by Cohn [7], and another is given by Gratzer [29]. The original paper on unsorted general algebra is by Birkhoff from 1935 [5]. Extensions to the many sorted case have been given by Higgins [34] and others, but the approach in this book follows that of Goguen and Meseguer [20], who were the first to prove a completeness theorem for the case where algebras are allowed to have empty carriers; the explicit use of quantifiers also comes from this work. The notation that we use follows [24], and was first developed by Goguen in lectures at the University of Chicago in 1969. An elegant treatment of related material at a somewhat more advanced level is given by the book of Mac Lane and Birkhoff [40], which is unfortunately out of print. A thorough treatment of both many sorted general algebra and OBJ3 is given in [15]. A comprehensive but sophisticated treatment of order sorted algebra is given in [22]. The user's manual for OBJ3 Version 2 is [26].

General algebra has many applications in Computing Science beyond those treated in this book. Some of these are concurrent processing [36], program derivation [4], hardware verification [15], program refinement [37], and computer security [49].

1.9 Exercises

Exercise 1 A *semiring* is a set, say with sort name `Elt`, which has two distinguished elements (say, "`0`" and "`1`"), and two binary operators (say, "`+`" and "`x`"), such that "`+`" is associative and commutative and has identity "`0`", and "`x`" is associative and has identity "`1`", and the following distributivity laws hold for all `a,b,c` of sort `Elt`:

```
a x (b + c)  =  (a x b) + (a x c)
(a + b) x c  =  (a x c) + (b x c) .
```

More concisely, the notion of semiring is specified by the following OBJ theory:

```
th SRNG is sort Elt .
  ops 0 1 : -> Elt .
  op  _+_ : Elt Elt -> Elt [assoc comm prec 4] .
  op  _x_ : Elt Elt -> Elt [assoc prec 3] .
  var A B C : Elt .
  eq  A + 0  =  A .
  eq  A x 1  =  A .
  eq  1 x A  =  A .
  eq  A x (B + C)  =  A x B + A x C .
  eq  (A + B) x C  =  A x C + B x C .
endth
```

We can introduce what we might call "natural multiplication" on semirings by introducing the operator

```
_*_ : Elt Nat -> Elt .
```

and defining it in such a way that `a * n` is the element `a` added to itself `n` times. This is captured by the following equations, where `A : Elt` and `M,N : Nat` :

```
A * 0  =  0 .
A * s N  =  (A * N) + A .
A * (M + N)  =  (A * M) + (A * N) .
```

These equations make use of the following definition of natural numbers:

```
obj NATP is
  sort Nat .
  ops 0 1 2 3 : -> Nat .
  op s_ : Nat -> Nat [prec 1] .
  eq 1 = s 0 .    eq 2 = s 1 .   eq 3 = s 2 .
  op _+_ : Nat Nat -> Nat [assoc comm idr: 0 prec 4] .
  op _*_ : Nat Nat -> Nat [assoc comm prec 3] .
  vars M N : Nat .
  eq  M + s N  =  s(M + N) .
  eq  M * 0  =  0 .
  eq  M * s N  =  M * N + M .
endo
```

Thus, for example, `1 * 3` is `1 + 1 + 1` . Note the overloading of the symbols "`0`" and "`+`" in the left sides of the above equations; these represent the operators from `NATP`, while the symbols in the right sides represent the operators from `SRNG`. This overloading is justified by the similarity between the operations on semirings and the arithmetic operations on numbers.

(a) In a similar vein, we can define "natural exponentiation,"

```
_**_ : Elt Nat -> Elt
```

in such a way that `a ** n` is the element `a` multiplied by itself (using `_x_`) `n` times. That is, fill in the elisions in the last two equations of the following module:

```
th SRNGNAT is pr SRNG .
              pr NATP .
  op  _*_ : Elt Nat -> Elt [prec 3] .
  op  _**_ : Elt Nat -> Elt [prec 2] .
  var A : Elt .
  var M N : Nat .
  eq  A * 0  =  0 .
  eq  A * s N  =  A * N + A .
  eq  A * (M + N)  =  A * M + A * N .
  eq  A ** 0  =  1 .
  eq  A ** s N  =  A ** N x ... .
  eq  A ** (M + N)  =  ... .
endth
```

Use `SRNGNAT` to prove the following, for all `a,b : Elt` and `m : Nat`:

```
a * 1  =  a .
(a + b) * 3  =  a * 3 + b * 3 .
a x (b * 3)  =  (a x b) * 3 .
a * (m * 3)  =  (a * m) * 3 .
a ** (m * 3) =  (a ** m) ** 3 .
```

(b) A commutative semiring is a semiring in which the operation `_x_` is commutative. Write an OBJ theory `CSRNG` that specifies commutative semirings in the same way that `SRNG` specifies semirings. Change the first line of the module `SRNGNAT` to

```
th SRNGNAT is pr CSRNG .
```

Use this module to prove the following, for all `a,b : Elt`:

```
(a x b) ** 3  =  a ** 3 x b ** 3 .
(a + b) ** 3  =  a ** 3  +  (a ** 2 x b) * 3  +
                 (a x b ** 2) * 3  +  b ** 3 .
```

□

Exercise 2 The built in OBJ module `QID` defines a sort `Id` of "quoted identifiers." Terms of sort `Id` are of the form `'A, 'B, ..., 'AA, ...`: i.e., they are strings prefixed with a quote (`'`). The following OBJ module defines a sort of natural number expressions which contain quoted identifiers.

```
obj EXP is pr QID .
  sort Exp .
  subsort Id < Exp .
  op 0 : -> Exp .
  op s_ : Exp -> Exp [prec 1] .
  op _+_ : Exp Exp -> Exp [prec 5] .
  op _*_ : Exp Exp -> Exp [prec 3] .
endo
```

(a) The following module defines an operation

```
subst : Exp Id Exp -> Exp
```

which takes an expression `E1`, a quoted identifier `X` and an expression `E2`, and returns the result of replacing all occurrences of `X` in `E2` by `E1`; i.e., `E1` is substituted for `X` in `E2`. Complete the following module by adding equations to it so that `subst` does in fact behave in the way described above.

```
obj SUBST1 is pr EXP .
  op  subst : Exp Id Exp -> Exp .
  vars E E1 E2 : Exp .
  vars X Y : Id .
  eq  subst(E,X,X)  =  E .
  cq  subst(E,X,Y)  =  Y   if  X =/= Y .
  ...
endo
```

(b) Given an expression `E1` and a quoted identifier `X`, we could define an operation `X := E1 [[_]]`, which, given an expression `E` as input, returns the expression `subst(E1,X,E)` as output. That is,

```
        var E : Exp .
(*)     eq  X := E1 [[E]]  =  subst(E1,X,E) .
```

In fact, we might think of `X := E1` as belonging to a sort of *substitutions*, as in the following module:

```
obj SUBST2 is pr EXP .
  sort Subst .
  op _:=_ : Id Exp -> Subst .
  op _[[_]] : Subst Exp -> Exp .
  vars E E1 E2 : Exp .
  vars X Y : Id .
  var S : Subst .
  eq ...
  ...
endo
```

Complete the module by adding equations so that equation `(*)` is true (without using `subst`!).

(c) We might even apply sequences of substitutions to a term. The following module defines a sort of sequences of substitution:

```
obj SUBST3 is pr EXP .
  sort Subst .
  op skip : -> Subst .
  op _:=_ : Id Exp -> Subst .
  op _;_ : Subst Subst -> Subst [assoc id: skip] .
  op _[[_]] : Subst Exp -> Exp .
  vars ... .
  eq (S ; X := E)[[X]] = ... .
  ...
endo
```

Complete the definition of the module by adding equations so that, for example, the following equation holds:

```
vars E E1 E2 : Exp .
eq ('X := E1 ; 'Y := E2)[[E]] =
        subst(E1,'X,subst(E2,'Y,E)) .
```

In general, a substitution of the form `s1 ; s2` substitutes first according to `s2` and then according to `s1`. This order may seem strange, but the reason for choosing this order should become clear in the following chapter, where we give a semantics for assignment in programming languages.

(d) Find substitutions `S1`, `S2`, `S3` and `S4` such that

```
S1 [[ 'X + s 'Y ]]  =  S2 [[ ('U * 'V) + 'U ]] .
S3 [[ ('X * s 'X) + s 'Y ]]  =  S4 [[ ('U * 'Y) + 'U ]] .
```

□

The exercise below makes use of the notion of homomorphism, which consists of a family of functions from the carriers of one algebra to the carriers of another, which "preserves the algebraic structure" in a sense made precise by the following definition.

Definition 25 Given two Σ-algebras A and B, a **Σ-homomorphism** $h : A \rightarrow B$ is a family of functions $h_s : A_s \rightarrow B_s$ for each sort $s \in S$, such that the following properties hold:

- for each constant operation $\sigma \in \Sigma_{[],s}$, $h_s(\sigma_A) = \sigma_B$;
- for each operation $\sigma \in \Sigma_{w,s}$ with $w = s_1 \ldots s_n$,

$$h_s(\sigma_A(a_1,\ldots,a_n)) \;=\; \sigma_B(h_{s_1}(a_1),\ldots,h_{s_n}(a_n))$$

  for all $a_i \in A_i$, $i = 1 \ldots n$.

□

Thus, a homomorphism can be thought of as interpreting each operation of the algebra A as the corresponding operation of the algebra B.

Exercise 3 The data type of binary trees over the natural numbers is defined by the following OBJ module:

```
obj BTREE is sort BTree .
  pr NAT .
  op tip_ : Nat -> BTree .
  op _++_ : BTree BTree -> BTree .
endo
```

Let BT be T_Σ, the initial Σ-algebra, where Σ is the signature of **BTREE**.

(a) Show that the identity function $id : BT \to BT$ is a homomorphism. (More precisely, we should say that the family of identity functions

$$\begin{aligned} id_{\texttt{BTree}} &: BT_{\texttt{BTree}} \to BT_{\texttt{BTree}} \\ id_{\texttt{Nat}} &: BT_{\texttt{Nat}} \to BT_{\texttt{Nat}} \end{aligned}$$

is a Σ-homomorphism.)

(b) Further examples of Σ-homomorphisms are given by the following OBJ module, which introduces operations to sum and count the tips of a tree:

```
obj HOMS is pr BTREE .
  ops h1 h2 : Btree -> Nat .
  var N : Nat .
  vars X Y : BTree .
  eq  h1(tip N)  =  N .
  eq  h1(X ++ Y)  =  h1(X) + h1(Y) .
  eq  h2(tip N)  =  1 .
  eq  h2(X ++ Y)  =  h2(X) + h2(Y) .
endo
```

Both of these operations can be thought of as Σ-homomorphisms from BT to some other "target" algebra; in each case, state what the target algebra is.

(c) Initial Σ-algebras enjoy the property that there is exactly one Σ-homomorphism from the initial algebra to any other Σ-algebra (indeed, this is the formal definition of "initial"; diligent readers may prove for themselves that term algebras are initial by induction on terms: see Section 3.3 of Chapter 3). This provides a means of proving functions equal: if they are both homomorphisms from an initial Σ-algebra to the same Σ-algebra, then they must both be equal to the unique homomorphism from the initial algebra to that target algebra. Consider, for example, the functions **h3** and **h4**, defined as follows:

```
open HOMS .
ops h3 h4 : BTree -> Nat .
op inc : BTree -> BTree .
var N : Nat .
vars X Y : BTree .
```

```
eq  inc(tip N)  =  tip(N + 1) .
eq  inc(X ++ Y)  =  inc(X) ++ inc(Y) .
eq  h3(X)  =  h1(inc(X)) .
eq  h4(X)  =  h1(X) + h2(X) .
close
```

Use initiality of BT to show that `h3` and `h4` are equal; that is, show that they are both Σ-homomorphisms from BT to the same target Σ-algebra.

□

2 Stores, Variables, Values, and Assignment

We begin our discussion of Algebraic Denotational Semantics with an examination of the single feature that characterises imperative programming languages: the assignment of values to variables. Ensuing chapters present the syntax and semantics of various other features found in programming languages, but the semantics of each of these features is based very squarely on the semantics of assignment. We intend to use this semantics to prove properties of programs, so we require a simple and tractable semantics that will allow us to prove such properties with a minimum of effort. For this reason, it is important to formulate the semantics of assignment as simply and elegantly as possible. However, we approach this formulation by a roundabout route. The key concept in Algebraic Denotational Semantics is that of a *store*: an abstract entity which associates integer values with the variables of our programming language. The first section presents a characterisation of stores which has been simplified to illustrate clearly the essential features of assignment. Section 2.2 then presents the characterisation of stores that we use in the remainder of the book, and uses this to formulate the semantics of a basic programming language whose syntax consists solely of variables, expressions and assignment.

2.1 Stores, Variables, and Values

Let us begin by examining the basic concept of storage that must underlie any imperative programming language. In this section we do not discuss a programming language *per se*, but we describe a class of models for a very basic form of computation based upon assignment to variables.

Intuitively, the values assigned to variables are held in a *store*, and programs modify stores by updating the values associated with the variables of the programming language. We can give this a precise algebraic semantics with a single OBJ module. This module describes abstract properties of the association of values to variables. It is a *theory* of storage that can be satisfied by a great variety of actual storage mechanisms, such as disks, caches, hash tables, and so on. This is important because we do not want our semantics to be tied to any particular form of implementation. The semantics of programs should be independent of the details of the machine on which they are executed.

First of all, we require a sort for variables that can be used in a programming language. Let us assume for the moment that we have such a sort, say `Var`. For simplicity, we assume that all variables take integer values. These values are held in a store, and we require some means of accessing the value that a store associates with a given variable. That is, we require an operation

```
_[[_]]  : Store Var -> Int
```

so that for any store `S` and variable `X`, `S[[X]]` denotes the integer value that `S` associates with `X`. (Square brackets are treated as special characters by OBJ3, which is why in this case we do not need to put spaces between the mixfix operator and its arguments, i.e., we can write `S[[X]]` instead of `S [[ X ]]`).

We also require some means of changing the value that a store associates with a given variable, for this will be the effect of an assignment in our programming language. In order to illustrate the concepts involved, we assume here that the only form of assignment is the assignment of the value of one variable to another; in the following section we describe a more general and realistic form of assignment. For the present, we content ourselves with an operation

```
_;_:=_  : Store Var Var -> Store .
```

Thus, given a store `S`, and variables `X` and `Y`, we can construct a new store

```
S ; X := Y .
```

We want to specify that this "updated" store differs from the original store `S` only in the value that it associates with the variable `X`; that is, we want to specify that the value of `X` in the updated store is the old value of `Y` (i.e., the value that `S` associates with `Y`) and that the value in the updated store for any variable other than `X` is the same as its value in `S`. We can make this precise by means of two equations. First, we say that the new value of `X` is the old value of `Y` with the following OBJ equation:

```
eq   S ; X := Y [[X]]  =  S[[Y]] .
```

and then, with the following conditional equation, we say that the values of all other variables are unchanged:

```
cq   S ; X := Y [[Z]]  =  S[[Z]]   if  X =/= Z .
```

This is exactly what our intuitions tell us the operational semantics of assignment should be, though it should be stressed that we are talking about models of assignment, rather than about assignment as a feature of a programming language.

This discussion of stores is formalised by the OBJ module given below, which presents a *theory* of stores, and therefore characterises a class of models.

```
th STORE is
  pr ZZ .
  dfn Var is QID .
  sort Store .
  op  _[[_]] : Store Var -> Int .
  op  _;_:=_ : Store Var Var -> Store .
  vars X Y Z : Var .
  var  S : Store .
  eq  S ; X := Y [[X]]  =  S[[Y]] .
  cq  S ; X := Y [[Z]]  =  S[[Z]]   if  X =/= Z .
endth
```

The sort of integers is imported from the module ZZ, which extends OBJ's built in integers with an equality predicate, "is", and some equations, such as distributivity of multiplication over addition, which we will need later on for doing proofs. The code for the module ZZ is given in Appendix A. The second line of the definition of STORE defines the sort Var to be OBJ's built in sort of "quoted identifiers". These quoted identifiers have the form 'A, 'B, ...,'Z, 'AA, ... Although the prefixed quotation mark does not, of course, appear in the variables of ordinary programming languages, it is very useful for distinguishing variables at the programming language level from variables in the language (usually OBJ) that we use to reason about programs. Remember that Var is a sort, which we shall use in following chapters to represent the variables of a programming language, while "var" is an OBJ keyword: the declaration

```
var X : Var .
```

declares X to be an OBJ variable which ranges over Variables. To emphasise the distinction between the sort Var and OBJ variables, we often refer to elements of sort Var as "program variables."

We might, in fact, view the module STORE as specifying a simple programming language, and we give an example below of a program written in this language. STORE also defines the language's semantics, in that it specifies how the constructs of the language act upon, or modify, stores (in this case, there is only one construct, the assignment). The beauty of the definition is that the only restriction imposed on the sort Store is that stores associate integer values with program variables, in a way that can be modified by assignments. Any implementation of stores that satisfies this, fairly minimal, requirement is acceptable.

Even with the very limited resources of this language, we can make, and prove, assertions about programs. Of course, these programs will not be terribly interesting, but we can, for example, write a program that swaps the values of two variables `'X` and `'Y`, assigning the value of `'X` to `'Y` and the value of `'Y` to `'X`. That is, given any store, `S`, we can construct a new store, `swap(S)`, with the values of `'X` and `'Y` interchanged. Our program, then, must satisfy the following sentence:

```
(∀ S : Store)  swap(S)[['X]] = S[['Y]]   and
               swap(S)[['Y]] = S[['X]] .
```

This is a *specification* of the program `swap`, and once we have found a suitable program, it should be possible to prove that it satisfies this specification, using the equations of the module `STORE`. The standard definition of `swap`, together with a proof of its correctness is given below:

```
open STORE .
op swap : Store -> Store .
eq swap(S)  =  S ; 'T := 'X ; 'X := 'Y ; 'Y := 'T .

red swap(S)[['X]] .   ***> should be: S[['Y]]
red swap(S)[['Y]] .   ***> should be: S[['X]]
close
```

The use of the (OBJ) variable `S` in the above reductions guarantees that the equalities hold for *all* stores: after all, the purpose of the OBJ variable declaration

```
var S : Store .
```

is to represent an arbitrary store. Thus we conclude that

```
swap(S)[['X]]  =  S[['Y]]
swap(S)[['Y]]  =  S[['X]]
```

for all `S` of sort `Store`, as desired.

When you reduce a term which contains a variable, OBJ responds with

```
Warning: in a reduction the term contains a variable.
```

This warning can be ignored, as OBJ performs the reduction nevertheless. An alternative way to prove a statement with a universal quantification involves declaring a new *constant* operator. For example, the following OBJ score, in which a new constant operator `s : -> Store` is declared, is an alternative way of proving the correctness of `swap`:

```
open STORE .
op swap : Store -> Store .
eq swap(S)  =  S ; 'T := 'X ; 'X := 'Y ; 'Y := 'T .
op s : -> Store .
red swap(s)[['X]] .  ***> should be: s[['Y]]
red swap(s)[['Y]] .  ***> should be: s[['X]]
close
```

The validity of this method of proving universally quantified statements is a consequence of the Theorem of Constants, as discussed in Section 1.6.3 above, and this is the method that we use in the remainder of this book. However, there are cases involving the use of OBJ's built-in inequality (=/=) where we should be very careful in applying the Theorem of Constants: such cases arise, for example, in the discussion in Chapter 7 of procedures that take program variables as parameters, so it is worthwhile to understand what could go wrong. This is the subject of the following subsection.

2.1.1 OBJ's built-in inequality

Suppose we wish to prove that `swap` does not change the values of any variables other than `'X`, `'Y` and `'T`. We might specify this property with the following sentence:

```
(∀ S : Store)(∀ Z : Var)
     Z ≠ 'X and Z ≠ 'Y and Z ≠ 'T
     ⇒  swap(S)[[Z]] = S[[Z]] .
```

Proving this amounts to proving that the following conditional equation follows from the equations of the module `STORE` and the definition of `swap`:

```
(∀ S : Store)(∀ Z : Var)
     swap(S)[[Z]] = S[[Z]]
       if Z =/= 'X and Z =/= 'Y and Z =/= 'T .
```

In order to prove this, we first introduce new constants for the universal quantifications:

```
op  s : -> Store .
op  z : -> Var .
```

Now, rewriting `swap(s)[[z]]` gives

```
s ; 'T := 'X ; 'X := 'Y ; 'Y := 'T [[z]]
```

by the definition of `swap`. We can only proceed by applying one of the two equations of `STORE`: which one can be applied depends on whether or not `'Y` is equal to `z`. If we *assume* that `z` is different from `'X`, `'Y` and `'T`, then we can proceed as follows:

```
     swap(s)[[z]]
=
     s ; 'T := 'X ; 'X := 'Y ; 'Y := 'T [[z]]
=          { assumption: z =/= 'Y }
     s ; 'T := 'X ; 'X := 'Y [[z]]
=          { assumption: z =/= 'X }
     s ; 'T := 'X [[z]]
=          { assumption: z =/= 'T }
     s[[z]]
```

This shows that `swap(s)[[z]] = s[[z]]` if `z =/= 'X` and `z =/= 'Y` and `z =/= 'T`, which is exactly what we wanted.

However, let us look more closely at the last equality in the above proof. Given the term `s ; 'T := 'X [[z]]`, the equation

```
eq  S ; X := Y [[X]]  =  S[[Y]] .
```

cannot be applied, because that would require matching the OBJ variable `X` to both `'T` and `z`. The only other equation is the conditional equation

```
cq  S ; X := Y [[Z]]  =  S[[Z]]    if  X =/= Z .
```

This can be applied only if the condition is satisfied when `X` is matched to `'T` and `Z` is matched to `z`, i.e. if `'T =/= z`. Section 1.6.2 explained that OBJ evaluates terms of the form `T1 =/= T2` by evaluating the left and right sides as far as possible and then comparing the results: if the results are identical, then `T1 =/= T2` gives the result `false`, and otherwise it gives the result `true`. In this example, `'T` and `z` cannot be reduced any further, and they are not identical. Therefore `'T =/= z` gives the result `true`, and the conditional equation is applied, giving:

```
s ; 'T := 'X [[z]]  =  s[[z]] .
```

Note that OBJ applies the conditional equation even without our assumption that `'T =/= z`. When we extend a signature with new constants to play the rôle of universally quantified variables, these new constants are automatically different from any other terms over the signature.

This is what we wanted in the above example, but now consider the following OBJ score:

```
obj NAT is sort Nat .
  op  0 : -> Nat .
  op  s_ : Nat -> Nat .
endo

open NAT .
op  x : -> Nat .
red  x =/= 0 .
close
```

The reduction of `x =/= 0` gives the result **`true`**, which, by the Theorem of Constants, might seem to prove that

$$(\forall x : \texttt{Nat})\ x \neq 0\ ,$$

which is obviously false. In fact, the Theorem of constants applies to *loose* semantics, i.e., to all models of a specification. The reduction above tells us that `x` and `0` have different normal forms, so the conclusion we should draw from the Theorem of Constants is that there is some model of `NAT` which does not satisfy the equation $(\forall x : \texttt{Nat})\ x = 0$.

The reason why the above reduction does not prove that all numbers are different from 0 lies in the nature of variables. Any variable *ranges over* a specific domain. This means that a variable cannot be equal to any particular element of its domain; and in particular, when we extend a signature Σ with a new constant, that constant is not equal to any given Σ-term. But this also means that we cannot say that a variable is different from any particular element of its domain, because any element of the domain may be substituted for the variable. Yet that is what happens in the above example: we make use of the fact that `x` is different from `0`, even though `0` belongs to the domain that `x` is intended to range over.

The solution to this complication is to examine all of the equations used in a rewriting sequence, and if a term of the form `x =/= t` is used, where `x` is a new constant that plays the rôle of a new variable, then `x =/= t` must be considered to be an assumption about the variable `x`. This is exactly what we did above in proving that `swap` only changed the values of the variables `'X`, `'Y` and `'T`. The assumptions all appear as antecedents in the statement

```
(∀ S : Store)(∀ Z : Var)
     Z ≠ 'X and Z ≠ 'Y and Z ≠ 'T
     ⇒  swap(S)[[Z]] = S[[Z]] .
```

Another way of avoiding this difficulty is just not to use OBJ's built-in equality when proving universally quantified statements, but to define explicitly an equality predicate. For example, we might add an equality predicate `_is_` to the natural numbers as defined above, as follows:

```
obj NAT is sort Nat .
  op  0 : -> Nat .
  op  s_ : Nat -> Nat .
  op  _is_ : Nat Nat -> Bool .
  vars X Y : Nat .
  eq  X is X  =  true .
  eq  s X is s Y  =  X is Y .
  eq  s X is 0  =  false .
  eq  0 is s X  =  false .
endo
```

It is possible to prove that for all ground terms `t` and `t'` of sort `Nat`, the Boolean term `t is t'` always reduces to either `true` or `false`, and that

```
t is t'  =  (t == t') .
```

So `_is_` agrees with `==` for ground terms. Moreover, when we extend signatures with new constants, we do not get 'wrong' answers. For example, in

```
open NAT .
op  x : -> Nat .
red  x is 0 .
close
```

the reduction gives `x is 0` as result, rather than `true` or `false`, so we avoid the contradiction obtained by using OBJ's built in inequality. Note, however, that because we now have terms of sort `Bool` that are neither `true` nor `false`, the module `BOOL` is no longer `protected` when we open `NAT` (cf. Section 1.7). Strictly speaking, we should explicitly state that we are extending `BOOL`:

```
open NAT .
ex BOOL .
```

```
op  x : -> Nat .
red  x is 0 .
close
```

In the following chapters, most of the proofs of program correctness involve reasoning about integer values. To facilitate such reasoning, and to avoid the complications concerning OBJ's built in inequality, the module `ZZ` declares an equality predicate `_is_` on the integers. When we `open` a module to prove some property of a program, we allow ourselves the liberty of omitting the caveat that we are `extending` the module `BOOL`. This does not affect OBJ3's operational semantics.

We might summarise this subsection by saying that reasoning with variables is a subtle process, with some pitfalls for the unwary. The Theorem of Constants states that variables are simply new constants about which nothing is assumed. The above discussion highlights the importance of the clause: "about which nothing is assumed". In particular, we may not assume that a variable, or a new constant which plays the rôle of a universally quantified variable, is equal to, *or different from,* any element of the domain over which the variable ranges. For OBJ, however, new constants are treated in the same way as "old" constants: both are different from all other terms unless the declared equations state otherwise. Thus, as in the last example, the new constant `x` is different from the constant `0`, and although we intend `x` to play the rôle of a variable, there is no way to tell OBJ that it is meant to be a variable. And so the command

```
red  x =/= 0 .
```

gives the result `true`.

These complications will only concern us in Chapter 7, where we consider procedures which take parameters of sort `Var`. Proving correctness of such procedures involves adding new constants to represent the parameter variables. Because these new constants are different from any other term of sort `Var`, the conditional equation

```
cq  S ; X := Y [[Z]]  =  S[[Z]]    if  X =/= Z .
```

might be applied when it should not be, as in the examples above. It is interesting to note that the discussion of variables in this section actually corresponds to the well-known guidelines for writing parameterised procedures that state that "global" variables used in the body of a procedure should not be passed as parameters to that procedure (see Section 7.1.2).

2.2 Assignment

The previous section characterised a simple form of assignment. Using that characterisation, we saw that we could write programs like `swap` by defining their effect on stores. But we did not define a programming language, and we considered only those assignments where a variable takes the value of another variable. This section presents the syntax of a basic programming language with a more general assignment, and gives it a semantics, again by describing its effects on stores. The language we describe is exceptionally simple: its only feature is assignment. The remainder of this book extends this language with many features, such as sequential composition, while-loops and arrays; but the semantics of each extension will be based on that of assignment, which is why we consider assignment first. Assignment is the basis of imperative programs.

Our assignment operation will allow us to write programs such as

```
'X := 2 * 'Y + 'X .
```

But before we can declare `_:=_` as an operation, we have to define a sort for expressions like `2 * 'Y + 'X`, which "look like" integers, but include program variables; they are like polynomials over the integers, but without axioms such as associativity of addition, etc. The syntax of expressions is defined by the following OBJ module, which says that an expression may be a program variable or an integer, or the sum, product or difference of two expressions:

```
obj EXP is pr ZZ .
  dfn Var is QID .
  sort  Exp .
  subsorts  Var Int < Exp .
  op  _+_  : Exp Exp -> Exp [prec 10] .
  op  _*_  : Exp Exp -> Exp [prec 8] .
  op  _-_  : Exp Exp -> Exp [prec 10] .
  op   -_  : Exp -> Exp [prec 1] .
endo
```

As in the previous section, the integers are imported from the module `ZZ`, and we use the sort of quoted identifiers for program variables.

We can now define the syntax of our programs with the following simple module, since for the moment we are interested in only one feature: assignment.

```
obj BPGM is pr EXP .
  sort BPgm .
  op  _:=_  : Var Exp -> BPgm [prec 20] .
endo
```

This completes the syntax of our programming language; we turn now to its semantics.

In order to give a semantics to this language, we define a theory of storage. The stores we consider here are much the same as those of the previous section: the only essential differences are that we introduce a more general model of assignment, and that we declare a particular store, `initial`, which represents, if you like, the state of an abstract computing machine just after it is plugged in and switched on. As before, we require stores to have an operation

```
op  _[[_]] : Store Var -> Int .
```

and (though this is an arbitrary choice) we shall say that in the initial state, the value associated with each program variable is `0`; that is, for all program variables, `X`,

```
initial [[X]]  =  0 .
```

An expression such as `2 * 'X + 'Y` is intended to have an integer value. Given an operation which assigns integer values to variables, we can assign integer values to any expression which contains variables. For example, if we assign the value `5` to `'X` and `2 to 'Y`, then the expression `2 * 'X + 'Y` should denote the value

```
2 * 5 + 2  =  12 .
```

Thus, we want to extend the operation `_[[_]]` to

```
op  _[[_]] : Store Exp -> Int .
```

which can be done by adding the following equations, where `S` is an OBJ variable ranging over stores, and `E1` and `E2` are OBJ variables ranging over expressions:

```
eq  S[[E1 + E2]]  =  (S[[E1]]) + (S[[E2]]) .
eq  S[[E1 * E2]]  =  (S[[E1]]) * (S[[E2]]) .
```

And similarly for the other operations on expressions. Because expressions in our language can also be integers, we need the equation

```
eq  S[[I]]  =  I .
```

where I is an OBJ variable ranging over integers. This equation states that the value represented by an integer is the integer itself; it does not depend upon the store.

To complete the semantics of our programming language, we need to state how stores are modified by assignment. In the previous chapter, we declared an operation

```
op  (_;_:=_) : Store Var Var -> Store .
```

We now replace this with an operation

```
op  _;_ : Store BPgm -> Store .
```

Hence, given a store S, a program variable X, and an expression E, we can form the basic program X := E , and using the above operation, the store S ; X := E . This store should differ from S only in the value that it assigns to the variable X, which should be S[[E]] , the value of E. That is, for any program variable Y,

```
eq  S ; X := E [[X]]  =  S[[E]] .
cq  S ; X := E [[Y]]  =  S[[Y]]   if X =/= Y .
```

This gives a complete semantics for our basic programming language. Its syntax uses two sorts, Exp and BPgm; the semantics of expressions was given by stating how the value of an expression depended on the values of the variables that occur in that expression; and the semantics of programs was given by stating how each syntactic construct of the language (i.e., assignment) modifies the values that stores associate with variables. Thus, putting it all together, we have the following characterisation of stores, expressions and programs:

```
th STORE is pr BPGM .
  sort Store .
  op initial : -> Store .
  op  _[[_]] : Store Exp -> Int [prec 65] .
  op      _;_ : Store BPgm -> Store [prec 60] .
  var  S : Store .
  vars E1 E2 : Exp .
  vars X Y : Var .
  var  I : Int .
  eq  initial [[X]]  =  0 .
  eq  S[[E1 + E2]]  =  (S[[E1]]) + (S[[E2]]) .
  eq  S[[E1 * E2]]  =  (S[[E1]]) * (S[[E2]]) .
```

```
    eq  S[[E1 - E2]]  =  (S[[E1]]) - (S[[E2]]) .
    eq  S[[- E1]]  =  -(S[[E1]]) .
    eq  S[[I]]  =  I .
    eq  S ; X := E1 [[X]]  =  S[[E1]] .
    cq  S ; X := E1 [[Y]]  =  S[[Y]]   if X =/= Y .
  endth
```

Note that whereas the syntax of the language is defined by means of *object* modules, the semantics of the language is defined by means of a *theory* of stores. This is because the syntax of the language is fixed by the operations declared in the modules **EXP** and **BPGM**, whereas a store can be anything that has the operations declared in the module **STORE** and satisfies the equations in that module.

The only programs that we can write in the basic programming language are single assignments, but we can combine these to define more complex operations mapping stores to stores. For example, the **swap** operation and its proof of correctness are much the same as in the previous section:

```
open STORE .
op swap : Store -> Store .
eq swap(S)  =  S ; 'T := 'X ; 'X := 'Y ; 'Y := 'T .
op s : -> Store .
red swap(s)[['X]] .  ***> should be: s[['Y]]
red swap(s)[['Y]] .  ***> should be: s[['X]]
red (swap(s)[['X]]) is (s[['Y]]) .
***> should be: true
red (swap(s)[['Y]]) is (s[['X]]) .
***> should be: true
close
```

The only difference is that the operation `_;_:=_` has here been decomposed into two operations, `_;_` and `_:=_`. Note that the last two reductions provide an alternative way of proving the correctness of swap, since the operation `_is_` is the same as equality on the integers.

The following chapters extend the semantics of assignment to other programming language constructs.

2.3 Exercises

Exercise 4 Consider the following OBJ proof score:

```
open STORE .
op  s : -> Store .
red (s ; 'X := 'Y [['X]]) == (s ; 'X := 'Y [['Y]]) .
close
```

By the Theorem of Constants, what does this prove? □

Exercise 5 In the same vein as the `swap` example above, specify, write and prove correct a program which "rotates" the values of three variables `'X`, `'Y` and `'Z`: that is, `'X` gets the value of `'Y`, `'Y` gets the value of `'Z`, and `'Z` gets the value of `'X`. □

Exercise 6 Show that for all stores `S`,

```
S[['X *('Y + 'Z)]]  =  S[['X * 'Y + 'X * 'Z]] .
```

□

Exercise 7 Consider the following OBJ declarations:

```
open STORE .
ops p1 p2 : Store -> Store .
eq  p1(S)  =  S ; 'Y := 'X + 'Y ; 'Z := 'Y + 'Z .
eq  p2(S)  =  S ; 'Z := 'Y + 'Z ; 'Z := 'X + 'Z .
close
```

(a) Show that for all `S` of sort `Store`,

```
p1(S)[['Z]]  =  p2(S)[['Z]] .
```

(b) Is it the case that for all `S` of sort `Store`, the equation

```
p1(S)[['Y]]  =  p2(S)[['Y]]
```

holds? Give a proof or a counterexample (and prove that it is a counterexample).

□

Exercise 8 The module `EXP` overloads the integer operations `+`, `*`, etc. What sorts can the following expressions have?

```
23 + 5
23 + 'X * 2 .
```

□

Exercise 9 Prove that the following program `swap1` also satisfies the specification of `swap`:

```
open STORE .
op  swap1 : Store -> Store .
eq  swap1(S) =
    S ; 'X := 'X + 'Y ; 'Y := 'X - 'Y ; 'X := 'X - 'Y .
close
```

□

Exercise 10 A major motivation for using algebra is that it is supposed to make it easier to reason about programs. Evaluate this claim with the evidence available at this point. □

3 Composition and Conditionals

In this chapter, we extend the syntax of programs by giving syntactic constructs for sequential composition and for conditionals. We also extend the semantics of the programming language by describing the effects that each of these constructs has on stores. Extending the syntax of programs is straightforward: we need only declare the desired operations; the semantics of the language is extended by giving equations that capture our intuitions about the behaviour of the syntactic constructs. As in the previous chapter, properties of programs may be proved by rewriting; in Section 3.3 below, we introduce a principle of structural induction over programs which allows us to prove properties of all programs, for example that all programs consisting of assignments, sequential composition and conditionals terminate.

To emphasise that we are extending the basic programming language with new constructs, we introduce a new sort, `Pgm`, which contains all the basic programs (i.e., assignments), and all of the extensions that we add here and in subsequent chapters. For example, let us extend our language straight away with a program, `skip`, whose intended semantics is that it does nothing: it leaves stores unaltered.

```
obj PGM is pr BPGM .
  sort Pgm .
  subsort BPgm < Pgm .
  op  skip : -> Pgm .
endo
```

Because of the subsort relation `BPgm < Pgm` , a program in this extended language is either a basic program, or the "do nothing" program, `skip`.

Having extended the syntax of programs, we now extend their semantics. The theory of stores given in the previous chapter posited an operation

```
_;_ : Store BPgm -> Store ,
```

which was used to describe the effect of a basic program on a store; we extend this operation to one which takes a `Pgm` as its second argument. However, we cannot be sure that the result of the extended operation will always be a store: when we extend the syntax of the programming language, we cannot know *a priori* that the new syntactic construct will always modify stores in a meaningful way. For example, until we have given a semantics to `skip`, we do not know if `initial ; skip` is a meaningful store or not: what should be the value of, say,

```
initial ; skip [['X]] ?
```

For this reason, just as we introduced `Pgm` as a supersort of `BPgm`, we introduce a new sort `EStore` as a supersort of `Store`, and overload the `_;_` operator with the following declaration:

```
op  _;_ : EStore Pgm -> EStore .
```

"`EStore`" stands for "Error Store": the intention is that `EStore` contains all the "well-defined" values of sort `Store`, plus some values that we are not interested in, which we might think of as error states. The concept of error states, however, only gains significance in Chapter 5, where we discuss the possibility of non-terminating loops.

The extension of stores, together with an equation which captures the intended semantics of `skip`, is given by the following OBJ module:

```
obj SEM is pr STORE .
           pr PGM .
  sort EStore .
  subsort  Store < EStore .
  op _;_ : EStore Pgm -> EStore [prec 60] .
  var S : Store .
  eq  S ; skip  =  S .
endo
```

We use an object module here to indicate that we are not changing our theory of stores, simply extending it to include new features of the programming language. What we are adding is a sort `EStore`, and we intend this to have an initial semantics, while `STORE` keeps its loose semantics. That is, we can think of `EStore` as containing, beside all values of sort `Store`, all the terms of the form `s ; p`, where `s` is some element of sort `Store` from some model of `STORE`, and `p` is a program that does not terminate on `s`. Termination of programs is discussed in Section 3.3 and Chapter 5 below, and the semantics of object modules importing theories is discussed more fully in Appendix A. In fact, there will be no new elements of sort `EStore` until we introduce while-loops in Chapter 5; in particular, we can see from the semantics of `skip` that this extension of the programming language does not in fact generate any new elements of sort `Store` or `EStore`. All of the terms that we can write of sort `EStore` can be rewritten as a term of sort `Store`; for example,

```
initial ; skip  =  initial .
```

This means that a syntactically ill-defined term such as

```
initial ; skip [['X]]
```

(`_[[_]]` requires a term of sort `Store` as its first argument, whereas `initial ; skip` has sort `EStore`), rewrites to a syntactically well-defined term. Thus,

```
initial ; skip [['X]]   =   initial [['X]]
```

and the latter term is syntactically well-defined.

This notion of a term being syntactically well-defined is central to our use of an error supersort `EStore` to handle non-terminating computations. In Appendix C we explain how OBJ extends an order sorted specification with a "retract operation"

```
op r:S'>S : S' -> S .
```

for every subsort relation `S < S'` in the specification, and also adds an equation

```
var X : S .
eq  r:S'>S(X)  =  X .
```

The retract operations can be thought of as signaling potential errors; the added equation states when no such signal is necessary. For example, consider the command

```
red  initial ; skip [['X]] .
```

OBJ will insert a retract to make the term well defined:

```
(r:EStore>Store(initial ; skip))[['X]] .
```

The equation defining the semantics of `skip` can be applied to the retract's argument, yielding

```
(r:EStore>Store(initial))[['X]] .
```

And now the added equation can be applied to remove the retract, to give

```
initial [['X]]
```

which further reduces to `0`.

This point is further discussed in Section 3.3 and Chapter 5 below, where we discuss the notions of terminating and non-terminating programs.

3.1 Sequential Composition

All that is needed to extend the syntax of programs with sequential composition is to decide upon a notation. We will write `P1 ; P2` for the sequential composition of programs `P1` and `P2`. This notation is fixed in the following module:

```
obj PGM1 is ex PGM .
  op _;_ : Pgm Pgm -> Pgm [assoc prec 50] .
endo
```

Note the use of `ex` in the first line of this module: it indicates that the sort of programs is being extended. Note also that sequential composition is declared to be an associative operation. Strictly speaking, associativity is a *semantic*, and not a *syntactic* property of programs. We declare composition to be associative for convenience, to avoid the need to add disambiguating parentheses in expressions such as:

```
'T := 'X ; 'X := 'Y ; 'Y := 'T .
```

However, this semantic property of composition is justified in that whichever way we parenthesise the above program, its effect upon a store will always be the same (see Exercise 15).

As for the semantics of sequential composition, we need only state how a composite program `P1 ; P2` modifies a store: the obvious way is first to let `P1` modify the store, and then let `P2` modify the resulting store. This is stated by the equation in the following module, which gives the semantics for the language extended with sequential composition.

```
obj SEM1 is pr SEM .
            pr PGM1 .
  var  S : Store .
  vars P1 P2 : Pgm .
  eq  S ; (P1 ; P2)  =  (S ; P1) ; P2 .
endo
```

This is just as simple as you could wish. The similarity of the composition rule to an equation for associativity means that we can miss out parentheses in an expression such as

```
initial ; 'T := 'X ; 'X := 'Y ; 'Y := 'T ,
```

since all possible ways of parenthesising the above expression give equal results. (However, the OBJ parser does not know this and will warn that such a term is ambiguous: this warning can be ignored.)

We use `obj` and `endo` in `SEM1` for the same reason they were used in `SEM`: we are not changing our theory of stores, because any abstract machine that can execute assignments (i.e., any model of `STORE`) can be extended to a machine that executes sequences of assignments. How to do this is described by the equation in `SEM1`. Similar remarks apply to our use of an object module to define the semantics of conditionals in the following section.

3.2 Conditionals

Before we can introduce an operation to allow us to write conditional programs such as

```
if 0 < 'X then 'Z := 'X else 'Z := - 'X fi ,
```

we need to define the syntax of *tests*, expressions such as `0 < 'X`, which look like boolean expressions but which may contain program variables. The following module defines the sort `Tst` of such expressions.

```
obj TST is pr EXP .
  sort Tst .
  subsort  Bool < Tst .

  op     _<_ : Exp Exp -> Tst [prec 15] .
  op    _<=_ : Exp Exp -> Tst [prec 15] .
  op    _is_ : Exp Exp -> Tst [prec 15] .

  op    not_ : Tst -> Tst [prec 1] .
  op   _and_ : Tst Tst -> Tst [prec 20] .
  op    _or_ : Tst Tst -> Tst [prec 25] .
endo
```

The subsort relation, `Bool < Tst` , means that OBJ's built in boolean values, `true` and `false`, are also tests (recall that the module `BOOL` is implicitly imported in all OBJ modules, unless it is explicitly excluded). The semantics of tests is defined analogously to the semantics of expressions: the meaning of an operation on tests is its corresponding boolean-valued operation:

```
obj SEMTST is pr SEM1 .
              pr TST .
  op  _[[_]] : Store Tst -> Bool .
  var S : Store .
  vars E1 E2 : Exp .
  vars T1 T2 : Tst .
  var  B : Bool .
  eq  S[[E1 < E2]]     =  (S[[E1]]) < (S[[E2]]) .
  eq  S[[E1 <= E2]]    =  (S[[E1]]) <= (S[[E2]]) .
  eq  S[[E1 is E2]]    =  (S[[E1]]) is (S[[E2]]) .
  eq  S[[T1 or T2]]    =  (S[[T1]]) or (S[[T2]]) .
  eq  S[[T1 and T2]]   =  (S[[T1]]) and (S[[T2]]) .
  eq  S[[not T1]]      =  not(S[[T1]]) .
  eq  S[[B]]  =  B .
endo
```

Now the syntax of conditional programs is defined by extending the language with the desired operation:

```
obj PGM2 is ex PGM1 .
            pr TST .
  op  if_then_else_fi : Tst Pgm Pgm -> Pgm [prec 40] .
endo
```

We give a semantics for this construct by stating how conditional programs modify stores. Consider the error store

```
S ; if T then P1 else P2 fi ,
```

where `S` is a store, `T` a test, and `P1` and `P2` are programs. Our intuitions about conditionals tell us that this should be equal to `S ; P1` if the value of `T` is `true` (that is, if `S[[T]] = true`), and equal to `S ; P2` otherwise. This is captured by the pair of conditional equations in the following module, which gives the semantics of conditional programs:

```
obj SEM2 is pr SEMTST .
            pr PGM2 .
  var  S : Store .
  var  T : Tst .
  vars P1 P2 : Pgm .
```

```
    cq  S ; if T then P1 else P2 fi  =  S ; P1
        if  S[[T]] .
    cq  S ; if T then P1 else P2 fi  =  S ; P2
        if  not(S[[T]]) .
  endo
```

By repeated application of the equations for conditionals, occurrences of the **if_then_else_fi** operator can be eliminated, leaving programs which consist solely of sequences of assignments. For example, the error store

```
initial ; 'X := 1
        ; if 'X <= 'Y
          then 'X := 2 * 'X
          else 'Y := 2 * 'Y
              ; if 'Y <= 'Z then 'Y := 'Y + 'Z
                             else skip fi
          fi
```

reduces to

```
initial ; 'X := 1 ; 'Y := 2 * 'Y
        ; if 'Y <= 'Z then 'Y := 'Y + 'Z
                      else skip fi
```

because

```
    initial ; 'X := 1 [['X <= 'Y]]
=         { reductions for Tst's }
    (initial ; 'X := 1 [['X]])
    <= (initial ; 'X := 1 [['Y]])
=         { further reductions }
    1 <= 0
=         { arithmetic }
    false
```

so the second of the conditional rules is applicable. Similarly, this error store in turn reduces, by application of the first of the conditional rules, to the store:

```
initial ; 'X := 1 ; 'Y := 2 * 'Y ; 'Y := 'Y + 'Z .
```

Thus programs which use the conditional construct can be reduced, by means of the conditional rules, to sequences of assignments, yielding expressions that are effectively like those of the simple programming language of Chapter 2: in this sense, the semantics of the conditional construct is reduced, by means of the conditional rules and the rule for sequential composition, to the semantics of assignment.

The programming language that we have so far defined is therefore not so very different from the simple language of Chapter 2. In particular, because in any given store the `if_then_else_fi` operator can be eliminated from programs by using the conditional rules, giving programs consisting only of sequences of assignments, it is clear that all programs terminate, in the sense that for any store `S` and program `P`, the error store `S ; P` can be rewritten to an expression of sort `Store`; the following section introduces the concept of structural induction and gives an inductive proof of this assertion. (Some readers may wish to take our word for it and skip Section 3.3.) The situation changes, however, in Chapter 5, where we extend the language with a construct for while-loops, and make precise what we mean by termination of programs.

3.3 Structural Induction

Because we have been using the keyword `obj` in defining the syntax of our programming language, the denotation of the module `PGM2` is the class of initial algebras over the signature of the module (cf. Section 1.6.2). One such initial algebra is the term algebra over the signature T_Σ, which by Theorem 19 we may consider to be "the" initial algebra: that is, it provides a convenient standard interpretation of the module `PGM2` in a uniform way. In this sense, the standard interpretation of the sort of programs is the set of terms $T_{\Sigma,\mathtt{Pgm}}$. Looking at the definition of the term algebra (Definition 7 in Section 1.3), we see that $T_{\Sigma,\mathtt{Pgm}}$ is the *least* set X which satisfies the following conditions.

`C1`(X)	$T_{\Sigma,\mathtt{BPgm}} \subseteq X$
`C2`(X)	`skip` $\in X$
`C3`(X)	$(\forall$ `p1,p2` $\in X)$ `p1 ; p2` $\in X$
`C4`(X)	$(\forall$ `t` $\in T_{\Sigma,\mathtt{Tst}})(\forall$ `p1,p2` $\in X)$ `if t then p1 else p2 fi` $\in X$

To say that $T_{\Sigma,\mathtt{Pgm}}$ is the least such set is to say that $T_{\Sigma,\mathtt{Pgm}}$ satisfies all four of these conditions, and if any set X also satisfies these conditions, then $T_{\Sigma,\mathtt{Pgm}}$ is smaller than X, that is, $T_{\Sigma,\mathtt{Pgm}} \subseteq X$.

From this characterisation of $T_{\Sigma,\mathtt{Pgm}}$, we can derive a principle of induction on programs which will allow us to prove properties that hold for all programs. Let `P` be a predicate on programs, and suppose that we want to show that P is true for all programs. First, define the set $\bar{P}$ by:

$$\bar{P} = \{p \in T_{\Sigma,\mathrm{Pgm}} \mid P(p)\}.$$

If $T_{\Sigma,\mathrm{Pgm}} \subseteq \bar{P}$, then it follows that $(\forall p \in T_{\Sigma,\mathrm{Pgm}})\ p \in \bar{P}$, or equivalently (writing `p : Pgm` for $p \in T_{\Sigma,\mathrm{Pgm}}$),

```
(∀ p : Pgm) P(p) ,
```

which is what we are interested in showing. From the definition of $T_{\Sigma,\mathrm{Pgm}}$, it follows that $T_{\Sigma,\mathrm{Pgm}} \subseteq \bar{P}$ if $\bar{P}$ satisfies the four conditions C1-4: this is the *principle of structural induction*.

Using a little set theory, and the definition of $\bar{P}$, we can rephrase those conditions as follows:

```
C1(P̄)    (∀ b : BPgm) P(b)
C2(P̄)    P(skip)
C3(P̄)    (∀ p1,p2 : Pgm) P(p1) and P(p2) ⇒ P(p1 ; p2)
C4(P̄)    (∀ t : Tst)(∀ p1,p2 : Pgm) P(p1) and P(p2)
                                  ⇒ P(if t then p1 else p2 fi) .
```

Thus a property P holds for all programs if: (C1) it holds for all assignments; (C2) it holds for the program skip; (C3) it holds for p1 ; p2 whenever it holds for p1 and p2; and (C4) it holds for if t then p1 else p2 fi whenever it holds for p1 and p2. We summarise this argument in the following proposition, which states the principle of structural induction for programs.

Proposition 26 Let P be a predicate on programs (usually called "the induction hypothesis"). Then P holds for all programs if the following conditions are satisfied:

```
(∀ b: BPgm) P(b) ;
P(skip) ;
(∀ p1,p2 : Pgm) P(p1) and P(p2) ⇒ P(p1 ; p2) ; and
(∀ t : Tst)(∀ p1,p2 : Pgm) P(p1) and P(p2)
                               ⇒ P(if t then p1 else p2 fi) .
```

□

We use this principle to prove the following property, which states that all programs modify stores in such a way as to produce a meaningful store as a result: that is, all programs "terminate." Note, however, that this property will no longer hold once we extend the language with while-loops! The statement that a program terminates is expressed as a sentence in first order logic (see Appendix B).

Proposition 27 `(∀ p : Pgm)(∀ S : Store)(∃ S' : Store) S ; p = S' .`
Proof: We use structural induction, where our induction hypothesis is:

```
P(p)  =  (∀ S : Store)(∃ S': Store) S ; p = S' .
```

We must show that the four conditions of Proposition 26 are satisfied.

- To show the first condition, let `b : BPgm` . For all stores `S`, we have that `S ; b` has sort `Store`, so we choose `S'` to be `S ; b` .
- To show the second condition, for all stores `S` we have `S ; skip = S` , so we choose `S'` to be `S`.
- To show the third condition, assume the induction hypothesis holds for programs `p1` and `p2`. The induction hypothesis for `p1` states that for any store `S`, there exists a store `S1` such that `S ; p1 = S1` , and the induction hypothesis for `p2` implies that there exists a store `S2` such that `S1 ; p2 = S2`. Thus, for any store `S`,

  ```
  S ; (p1 ; p2)  =  (S ; p1) ; p2  =  S1 ; p2  =  S2
  ```

  so we choose `S'` to be `S2`.
- The fourth condition is left as an exercise for the reader (Exercise 14).

□

In Chapter 5 we introduce while loops, and with them, the possibility of non-terminating computations. In that context, we will see states and programs that violate the above proposition.

3.4 Exercises

Exercise 11 Consider the following specification for a program `sqtwo`, which sets the variable `'Z` to the square of `'X + 2`:

```
(∀ S : Store)  S ; sqtwo [['Z]]  =  S[[('X + 2)*('X + 2)]] .
```

(a) Give a basic program (a single assignment) that satisfies this specification.
(b) Prove that the following definition also satisfies the specification:

```
sqtwo = 'Z := 'X + 4 ; 'X := 'X * 'Z ; 'Z := 'X + 4 .
```

□

Exercise 12 Prove that the following program sets `'Z` to the square of `'X + 'Y`:

```
'Z := 'X + 'Y ; 'X := 'Z * 'X ; 'Y := 'Z * 'Y ; 'Z := 'X + 'Y .
```

□

Exercise 13 The module `EXP` contains only four operations for constructing expressions: it is, however, a simple matter to extend the syntax, and semantics, of expressions by introducing further operations.

(a) Integer division is represented in OBJ3 by the operation

```
op _quo_ : Int NzInt -> Int .
```

where the sort `NzInt` is the subsort of non-zero integers. For example, `17 quo 4 = 4`. Extend the module `EXP` with an operation

```
op _div2 : Exp -> Exp .
```

and give an equation which states that the semantics of `div2` is integer division by 2. (OBJ3 accepts `2` as having sort `NzInt`.)

(b) Remainder upon integer division is represented in OBJ by the operation

```
op _rem_ : Int NzInt -> Int .
```

Extend the module `EXP` with an operation

```
op _mod2 : Exp -> Exp .
```

and give an equation which states that the semantics of `mod2` is remainder upon integer division by `2`.

(c) Extend the module `TST` with operations

```
op even_ : Exp -> Tst .
op  odd_ : Exp -> Tst .
```

and write equations which give the obvious semantics for these operations. Run some test cases in OBJ.

□

Exercise 14 Complete the proof of Proposition 27 by proving the following statement (the fourth condition for induction):

```
(∀ t : Tst)(∀ p1,p2 : Pgm) P(p1) and P(p2)
                    ⇒ P(if t then p1 else p2 fi) .
```

Hint: in your proof, consider separately the case where the value of `t` is `true`, and the case where the value of `t` is false. □

Exercise 15 Without using the associativity of sequential composition, show that for all stores `S` and all programs `P1`, `P2` and `P3`,

```
S ; ((P1 ; P2) ; P3)  =  S ; (P1 ; (P2 ; P3)) .
```

This justifies our declaring composition to be associative, in that whichever way a composition of programs is parenthesised, the effect upon a store is the same. In a similar vein, how would you justify declaring the operation

```
_+_ : Exp Exp -> Exp
```

to be associative and commutative? □

Exercise 16 State the principle of structural induction for the sort `Exp`.

(a) Modify your answer to Exercise 2 of Chapter 1 to define an operation

```
subst : Exp Var Exp -> Exp
```

so that `subst(E1,X,E2)` gives the result of substituting `E1` for the program variable `X` in `E2`.

(b) Give an inductive proof that for all stores `S`, all program variables `X`, and all expressions `E1` and `E2`,

```
S ; X := E1 [[E2]]  =  S[[ subst(E1,X,E2) ]] .
```

(If you use OBJ in your proof, bear in mind the warning in Section 2.1.1.)

□

4 Proving Program Correctness

The semantics of our programming language allows us to make and prove assertions about the behaviour of programs written in the language. Moreover, because the semantics is presented by means of OBJ equations, we can reason about the behaviour of programs using equational logic, using in particular OBJ's rewriting mechanism to perform elementary deductions in our proofs and even to verify the correctness of our proofs. This chapter defines the notion of program correctness and provides some examples of proofs written in, and verified by, OBJ.

Some programs are intended to be evaluated only when some condition holds; for example, a program which sets `'Z` to the value of `'X` divided by `'Y` should only be evaluated if the value of `'Y` is not zero. We call such a condition a *precondition*. The requirement that, after evaluating the program, `'Z` holds the value of `'X` divided by `'Y`, is called the *postcondition*.

A *specification* for a program is given by a pair of predicates, one of which is the precondition, and the other the postcondition. The postcondition states what we expect of the program; the precondition states under what circumstances the program behaves as specified. A program is *correct* with respect to a given pre- and postcondition if evaluation of the program in a store that satisfies the precondition results in a store that satisfies the postcondition.[1] In more formal notation, this says that a program `p` is correct with respect to precondition `pre` and postcondition `post` iff

```
(∀ S : Store) pre(S) ⇒ post(S ; p) .
```

Note that this statement of correctness is a sentence of first order logic, which extends equational logic with formal notation for implication, universal quantification, etc. A review of first order logic is given in Appendix B.

In practice, we will need the more general definition of correctness given in Definition 28 below. But first we give some further motivation for specifying programs using preconditions and postconditions. In particular, preconditions are useful for programs such as while-loops that might not terminate, since if a loop does not terminate, it does not make sense to judge whether evaluation of the program in a given store makes the postcondition true. For example, our intuition says that the program

[1] This formalises the case of a program that starts with a given store and runs to completion. But of course, there are programs, like operating systems, that may receive new inputs at any time while they are running; such programs are often called *reactive systems*. There are also systems, and again operating systems are an example, that are *not supposed* to halt, but rather to continue producing outputs into the indefinite future. This book does not address such programs, although it would certainly be possible to do so with the kind of approach taken here, using equational logic, rewriting and OBJ, supplemented by some further theory.

```
fact  =  'X := 'Y ; 'C := 1 ;
         while not('X is 0) do 'C := 'C * 'X ; 'X := 'X - 1 od
```

only terminates on stores `S` such that `0 <= S[['Y]]`. If `S` satisfies this condition, then upon termination we would expect `'C` to hold the factorial of the value initially held in `'Y`; i.e., that

```
(S ; fact [['C]])  is  (S[['Y]])!
```

where `_!` denotes the factorial operation (see Section 5.1 below). But if `S` is such that `S[['Y]] < 0`, the program will loop indefinitely, so that `S ; fact [['C]]` does not even denote an integer value. Therefore it is reasonable to expect that the precondition for **fact** would provide a sufficient condition for the program to terminate. For example, we might choose as precondition:

```
pre(S)  =  0 <= S[['Y]] .
```

Since the program is intended to compute the factorial of `'Y`, we might propose the following postcondition:

```
post(S) =  (S[['C]])  is  (S[['Y]])! .
```

According to the definition of correctness given above, the program **fact** is correct with respect to this precondition and postcondition iff

```
(∀ S : Store) 0 <= S[['Y]] ⇒
  (S ; fact [['C]])  is  (S ; fact [['Y]])! .
```

However, in this case the specification of **fact** given by **pre** and **post** is somewhat weak, for the following program also satisfies this specification:

```
fact'  =  'Y := 0 ; 'C := 1 .
```

The reader should, at this point, prove that **fact'** is correct with respect to **pre** and **post** as above, using the equality `0! = 1`. Clearly, we do not want to allow this solution to the problem of setting `'C` to the factorial of `'Y`: we want to specify that, upon termination, `'C` holds the factorial of the *initial* value of `'Y`. A more precise specification is given by the following pre- and postconditions,

```
pre(y,S)   =  (S[['Y]]) is y  and  0 <= y .
post(y,S)  =  (S[['C]])  is  y ! .
```

where **y** represents an *arbitrary integer* (such a **y** is usually referred to in the literature as a "specification constant" or "ghost variable"). The correctness of the program **fact** with respect to this specification is the statement:

```
(∀ y : Int)(∀ S : Store) pre(y,S) ⇒ post(y, S ; fact) .
```

Some straightforward predicate calculus shows that this is equivalent to:

```
(∀ S : Store) 0 <= S[['Y]] ⇒ (S ; fact [['C]]) is (S[['Y]])! .
```

So our general definition of correctness of programs with respect to specifications that use specification constants is as follows:

Definition 28 **Preconditions** and **postconditions** are predicates that take some number of integers (specification constants) and a store and return a boolean value. A program `p` is **correct** with respect to a given precondition `pre` and postcondition `post` which use the specification constants `x1,...,xn` iff the following holds:

```
(∀ x1,...,xn : Int)(∀ S : Store)
  pre(x1,...,xn,S) ⇒ post(x1,...,xn, S ; p) .
```

□

Example 29 Now that our language has sequential composition, we can write `swap`, which exchanged the values held in `'X` and `'Y` as a `Pgm`:

```
swap  =  'T := 'X ; 'X := 'Y ; 'Y := 'T .
```

If we introduce constants `x` and `y` to represent the initial values of `'X` and `'Y` respectively, then `swap` can be specified by the following pre- and postconditions:

```
pre(x,y,S)  =  S[['X]] is x  and  S[['Y]] is y .
post(x,y,S) =  S[['X]] is y  and  S[['Y]] is x .
```

To prove the correctness of `swap` with respect to this specification, we need to show

```
(∀ x,y : Int)(∀ S : Store)
  S[['X]] is x  and  S[['Y]] is y
  ⇒  (S ; swap [['X]]) is y  and  (S ; swap [['Y]]) is x.
```

(A little predicate calculus shows that this is equivalent to

```
(∀ S : Store)  S ; swap [['X]]  =  S [['Y]]    and
               S ; swap [['Y]]  =  S [['X]] .
```

which was the specification given in Chapter 2.)

Recall the discussion on the Theorem of Constants at the end of Chapter 2: a universal quantification is proved in OBJ by adding new constants, so we would add constants `x` and `y` of sort `Int`, and `s` of sort `Store`. To prove the implication, we assume the antecedent `pre(x,y,s)` by adding the equalities as OBJ equations, and then we perform reductions to prove the consequent `post(x,y, s ; swap)`. The OBJ proof score would look as follows:

```
open SEM2 .
let swap = 'T := 'X ; 'X := 'Y ; 'Y := 'T .
op  s : -> Store .
ops x y : -> Int .

*** assume pre(x,y,s) ***
eq  s[['X]]  =  x .
eq  s[['Y]]  =  y .

*** prove post(x,y,s) ***
red (s ; swap [['Y]]) is x .   ***> should be: true
red (s ; swap [['X]]) is y .   ***> should be: true
close
```

□

Note that in this example the assumption that the precondition holds is effected by adding the equations

```
eq  s[['X]]  =  x .
eq  s[['Y]]  =  y .
```

In other words, we consider the "=" in these equations to be equivalent to the predicate `_is_` (a detailed discussion of why we can do this is given in Appendix A). This distinction between = and `_is_` reflects a distinction we generally make in OBJ proofs between assumptions and goals.

Our approach to properties of programs is traditional, in that we use first order logic for preconditions, postconditions, and invariants. This raises the issue of how to handle first order sentences in the context of an algebraic semantics. Our approach is to use standard rules of deduction to translate first order sentences into sequences of declarations and reductions. Predicates are represented as `Bool`-valued operations. Assumptions and goals must be treated differently: assumptions become declarations, while goals become reductions (generally in the context of some specifically constructed declarations). For example, an assumption that is a conjunction of sentences is represented by giving one declaration for each sentence.

Universal quantifiers in goals are handled by introducing new constants (this is valid by the Theorem of Constants). Existential quantifiers in assumptions are handled by introducing so-called Skolem functions. The result of all this is what we call an OBJ *proof score*, that is, an OBJ program such that if its reductions all produce `true` when expected, then the desired theorem has in fact been proved.

Using pre- and postconditions may make specifications slightly more complicated, in that we may need to introduce ghost variables to denote initial values of variables, but preconditions are necessary for while-loops that do not always terminate. Moreover, pre- and postconditions allow modularity in correctness proofs, as illustrated by the example proofs in the following two sections.

4.1 Example: Absolute Value

The task of setting `'Z` to the absolute value of the variable `'X` is specified by the following pre- and postconditions, which use the ghost variable `x`,

```
pre(x,S)  =  S[['X]] is x
post(x,S) =  S[['Z]] is abs(x)
```

where `abs` is the *mathematical* function which returns the absolute value of a given integer. This function is specified by the following OBJ theory:

```
obj ABS is pr ZZ .
  op abs : Int -> Int .
  var I : Int .
  cq  abs(I)  =  I    if  0 <= I .
  cq  abs(I)  =  - I  if  I < 0 .
endo
```

A program which satisfies the specification given by `pre` and `post` is:

```
absx  =  if 0 <= 'X then 'Z := 'X else 'Z := - 'X fi .
```

According to Definition 28, to prove the correctness of this program we must show that

```
(∀ x : Int)(∀ S : Store) pre(x,S) ⇒ post(x, S ; absx) .
```

In order to do this, we introduce constants `x` of sort `Int` and `s` of sort `Store`, and we assume the precondition by adding the equation

```
eq  s[['X]]  =  x .
```

Now we must prove that the postcondition holds for `s ; absx` by showing that

```
(s ; absx [['Z]]) is x .
```

We proceed by case analysis on the value of **x**: either `0 <= x` or `x < 0`.

If `0 <= x` , then `abs(x) = x` and `s[[0 <= 'X]]` is **true**, so

```
s ; absx  =  s ; 'Z := 'X
```

by the semantics of conditionals. This justifies the first step in the following calculation:

```
     s ; absx [['Z]]
=
     s ; 'Z := 'X [['Z]]
=
     s[['X]]
=
     x
=          { 0 <= x }
     abs(x)
```

And so the postcondition holds when `0 <= x` . The proof that the postcondition also holds when `x < 0` is similar, and is left as an exercise for the reader.

Once the structure of the proof was decided upon, the steps necessary to complete the proof were trivial; indeed, they may just as well be entrusted to OBJ's rewriting mechanism. The following score outlines OBJ's verification of the proof:

```
obj ABSX is pr SEM2 .
  let absx = if 0 <= 'X then 'Z := 'X else 'Z := - 'X fi .
endo

th PROOF is pr ABSX .
            pr ABS .
  op  s : -> Store .
  op  x : -> Int .
  *** assume pre(x,s) ***
  eq  s[['X]]  =  x .
endth
```

```
*** prove post(x, s ; absx) by case analysis ***
*** case  0 <= x ***
open PROOF .
eq  0 <= x  = true .
red (s ; absx [['Z]]) is abs(x) .      ***> should be: true
close

*** case  x < 0 ***
open PROOF .
eq  x < 0  = true .
red (s ; absx [['Z]]) is abs(x) .      ***> should be: true
close
```

We use a theory module for this proof because we make use of the Theorem of Constants. The constants `s` and `x` stand for the universally quantified variables in the statement of correctness for `absx`. These are intended to represent an arbitrary store and integer, respectively, so they must be interpreted loosely. The proof is valid for any model of `PROOF`, that is, it is valid for any interpretation of `s` and `x`.

Note the way in which the module `PROOF` is `open`ed and `close`d twice, to prevent interference between the two conflicting assumptions $0 \leq$ `x` and `x` < 0. This is a good example of the way we use OBJ's module facilities to structure our proof scores.

The proof is also a good example of the general structure of proofs in OBJ, which is illustrated in Figure 4.1. The proof uses the semantics of programs defined in `SEM2`, on top of which is the definition of the program given in `ABSX`. The proof also uses the mathematical operation `abs`, and the case analysis structure of the proof is a valid means of proving sentences in first order logic (see Appendix B). In general, the structure of all of the OBJ proof scores in this book follows the rules of inference of first order logic; we prove universally quantified sentences by introducing constants for the quantified variables, we prove implications by making declarations that correspond to assumptions and performing reductions to prove goals, as described in Example 29 above, and so on. Thus, first order logic is the "background" for our proof scores. All of the proofs in this book use the semantics of programs, on top of which we generally define some program that we want to prove correct. In general, the specification of the program uses some mathematical operations, such as factorial, absolute value, etc., and sometimes, though not in the case of `absx`, we need some lemmas concerning these operations. Typically, we simply introduce these lemmas as they are needed in our proof of program

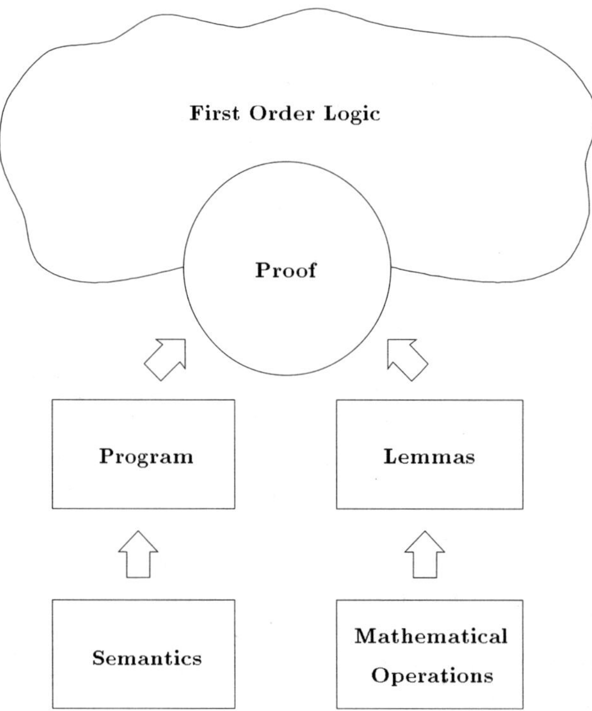

Figure 4.1
The general structure of OBJ proofs

correctness, but it is possible to use OBJ to prove these lemmas.

This general structure of proof scores is again illustrated by the example in the following section.

4.2 Example: Computing the Maximum of Two Values

The task of setting `'Z` to the maximum of the values held in the variables `'M` and `'N` is specified by the following pre- and postconditions, using the specification constants `m` and `n`:

```
pre(m,n,S)  =  (S[['M]]) is m  and  (S[['N]]) is n .
post(m,n,S) =  (S[['Z]]) is (m max n) .
```

where the integer function `max` used in the postcondition is specified by the following:

```
obj MAX is pr ZZ .
  op _max_ : Int Int -> Int .
  vars M N : Int .
  cq  M max N  =  M   if  N <= M .
  cq  M max N  =  N   if  M <= N .
endo
```

We claim that the following program computes the maximum value of two variables `'M` and `'N`:

```
maxp  =  if 'N <= 'M then 'Z := 'M else 'Z := 'N fi .
```

That is, according to Definition 41, we claim that

```
(∀ m,n : Int)(∀ S : Store)
  (S[['M]]) is m  and  (S[['N]]) is n
  ⇒  (S ; maxp [['Z]]) is (m max n)
```

An OBJ proof which proceeds by straightforward case analysis (either `n <= m` or `m < n`) is given below. This proof corresponds closely to the structure of the program `maxp`.

```
obj MAXP is pr SEM2 .
  let maxp  =  if 'N <= 'M then 'Z := 'M else 'Z := 'N fi .
endo

th PROOF is pr MAXP .
            pr MAX .
  op s : -> Store .
  ops m n : -> Int .
  *** assume pre(m,n,s) ***
  eq s [['M]] = m .
  eq s [['N]] = n .
  op post : Int Int Store -> Bool .
  var S : Store .
  vars M N : Int .
  eq post(M,N,S)  =  (S[['Z]]) is (M max N) .
endth
```

```
*** prove post(m,n, s ; maxp) by case analysis ***
*** case 1: n <= m ***
open PROOF .
eq  n <= m  =  true .
red post(m,n, s ; maxp) .    ***> should be: true
close

*** case 2: m < n ***
open PROOF .
eq  m < n  =  true .
red post(m,n, s ; maxp) .    ***> should be: true
close
```

The operations m and n, as well as handily abbreviating s[['M]] and s[['N]], play the role of the specification constants in the definitions of pre and post. The Theorem of Constants ensures that what is proven by the above OBJ score yields the universally quantified statement of the correctness of maxp:

$$(\forall\ \texttt{m,n : Int})(\forall\ \texttt{S : Store})\ \texttt{pre(m,n,S)} \Rightarrow \texttt{post(m,n, S ; maxp)}\ .$$

4.3 Exercises

Exercise 17 Specify, write and prove correct a program which sets 'Z to the minimum of the values of 'M and 'N. □

Exercise 18 Define the predicate P by: for all integers n and stores S,

```
P(n,S)   =   (S[['U * 'X + 'V * 'Y]])  is  n .
```

Define the program euc by

```
euc  =  if 'X < 'Y
        then 'Y := 'Y - 'X ; 'U := 'U + 'V
        else if 'Y < 'X then 'X := 'X - 'Y ; 'V := 'U + 'V
                        else skip fi
        fi .
```

Show that euc is correct when P(n,S) is both the precondition and the postcondition. □

Exercise 19 Specify, write and prove correct a program which sets `'P` to the maximum of the values of `'X`, `'Y` and `'Z`. □

Exercise 20 Show that the program p, defined by

```
p  =  if 'X <= 'Y then 'P := 'X
                  else if 'Y <= 'Z then 'P := 'Z
                                   else 'P := 'Y fi
      fi ,
```

is correct with respect to the following pre- and postconditions:

```
pre(x,y,z,S)  =  (S[['X]]) is x  and  (S[['Y]]) is y  and
                 (S[['Z]]) is z  and  z <= x .
post(x,y,z,S) =  (S[['P]])  is  (x min y) max z .
```

where `_min_` returns the minimum of two integers. □

5 Iteration

We now turn our attention to the iterative construct, `while_do_od` . We first give an operational account of how we expect programs of the form `while T do P od` to behave, and we then formalise this account by giving equations which define the semantics of such programs. Adding the iterative construct raises the issue of termination of programs. In Section 5.2 we give a formal definition of termination, and present a method for proving that programs terminate. This method, together with the notion of "invariant" examined in Section 5.1, leads to a proof rule for proving the correctness of programs with while-loops.

Following the by now familiar procedure, we first extend the syntax of our programming language with a construct for while-loops:

```
obj PGM3 is ex PGM2 .
  op  while_do_od : Tst Pgm -> Pgm .
endo
```

We refer to programs of the form `while T do P od` as **while-loops**, or just **loops**; the test `T` is called the **guard** of the loop, and the program `P` the **body** of the loop.

Intuitively, we want to say that a program of the form `while T do P od` iterates the program `P` as long as the guard `T` remains true. That is, in a given store `S`, if `S[[T]]` evaluates to `true`, then

```
S ; while T do P od  =  S ; P ; while T do P od
```

while if `S[[T]]` evaluates to `false`, then

```
S ; while T do P od  =  S .
```

The semantics of while-loops is therefore given by the two conditional equations in the following module:

```
obj SEM3 is pr SEM2 .
            pr PGM3 .
  var S : Store .  var T : Tst .  var P : Pgm .
  cq  S ; while T do P od  =  S ; P ; while T do P od
      if  S[[T]] .
  cq  S ; while T do P od  =  S
      if not(S[[T]]) .
endo
```

We claimed in Chapter 3 that the rules for conditionals could always be applied in a given store to remove all occurrences of the conditional construct, with the consequence that programs using the conditional construct could always be reduced to a sequence of assignments. Thus for all stores `S` and all programs `P`, the error-store `S ; P` could be rewritten to a term of sort `Store`. This no longer holds now that we have introduced the iterative construct, because the first of the above equations contains an occurrence of `while T do P od` in its right side, which admits the possibility that an occurrence of the iterative construct can never be eliminated by rewriting. Roughly speaking, these equations will produce a non-terminating rewrite sequence if evaluation of the program begins in a store that makes `T` true, and if `T` still holds after every iteration of `P`. For example, for any store `S`, `S[[true]]` is equal to `true`, so

```
S ; while true do skip od
```

will always rewrite by the first of these equations to

```
S ; skip ; while true do skip od
```

which will rewrite again to the original term

```
S ; while true do skip od .
```

Clearly, this cycle of rewriting will continue indefinitely, so the term remains of sort `EStore`, and cannot be rewritten to a term of sort `Store`. This is what we mean when we say the program does not terminate.

In summary, this construct represents a great change to our programming language, because it introduces the possibility of non-terminating programs. Termination is discussed fully in Section 5.2 but first, Section 5.1 outlines a method for proving the correctness of while-loops.

5.1 Invariants

In this section, we will ignore the question of termination, and outline a technique for proving properties of loops. This technique is based on the idea of *invariants*, which are properties that are preserved by the body of a loop in the sense that if the property is true of the store before the body is evaluated, then it will also be true of the store that results after the body has been evaluated.

To illustrate invariants in action, we consider a program that computes the factorial of the value held in the program variable 'N. The factorial function, denoted by a postfix exclamation mark, is specified by the following OBJ theory:

```
obj FAC is ex ZZ .
  op  _! : Int -> Int [prec 1] .
  var  I : Int .
  eq  0 !  =  1 .
  cq  I !  =  I * (I - 1)!     if  0 < I .
endo
```

We will use this in our specification and proof of a program to compute factorials, which is why we declare _! as an operation on integers, since we want to write terms such as (s[['C]])! for an arbitrary store s in our proof. However, the equations in FAC only define factorials of natural numbers. We use ex ZZ in this module to indicate that we are extending the specification of integers in ZZ with terms of the form I !, where I denotes a negative number.

The specification for a program to compute the factorial function is given by the following pre- and postconditions:

```
pre(n,S)  =  (S[['N]]) is n  and  0 <= n .
post(n,S) =  (S[['X]]) is n ! .
```

and the program, which is different from the factorial program in Chapter 4, is defined as follows:

```
obj FACP is pr SEM3 .
  let init  = 'C := 0 ; 'X := 1 .
  let guard = 'C < 'N .
  let body  = 'C := 'C + 1 ; 'X := 'X * 'C .
  let facp  = init ; while guard do body od .
endo
```

By running through a few iterations of body in our heads, we see that the program works by keeping 'X equal to 'C !, and incrementing the value of 'C until 'C is n, the initial value of 'N. We might describe how this algorithm works as follows:

(a) set 'C to 0 and 'X to 1 so that, initially, 'X is 'C !; then

(b) increment 'C and keep 'X equal to 'C ! until 'C is n.

Because 'X begins, and remains, equal to 'C !, and because when the program terminates (if it terminates), 'C is equal to n, upon termination we have

```
'X  =  'C !  =  n ! .
```

The aim of this section is to formalise this reasoning, while the next section will show that such reasoning can be used in a proof rule for while-loops.

We call the statement that **'X** is 'C ! an "invariant" of the loop. Of course, the statement must be made relative to some store S. The statement is therefore a predicate on stores:

```
inv(S)  =  (S[['X]]) is (S[['C]])! .
```

This is too weak, because the equations of the module **FAC** define the factorial function only on non-negative integers. So we strengthen **inv** to

```
inv(S)  =  (S[['X]]) is (S[['C]])!  and  0 <= (S[['C]]) .
```

The general notion of an invariant is defined as follows.

Definition 30 An **invariant** of a loop `while T do P od` is a predicate I on stores such that for all stores S, if I(S) and S[[T]] hold, then I(S ; P) holds too. □

Thus, in our example, we are claiming that for all stores S, if **inv**(S) and

```
S[['C < 'N]]
```

hold, then **inv**(S ; **body**) holds. We will prove this later; for the present, let us see how we can use this insight to argue that the program **facp** meets its specification.

The equations that define the semantics of while-loops suggest that a program **while** T do P od iterates the body P as long as the guard T holds, and terminates if it reaches a state in which the guard no longer holds. Given that the loop terminates when run in a store S, we might expect that

```
S ; while T do P od
```

rewrites to some store

```
S'  =  S ; P ; P ; ... ; P
```

i.e., S followed by some number of iterations of P; moreover, the program terminates because eventually the guard T becomes false, so not(S'[[T]]) is **true**, and the guard will hold after each iteration of P except the last. Now if I is an invariant of the loop, and if I(S) holds, then I will hold after each iteration of P: in particular, I(S') will be true, and therefore

```
I(S ; while T do P od)
```

will hold. In other words, the invariant and the negation of the guard both hold upon termination of the loop.

Suppose that the correctness of the loop was specified by means of predicates `pre` and `post`, and suppose that the precondition implies the invariant, and that the conjunction of the invariant and the negation of the guard implies the postcondition. Then we can argue for the correctness of the loop as follows:

> If we begin in a store which satisfies the precondition, then the invariant will hold initially; if the loop terminates, then the invariant and the negation of the guard will hold upon termination, and therefore the postcondition will hold.

Similarly, for a program of the form

```
init ; while T do P od
```

we can use the same reasoning if, for all stores `S`,

```
pre(S) ⇒ I(S ; init)
```

for then `init` establishes the invariant, so the invariant will hold before evaluation of the loop begins.

We summarise this reasoning in the following proof rule for while-loops:

> **Proof Rule (partial correctness of while-loops)**
> A program `init ; while T do P od` is correct with respect to precondition `pre` and postcondition `post` *if the precondition ensures that the program terminates*, and if there is a predicate `inv` that satisfies the following three conditions:
>
> - `inv` holds initially:
>   `(∀ S : Store) pre(S) ⇒ inv(S ; init) .`
> - `inv` and the negation of the guard imply the postcondition:
>   `(∀ S : Store) inv(S) and not(S[[T]]) ⇒ post(S) .`
> - `inv` is an invariant of the loop:
>   `(∀ S : Store) inv(S) and S[[T]] ⇒ inv(S ; P) .`

Using this proof rule, we can demonstrate the correctness of a program by finding an invariant which satisfies the three conditions of the rule, assuming that the program terminates. This notion of program correctness, dependent on the assumption of termination, is often called "*partial correctness*".

We now show how the rule can be used to prove the partial correctness of our factorial program. In order to use the proof rule, we must prove that **inv** satisfies three conditions: that it holds initially, that it and the negation of the guard imply the postcondition, and that it is indeed an invariant of the loop. If we attempt these proofs, we soon find that the second condition is not met! The postcondition is:

```
(S[['X]]) is n !
```

but **inv** and the negation of the guard give

```
(S[['X]]) is (S[['C]])!  and  0 <= (S[['C]])  and
(S[['N]]) <= (S[['C]]) .
```

We want to be able to conclude that `S[['C]]` is equal to `n`; to this end, we must strengthen **inv** again:

```
inv(S)  =  (S[['X]]) is (S[['C]])!  and  0 <= (S[['C]])  and
           (S[['C]]) <= (S[['N]])  and  (S[['N]]) is n .
```

Now from `inv(S)` and `not(S[[guard]])` we obtain

```
(S[['C]]) <= (S[['N]])  and  (S[['N]]) <= (S[['C]])
```

and therefore

```
(S[['C]]) = (S[['N]]) .
```

Moreover, from `(S[['N]]) is n` , we get

```
S[['X]]  =  (S[['C]])!  =  (S[['N]])!  =  n !
```

as desired. This proves the second of the three conditions of the proof rule. The other two conditions are straightforward to prove: as a summary, we give an OBJ score that proves all three conditions, and therefore demonstrates the partial correctness of the program `facp`:

```
th PROOF is pr FAC .
            pr FACP .
   op s : -> Store .
   op n : -> Int .
   ops inv post : Store -> Bool .
   var S : Store .
```

```
  eq  inv(S)  =  (S[['X]]) is (S[['C]])! and
                 0 <= (S[['C]])  and  (S[['C]]) <= (S[['N]])
                 and  (S[['N]]) is n .
  eq  post(S) =  (S[['X]]) is n ! .
endth

open PROOF .
*** assume pre(s) ***
eq  s[['N]]  =  n .
eq  0 <= n  = true .
*** 1st condition: inv holds initially ***
red  inv(s ; init) .    ***> should be: true
close

openr PROOF .
*** assume inv(s) ***
eq  s[['X]]  =  (s[['C]])! .
eq  0 <= (s[['C]])  =  true .
eq  s[['N]]  =  n .
eq  (s[['C]]) <= n  =  true .
close

open PROOF .
*** assume negation of guard ***
eq  n <= (s[['C]])  =  true .
*** therefore, since  s[['C]] <= n : ***
eq  s[['C]]  =  n .
*** 2nd condition: postcondition follows ***
red  post(s) .    ***> should be: true
close

open PROOF .
*** assume guard ***
eq  (s[['C]]) < n  =  true .
*** 3rd condition: inv is invariant ***
red  inv(s ; body) .    ***> should be: true
close
```

Note the use of openr after the proof of the first condition. This makes the assumption of the invariant valid throughout the remainder of the proof, where it is used in the proof of the second and third conditions of the proof rule. Note also that in proving the second condition of the proof rule, it was necessary to add the equation `s[['C]] = n` . This equality is a consequence of `n <= s[['C]]` (the negation of the guard) and `s[['C]] <= n` (from the assumption of the invariant), but the equality is, nevertheless, not available as an OBJ equation unless we explicitly add it to the proof script. This equation plays the rôle of a lemma in the proof, and could be proved in OBJ using properties of <=, =>, and =.

5.1.1 Example: greatest common divisor

We seek to construct a program which computes the greatest common divisor, `gcd(x,y)`, of two integers x and y, both greater than 0 (we follow standard practice in assuming that gcd is only defined on the positive integers). Thus, the precondition for our program is

```
pre(x,y,S)  =  S[['X]] is x  and  S[['Y]] is y  and
               0 < x  and  0 < y
```

and the postcondition is

```
post(x,y,S)  =  (S[['X]])  is  gcd(x,y) .
```

where gcd is defined as follows:

```
obj GCD is pr ZZ .
  op gcd : Int Int -> Int  [comm] .
  vars I J : Int .
  cq  gcd(I,I)  =  I   if  0 < I .
  cq  gcd(I,J + (- I))  =  gcd(I,J)   if  0 < I  and  I < J .
endo
```

This does not admit a trivial solution, so we seek a solution using a while-loop. The construction of this loop will ultimately be justified by properties of the operation gcd; the simplest property of gcd is that for all I,

```
gcd(I,I)  =  I .
```

That is, the task of computing `gcd(x,y)` is trivial when `x = y`. We shall attempt to use a loop to reduce the task of computing `gcd(x,y)` to the trivial case when `x = y` by considering a loop of the form

```
while not('X is 'Y) do ... od
```

having the invariant

```
inv(S)  =  gcd(S[['X]],S[['Y]]) is gcd(x,y)  and
           0 < (S[['X]])  and  0 < (S[['Y]]) .
```

Clearly, the invariant and the negation of the guard imply the postcondition; moreover, the invariant follows immediately from the precondition. Thus, the first and third conditions of the proof rule are satisfied, and we need only find a body for the loop which keeps `inv` invariant.

In order for the loop to make any progress, the body of the loop should reduce the difference between `'X` and `'Y`. Moreover, since `gcd(m,n)` is at most `m` and also at most `n`, the difference between `'X` and `'Y` should be reduced by decreasing the greater of `'X` and `'Y`. Thus we should consider the two cases: (a) `'X < 'Y`, and (b) `'Y < 'X`. (In fact, the two cases should be symmetric, since `gcd` is a commutative operator.) Again, we turn to properties of `gcd` to provide a line of attack. For the case (a), we require a property of the form

```
gcd(I,J)  =  gcd(I,J - J')   for some J' < J .
```

And fortunately, we know that subtraction of multiples preserves divisor properties, i.e., a standard property of `gcd` is that

```
gcd(I,J)  =  gcd(I,J - I)   if  I < J .
```

(The condition `I < J` ensures that we always take the `gcd` of positive integers.) This justifies the following fragment of code:

```
if 'X < 'Y then 'Y := 'Y - 'X else ... fi
```

for if `gcd(S[['X]],S[['Y]]) = gcd(x,y)` and `S[['X]] < S[['Y]]`, then by the above property of `gcd`,

```
gcd(S ; 'Y := 'Y - 'X [['X]], S ; 'Y := 'Y - 'X [['Y]])
=  gcd(x,y) .
```

Moreover, because `gcd` is commutative, the assignment `'X := 'X - 'Y` also preserves the invariant `inv` in the case (b), which gives us the `else` part of the program fragment above.

We have now arrived at the program:

```
while not('X is 'Y)
do  if 'X < 'Y then 'Y := 'Y - 'X else 'X := 'X - 'Y fi  od .
```

Notice that the desire to do a correctness proof led us towards a formulation of our program. We restate the proof in OBJ as follows:

```
obj GCDP is pr SEM3 .
  let body = if 'X < 'Y then 'Y := 'Y - 'X
                       else 'X := 'X - 'Y fi .
  let gcdp = while not('X is 'Y) do body od .
endo

th PROOF is pr GCDP .
            pr GCD .
  ops x y : -> Int .
  ops inv post : Store -> Bool .
  var S : Store .
  eq  post(S)  =  (S[['X]]) is gcd(x,y) .
  eq  inv(S)  =  gcd(S[['X]],S[['Y]]) is gcd(x,y)  and
                 0 < (S[['X]])  and  0 < (S[['Y]]) .
  op  s : -> Store .
endth

*** show inv holds initially ***
open PROOF .
*** assume precondition ***
eq  s[['X]]  =  x .
eq  s[['Y]]  =  y .
eq  0 < x  =  true .
eq  0 < y  =  true .
red inv(s) .   ***> should be true
close

*** assume inv(s) ***
openr PROOF .
eq  gcd(s[['X]], s[['Y]])  =  gcd(x,y) .
eq  0 < (s[['X]])  =  true .
eq  0 < (s[['Y]])  =  true .
close
```

```
*** assume not(guard); show postcondition ***
open PROOF .
eq  s[['Y]]  =  s[['X]] .
*** lemma: ***
red inv(s) .     ***> gives:  (s[['X]]) is gcd(x,y)
*** therefore, since inv(s) is true by assumption ***
eq  s[['X]]  =  gcd(x,y) .
red post(s) .    ***> should be:  true
close

*** assume guard ***
openr PROOF .
eq  not((s[['X]]) is (s[['Y]]))  =  true .
close

*** show inv invariant ***
*** case 'X < 'Y: ***
open PROOF .
eq  (s[['X]]) < (s[['Y]])  =  true .
red inv(s ; body) .             ***> should be true
close

*** case not('X < 'Y): ***
open PROOF .
eq  (s[['X]]) < (s[['Y]])  =  false .
*** hence, since not('X is 'Y): ***
eq  (s[['Y]]) < (s[['X]])  =  true .
red inv(s ; body) .             ***> should be true
close
```

Note that we required an additional lemma to prove that the postcondition follows from the invariant and the negation of the guard. We first assumed the invariant, then the negation of the guard. Together, these entail

(1)   `(s[['X]]) is gcd(x,y)` ,

as is shown by executing the command

```
red inv(s) .
```

Moreover, because `inv(s)` is true (by assumption) and because `inv(s)` is equal to `(1)`, then `(1)` is also true, which justifies adding the equation

```
eq  s[['X]]  =  gcd(x,y) .
```

at that point in the proof.

5.2 Termination

In the previous section, we gave a proof rule for the partial correctness of while-loops, whereby a program can be shown to meet a specification on the assumption that the program terminates; in this section we give a formal definition of termination, and present a method for proving termination of while-loops. This is then used to provide a proof rule for proving correctness and termination of while-loops. This notion of correctness, which requires a proof that the program terminates, is often referred to in the literature as "*total correctness*", to distinguish it from the notion of partial correctness considered in the previous section.

We begin with the definition of termination.

Definition 31 A program `P` **terminates** on store `S`, written `P↓S`, iff `S ; P` is equal to a term of sort `Store`; that is,

```
P↓S  iff  (∃ S' : Store) S ; P = S' .
```

□

Thus, a program terminates on a store if running the program on the store produces a result of sort `Store`. One way to show that a program terminates on a store is to rewrite the program to a finite sequence of assignments:

Example 32 Consider the program

```
loop = while not('X is 3) do 'X := 'X + 1 od .
```

If `S` is such that `S[['X]] = 0` , then `S ; loop` rewrites to

```
S ; 'X := 'X + 1 ; 'X := 'X + 1 ; 'X := 'X + 1
```

which can be parsed as having sort `Store`, and so `loop↓S`. □

In Chapter 4 we suggested that the precondition for a program should supply a sufficient condition for that program to terminate. Therefore, we are interested in proving that a program terminates on any store that satisfies a given condition. We formalise this notion by extending the notation of Definition 31.

Definition 33 Let `I` be a predicate on stores and let `P` be a program. Then define

$$\texttt{P}\!\downarrow\!\texttt{I} \quad \text{iff} \quad (\forall\ \texttt{S : Store})\ \texttt{I(S)} \Rightarrow \texttt{P}\!\downarrow\!\texttt{S}\ .$$

□

Looking again at the program `loop` of Example 32 above, we would expect that it terminates on all stores where `'X` has a value no greater than `3`; that is, $\texttt{loop}\!\downarrow\!\texttt{I}$, where

```
I(S)  =  (S[['X]]) <= 3 .
```

The reasoning behind this expectation is that if `'X` begins with a value not greater than `3`, then the body of the loop increases the value of `'X` repeatedly until `'X` is equal to `3`. Thus the value of `3 - 'X` is the number of times that the body of the loop is evaluated: each time the body of the loop is evaluated, the value of `'X` increases by 1, and so the value of `3 - 'X` decreases by 1; moreover, this value cannot decrease indefinitely, since `I` is an invariant of the loop (prove this), and if `I` holds, then the value of `3 - 'X` cannot be less than `0`.

The expression `3 - 'X` can be viewed as a function `M` from stores to integers:

```
M(S)  =  S[[3 - 'X]] .
```

We call such functions **measure functions** when they are used to argue for the termination of a loop (they provide a "measure" of how close a loop is to termination). Given a measure function and an invariant of a loop, we can argue that the loop terminates if evaluation of the body of the loop decreases the value of the measure function, and if the measure function cannot decrease indefinitely: that is, if the measure function is bounded below. More specifically, suppose that `inv` is an invariant of the loop `while T do P od`. Since we are interested in the correctness of the program, we need only consider the situation where the body of the loop is evaluated in stores which satisfy `inv` and which make the guard true. Therefore, we need only require that the measure function decreases and is bounded below on such stores.

The following theorem formalises this reasoning. The condition of the theorem takes `0` as a lower bound for the measure function, so that while a measure function may in general return arbitrary integer values, its values on stores that satisfy the invariant and make the guard true should be non-negative. The choice of `0` as a lower bound is an arbitrary one: any constant integer is also suitable as a lower bound; all that is essential to the proof of the theorem is that there is some lower bound. The proof of the theorem, which uses well-founded induction, is given in Appendix B.

Theorem 34 Let `inv` be a predicate on stores, let `M` be an integer valued function on stores, let `P` be a program, and let `loop = while T do P od`. Then `P↓inv`, and `inv` an invariant of the loop, and `M` bounded below and strictly decreasing, imply `loop↓inv` and `loop` terminates in a store which makes the invariant and the negation of the guard true. Formally:
if

```
(∀ S : Store) inv(S) and S[[T]]
              ⇒  P↓S  and  inv(S ; P)  and
                 0 <= M(S)  and  M(S ; P) < M(S)
```

then

```
(∀ S : Store) inv(S)
              ⇒  loop↓S  and  inv(S ; loop)  and
                 not(S ; loop [[T]]) .
```

□

Note that, by Definition 33, the conclusion of the theorem entails that `loop↓inv`.

A consequence of this theorem is the following proof rule:

Proof Rule (total correctness of while-loops)
A program `init ; while T do P od` is correct with respect to precondition `pre` and postcondition `post` if there is a predicate `inv` and an integer valued function `M` that satisfy the following three conditions:

- `inv` holds initially:

  ```
  (∀ S : Store) pre(S) ⇒ inv(S ; init) .
  ```

- `inv` and the negation of the guard imply the postcondition:

  ```
  (∀ S : Store) inv(S) and not(S[[T]]) ⇒ post(S) .
  ```

- `inv` is an invariant of the loop, and the program terminates:

  ```
  (∀ S : Store) inv(S) and S[[T]]
                ⇒  P↓S  and  inv(S ; P)  and
                   0 <= M(S)  and  M(S ; P) < M(S) .
  ```

Example 35 We close this section by proving the termination of the greatest common divisor program from Section 5.1.1, assuming that the invariant `inv`, etc., are as defined in that section. The measure function we use is

```
M(S)  =  S[['X + 'Y]] ,
```

since the body of the loop decreases either **'X** or **'Y**. The proof of termination extends the module **PROOF** of Section 5.1.1; the use of **openr** in that proof means that the assumption of the invariant and of the guard are still valid. We need only show that, under those assumptions, the measure function is bounded below, and strictly decreasing. To show that **M** is strictly decreasing, we repeat the case analysis in the proof of correctness.

```
openr PROOF .
op  M : Store -> Int .
eq  M(S)  =  S[['X + 'Y]] .
red  0 <= M(s) .    ***> should be: true
close

***> case 'X < 'Y:
open PROOF .
eq  (s[['X]]) < (s[['Y]])  =  true .
red  M(s ; body) < M(s) .    ***> should be: true
close

***> case not('X < 'Y):
open PROOF .
eq  (s[['X]]) < (s[['Y]])  =  false .
red  M(s ; body) < M(s) .    ***> should be: true
close
```

□

5.3 Exercises

Exercise 21 Show that if predicates `I` and `J` are both invariants of a given loop, then so too is `I&J`, defined by

```
I&J(S)  =  I(S) and J(S) .
```

□

Exercise 22 This exercise concerns the correctness of the following program to compute the integer division of the value of **'N** by 2:

```
div2  =  'X := 'N ; 'Y := 0 ;
         while  1 < 'X
         do 'X := 'X - 2 ; 'Y := 'Y + 1 od .
```

The precondition for this algorithm is

```
pre(n,S)  =  (S[['N]]) is n  and  0 <= n
```

and the postcondition is

```
post(n,S)  =  n is 2 * (S[['Y]]) + (S[['X]])  and
              0 <= (S[['X]])  and  (S[['X]]) <= 1 .
```

(a) Show that the predicate `I`, defined by

```
I(S)  =  (S[[2 * 'Y + 'X]]) is n ,
```

is an invariant of the loop.

(b) Show that the predicate `J`, defined by

```
J(S)  =  0 <= (S[['X]]) ,
```

is also an invariant of the loop.

(c) Prove the partial correctness of `div2`.

□

Exercise 23 Write, specify and prove correct a program to compute `sum(n)`, the sum of the integers from 0 up to `n`, where `n` is the initial value of the variable `'N`. The function `sum` is specified by the following OBJ theory:

```
obj SUM is ex ZZ .
  op sum_ : Int -> Int [prec 1] .
  var I : Int .
  cq  sum I  =  0   if  I <= 0 .
  cq  sum I  =  I + sum(I - 1)    if  0 < I .
endo
```

Hint: the function `sum` is very similar to the factorial function. □

Exercise 24 In each part of this question, you are asked to prove the partial correctness of a program which computes the square of a given number without using multiplication. The specification for each of these programs is:

```
pre(n,S)  =  S[['N is n  and  0 <= n]] .
post(n,S) =  S[['X is (n * n)]] .
```

(a) Prove the correctness of the following program:

```
'C := 0 ; 'X := 0 ;
while  'C < 'N
do  'X := 'X + 'N ; 'C := 'C + 1  od .
```

Use the following invariant in your proof:

```
inv(S) = S[['X is 'C * 'N  and  'N is n  and  'C <= 'N]] .
```

(b) Find an invariant and use it to prove the correctness of the following program:

```
'C := 'N ; 'X := 0 ;
while  0 < 'C
do  'X := 'X + 'N ; 'C := 'C - 1  od .
```

(c) Complete the following program and prove it correct:

```
C := 0 ; 'X := ... ; 'Y := ... ;
while  'C < 'N
do 'Y :=  ... ; 'X := ... ; 'C := 'C + 1 od .
```

Hint: use the variable `'Y` to keep the value of `2 * 'C + 1`.

□

Exercise 25 The Fibonacci sequence is $1, 1, 2, 3, 5, 8, 13, \ldots$, where each number after the first two is the sum of the preceding two numbers. The function `fib`, which computes the nth number in this sequence, is specified by the following OBJ module:

```
obj FIB is ex ZZ .
  op  fib : Int -> Int .
  eq  fib(0)  =  0 .
  eq  fib(1)  =  1 .
  var I : Int .
  cq  fib(I)  =  fib(I - 2) + fib(I - 1)    if  1 < I .
endo
```

Complete and prove correct the following program, which sets `'X` to `fib(n)`, where `n` is the initial value of the variable `'N`, which is non-negative:

```
'C := 0 ; 'X := ... ; ... ;
while  'C < 'N
do  ... ; 'X := ... ; 'C := 'C + 1  od .
```

Hint: use the variable `'Y` to keep the value .... □

Exercise 26 Write an OBJ module which defines a function `facs : Int -> Int` such that for all integers `n`,

$$\texttt{facs(n)} = \sum_{i=0}^{\texttt{n}} i\,!$$

i.e., `facs(n) = 0 ! + 1 ! + ... + n ! .`

Use your definition to specify, write and prove correct a program which sets `'X` to `facs(n)`, where `n` is the initial value of `'N`.
Hint: two possible invariants are:

```
inv(S)  =  (S[['F]]) is (S[['C]])!
           and  (S[['X]]) is facs(S[['C]])
           and ...
```

and

```
inv(S)  =  facs(S[['Y]]) + (S[['Y]])! * (S[['X]]) is facs(n)
           and ...
```

□

Exercise 27 A major motivation for using algebra is that it is supposed to make it easier to reason about programs. Evaluate this claim with the evidence available at this point. □

6 Arrays

The only data type supported by our programming language as it now stands is the integers: the programs we can write all compute integer values by means of assignments to variables. In this chapter we extend the syntax of our programming language with arrays, so we can write programs that manipulate arrays by means of assignments to array variables. We give a semantics to such programs using an abstract data type of arrays.

We can think of an array as a series of numbered pigeon-holes, each pigeon-hole containing an integer value. The value in the `i`th pigeon-hole of an array `a` can be denoted `a[i]`. For example, we can picture an array `a` with value `5` in the pigeon-hole numbered `0`, with `6` in the pigeon-hole numbered `1`, and with `4` in the pigeon-hole numbered `2` as follows:

0	1	2
5	6	4

In more conventional notation, we would write `a[0] = 5` and `a[1] = 6` and `a[2] = 4`. We can assign a new value to a pigeon-hole; for example, the program `a[0] := a[2]` should change the array pictured above into the array `a'`:

0	1	2
4	6	4

That is, `a'[0] = 4`, and the values in `a'[1]` and `a'[2]` remain unchanged. Note that in the assignment `a[0] := a[2]`, the terms `a[0]` and `a[2]` play very different rôles: `a[2]` refers to the *value* in the second pigeon-hole of `a`, i.e., `4` (we say that `4` is the second *element* of the array), whereas `a[0]` refers to the `0`th pigeon-hole itself, to which the value `4` is assigned (we call such pigeon-holes *components* of the array).

The above paragraphs convey some intuitions behind programming with arrays; however, we have been guilty of confusing syntax with semantics. An array is not a feature of a programming language; rather, it is a mathematical entity belonging to an abstract data type (this abstract data type is defined by the module **ARRAY** below). The pictures of numbers in pigeon-holes are a convenient and often used representation of arrays. Programs, on the other hand, are syntactic entities: in the program

```
a[0] := a[2]
```

`a` is an "array variable," which in any given store, denotes an array, just as the program variable `'X` denotes an integer value in any given store. The distinction between array variables and arrays is exactly the same as the distinction between program variables and integers. This is an important distinction, but one that many textbooks gloss over.

Before we give the syntax and semantics of programs that manipulate arrays, we give a precise characterisation of what arrays are. From the preceding discussion, it is clear that the salient features of arrays are that they store integer values in components, and that these values can be updated; in this respect, an array is very like a store. To capture the fact that arrays store values in numbered components, we introduce an operation

```
op _[_] : Array Int -> Int .
```

so that if `A` is an array and `I` an integer, then `A[I]` denotes the integer value held in the `I`th component of `A`. To represent modifications to arrays, we introduce an operation

```
op _[_<-_] : Array Int Int -> Array .
```

with the intention that, for a given array `A` and integers `I` and `J`, `A[I <- J]` denotes the array `A` with the value in the `I`th component set to `J`. For example, if `A` is the array

0	1	2
5	6	4

then the array denoted by `A[0 <- 4]` is

0	1	2
4	6	4

The array `A[0 <- 4]` differs from the array `A` only in the value held in the `0`th component. That is, we have

```
(A[0 <- 4])[0]  =  4
```

and

```
(A[0 <- 4])[K]  =  A[K]
```

for all integers `K` $\neq$ `0` (compare this with the effect of assignments upon stores). These equations are generalised in the following OBJ specification of arrays. Note that we introduce a distinguished array `zero` which stores the value `0` in each of its components: we will use this as the value of array variables in the initial store.

```
obj ARRAY is pr ZZ .
  sort Array .
  op  zero : -> Array .
  op  _[_] : Array Int -> Int [prec 5] .
  op  _[_<-_] : Array Int Int -> Array .
  var A : Array .
  var I J K : Int .
  eq  zero[I]  =  0 .
  eq  (A [ I <- J ])[I]  =  J .
  cq  (A [ I <- J ])[K]  =  A[K]    if  not(I is K) .
endo
```

Note that the arrays defined here are indexed by the set of all integers, and can therefore be thought of as extending infinitely in both directions. While this does not reflect what most programming languages do, it is a convenient simplification that will do no harm. This is discussed in more detail at the end of this section.

Turning now to the syntax of programs that manipulate arrays, we introduce new sorts `Arvar` and `Arcomp` to our programming language for arrays and components of arrays. We call objects of sort `Arvar` "array variables"; in the semantics that we give below, a store assigns an array to an array variable. The features of arrays in which we are interested are: (a) that the `i`th component of an array `a` can be accessed, so that the expression `a['X]` denotes, in a given store, an integer value; and (b) that array components can be modified by programs like

```
a['X] := 2 * a['X + 1] .
```

As always, it is easy to extend the syntax of the programming language by adding operations

```
op  _[_] : Arvar Exp -> Arcomp .
op  _:=_ : Arcomp Exp -> Pgm .
```

The reason for introducing the name `Arcomp` rather than just declaring

```
op  _[_] : Arvar Exp -> Exp .
```

is that we want to assign values to array components, and an assignment operator of type

```
op  _:=_ : Exp Exp -> Pgm .
```

would not be feasible! However, in order to regard terms like `a['X + 1]` as expressions when they occur in the right side of an assignment, we declare the subsort relation:

```
subsort  Arcomp < Exp .
```

Thus an **Arcomp** such as `a['X]` can be viewed either as a component to which values may be assigned, or as an expression denoting an integer.

Finally, we need some array variables. For the sort **Var** of program variables, we used OBJ's built in sort of quoted identifiers; we could do something similar for array variables, but in the examples below we will never need more than three array variables, so we just declare constants `a`, `b` and `c` to be array variables.

We package all this neatly up in the following OBJ module:

```
obj ARRPGM is ex PGM3 .
  sorts  Arvar Arcomp .
  subsort  Arcomp < Exp .
  ops a b c : -> Arvar .
  op  _[_] : Arvar Exp -> Arcomp [prec 1] .
  op  _:=_ : Arcomp Exp -> BPgm [prec 20] .
endo
```

Now `a['X] := 2 * a['X + 1]`, for example, is a syntactically correct program; but we still have to specify what such programs mean. Having extended the syntax of the language, we must now extend its semantics.

We intend the denotation of an **Arvar** in a given store to be an array. It may seem odd that we don't use the term "array" for the entities of the programming language, but our usage is consistent with our referring to `'X + 2` as an "expression" rather than an "integer": in the program `'X := 0 ; a['X] := 4`, for example, `a['X]` is merely an expression of the programming language, and it denotes an array component only in relation to a given store, just as the expression `'X + 2` only denotes an integer in relation to a given store. How then do we signify the array denoted by an array variable? As before, we overload the `_[[_]]` operator by declaring

```
op  _[[_]] : Store Arvar -> Array .
```

Suppose that, in a given store `s`, the array `A = s[[a]]` is

0	1	2
5	6	4

then if `s[['X]] = 0`, when we regard `a['X]` as as expression the only reasonable choice for the integer value `s[[ a['X] ]]` is 5; that is,

```
s[[ a['X] ]]  =  5  =  A[0]  =  (s[[a]])[ s[['X]] ] .
```

(Note the various typings associated with the operators `_[[_]]` and `_[_]` here.) The general case is covered by the following equation:

```
var AV : Arvar .
var E : Exp .
var S : Store .
eq  S[[ AV[E] ]]  =  (S[[AV]])[ S[[E]] ] .
```

Moreover, if `a`, `s` and `A` are as above, then after evaluating the program `a['X] := 4` in the store `s`, we should have `a` denote the array `A[0 <- 4]`, i.e., the array

```
(s ; a['X] := 4)[[a]]
```

should be `A[0 <- 4]`:

0	1	2
4	6	4

Thus we have:

```
(s ; a['X] := 4)[[a]]  =  A[0 <- 4]
                       =  (s[[a]])[ s[['X]] <- s[[4]] ] .
```

The general equation covering such cases is:

```
var AV : Arvar .
var E E' : Exp .
var S : Store .
eq  S ; AV[E] := E' [[AV]]  =  (S[[AV]])[ S[[E]] <- S[[E']] ] .
```

Also, if `a` and `a'` are different array variables, then the assignment `a['X] := 4` shouldn't affect the array denoted by `a'`:

```
var AV AV' : Arvar .
var E E' : Exp .
var S : Store .
cq  S ; AV[E] := E' [[AV']]  =  S[[AV']]   if  AV =/= AV' .
```

(This is similar to the equations for assignment to program variables.)

In summary, our semantics for array expressions is given by the following OBJ module, which contains two further equations stating that assignment to array components doesn't affect the value of variables, and vice-versa:

```
obj SEMARR is pr ARRAY .
              pr ARRPGM .
              pr SEM3 .
  op  _[[_]] : Store Arvar -> Array [prec 65] .

  var AV AV' : Arvar .
  var X : Var .
  var E E' : Exp .
  var S : Store .

  eq  initial [[AV]]  =  zero .
  eq  S[[ AV[E] ]]  =   (S[[AV]])[ S[[E]] ] .
  eq  S ; AV[E] := E' [[AV]]  =
      (S[[AV]])[ S[[E]] <- S[[E']] ] .
  cq  S ; AV[E] := E' [[AV']]  =  S[[AV']]    if  AV =/= AV' .

  eq  S ; X := E [[AV]]  =  S[[AV]] .
  eq  S ; AV[E] := E' [[X]]  =  S[[X]] .
endo
```

Finally, we note that in a programming language such as Pascal, an array always has a fixed size. For example, the Pascal declaration

```
array a[0..n] of int ;
```

creates an array with `n+1` components:

```
 0  1          n
|  |  |  ...  |  |
```

whereas in our programming language, we "create" an array by making the OBJ declaration

```
op  a : -> Arvar .
```

but the array denoted by `a` in any store has no fixed size, since for any array `A`, we can write `A[I]` for *any* integer `I`. We may picture `A` as having infinitely many components, stretching off in both directions:

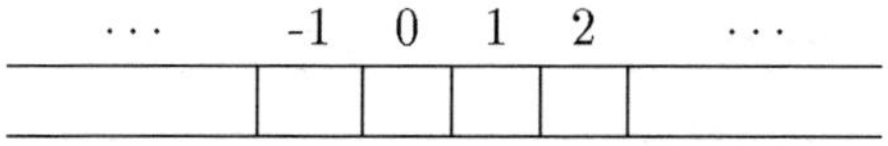

... -1 0 1 2 ...

While it is possible to define arrays of fixed size in OBJ, we prefer the simplicity of the definition given above. In practice, we consider only programs that manipulate finite segments of arrays. If `A` is an array and `l` and `u` integers, then by the array segment `A[l..u]` we mean that portion of the array `A` containing the components `A[l]`, `A[l+1]`, ..., `A[u-1]`; i.e., all components `A[i]`, where `l <= i < u` (the component `A[u]` is not included in this segment):

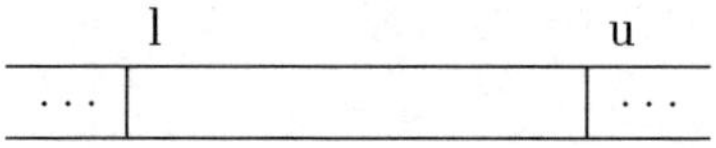

l u

... ...

Sometimes we will abuse this notation and talk of an array segment `a[l..u]` to mean the array segment `(s[[a]])[l..u]` in some given store `s`.

6.1 Some Simple Examples

This section works through a few simple examples, with the aim of strengthening the reader's intuitions about our definition of arrays.

Consider the program `p1` defined in the following OBJ module.

```
obj EG1 is pr SEMARR .
  let p1 = a[0] := 5 ; a[1] := 6 .
endo
```

For any store `s`, the array `A = s ; p1 [[a]]` will look like:

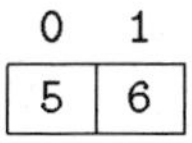

0	1
5	6

We can check this by evaluating `A[0]` and `A[1]`, which should give the values 5 and 6, respectively. For example, to check that `A[0] = 5` :

```
open EG1 .
op s : -> Store .
red s ; p1 [[ a[0] ]] .
close
```

The main steps in the above reduction are:

```
    s ; p1 [[ a[0] ]]
=
    (s ; p1 [[a]])[ s ; p1 [[0]] ]
=
    (s ; a[0] := 5 ; a[1] := 6 [[a]])[0]
=
    ((s ; a[0] := 5 [[a]])
     [ s ; a[0] := 5 [[1]] <- s ; a[0] := 5 [[6]] ])[0]
=
    ((s ; a[0] := 5 [[a]])[1 <- 6])[0]
=
    (((s[[a]])[ s[[0]] <- s[[5]] ])[1 <- 6])[0]
=
    ((s[[a]])[0 <- 5])[0]
=
    5 .
```

Now consider the program p2:

```
obj EG2 is pr SEMARR .
  let p2 = a['X] := a['Y] .
endo
```

We can show that for any store s, we have

```
s ; p2 [[ a['X] ]]  =  s[[ a['Y] ]]
```

by calculating as follows:

```
    s ; p2 [[ a['X] ]]
=
    (s ; p2 [[a]])[ s ; p2 [['X]] ]
=
    (s ; a['X] := a['Y] [[a]])[ s ; a['X] := a['Y] [['X]] ]
=
    (s ; a['X] := a['Y] [[a]])[ s[['X]] ]
=
    ((s[[a]])[ s[['X]] <- s[[ a['Y] ]] ])[ s[['X]] ]
=
    s[[ a['Y] ]] .
```

We can also show that `p` doesn't affect the value of `a['Y]`, though for this we need to make a case analysis. The first case is `s[['X]] = s[['Y]]` :

```
    s ; p2 [[ a['Y] ]]
=       { as above }
    ((s[[a]])[ s[['X]] <- s[[ a['Y] ]] ])[ s[['Y]] ]
=       { s[['X]] = s[['Y]] }
    s[[ a['Y] ]] .
```

And the second case is `not(s[['X]] is s[['Y]])` :

```
    s ; p2 [[ a['Y] ]]
=       { as above }
    ((s[[a]])[ s[['X]] <- s[[ a['Y] ]] ])[ s[['Y]] ]
=       { not(s[['X]] is s[['Y]]) }
    (s[[a]])[ s[['Y]] ]
=
    s[[ a['Y] ]] .
```

We define now a subroutine, `swap(AV,E1,E2)`, that swaps the values held in `AV[E1]` and `AV[E2]`:

```
obj SWAP is pr SEMARR .
  op swap : Arvar Exp Exp -> Pgm .
  var AV : Arvar .
  var E1 E2 : Exp .
  eq  swap(AV,E1,E2) =
        'T := AV[E1] ; AV[E1] := AV[E2] ; AV[E2] := 'T .
endo
```

Given a store `s` and an array variable `a`, we can reduce `s ; swap(a,1,2) [[a]]` to obtain

```
((s[[a]])[ 1 <- s[[ a[2] ]] ])[2 <- s[[ a[1] ]] ].
```

Thus, for example, if the array `A = s[[a]]` is

0	1	2
5	6	4

then the array `A' = s ; swap(a,1,2) [[a]]` is

0	1	2
5	4	6

We will use the subroutine **swap** in the following section, where we simply regard `swap(AV,E1,E2)` as an abbreviation for the program

```
'T := AV[E1] ; AV[E1] := AV[E2] ; AV[E2] := 'T .
```

Procedures are considered in detail in Chapter 7.

6.2 Exercises

Exercise 28 Consider the following OBJ code:

```
obj EG3 is pr SEMARR .
  let p3 = a[0] := 5 ; a[1] := 6 ; a[2] := 4 .
endo

open EG3 .
op s : -> Store .
let A = s ; p3 [[a]] .
close
```

Show that `A[0] = 5` , `A[1] = 6` and `A[2] = 4` . What is the value of `A[3]`? Show that

```
s ; p3 ; a[0] := a[2] [[ a[0] ]]  =  4 .
```

□

Exercise 29 Let `A = s[[a]]` be the array

0	1	2	3	4	5	6
5	6	4	6	5	4	6

What are the arrays `A1 = s ; a[a[0]] := a[0] + 1 [[a]]` and `A2 = s ; a[a[0]] := a[a[0] + 1] [[a]]` ? □

Exercise 30 Given the array `A = s[[a]]` :

0	1	2
5	6	4

evaluate `A' = s ; swap(a,1,2) [[a]]` , and show that `A'[0] = 5` , `A'[1] = 4` and `A'[2] = 6`. Evaluate the following:

```
A'' = s ; swap(a,1,2) ; swap(a,0,1) [[a]]
```

□

Exercise 31 Write an OBJ theory that specifies a sort `BArray` of arrays whose components hold Boolean values. □

6.3 Specifications and Proofs

In specifying and proving properties of programs that manipulate arrays, we often want to state that some property holds for each component in a segment of an array. For example, suppose we want to set `'M` to the value of the maximum element in an array segment `a[l..u]` where `l` and `u` are some fixed integers. We might specify this directly, using a universal quantification, as follows:

```
pre(S,a0,l,u)  =  (S[[a]] == a0)  and  l < u .
post(S,a0,l,u) =  (S[[a]] == a0)  and
                  (∀ i : l <= i < u) a0[i] <= S[['M]] .
```

Here, `a0` is a specification constant ranging over arrays, and is used to denote the initial value of the array variable `a`. A program which is correct with respect to this specification is:

```
th MAXP is pr SEMARR .
  ops l u : -> Int .
  eq  l < u  =  true .
  let init = 'X := l + 1 ; 'M := a[l] .
  let body = if 'M < a['X] then 'M := a['X] else skip fi ;
             'X := 'X + 1 .
  let maxp = init ; while 'X < u do body od .
endth
```

We use the keyword `th` to capture the idea that `maxp` is a correct program for all integers `l` and `u` such that `l < u`. We can prove the partial correctness of `maxp` by using the following invariant:

```
inv(S)  =  inv1(S) and inv2(S)
```

where

```
inv1(S)  =  S[['X]] <= u   and   (S[[a]] == a0)
inv2(S)  =  (∀ i : 1 <= i < S[['X]]) a0[i] <= S[['M]] .
```

To prove the partial correctness of **maxp** using the proof rule of the previous chapter, we need to show three things: that **init** establishes **inv**; that **inv** and the negation of the guard imply the postcondition; and that **inv** is an invariant of the loop. We show only the third, leaving the first two proof obligations for the reader (Exercise 34).

To prove that **inv** is an invariant of the loop, we must show that for all stores **s**, if **inv(s)** holds and **s** makes the guard true, then **inv(s ; body)** holds. To prove this, we add a new constant **s** of sort **Store** and declare equations which correspond to the assumptions that the guard is true and the invariant holds. These are given in the following module.

```
th PROOF is pr MAXP .
  op s : -> Store .
  op a0 : -> Array .
  *** assume guard ***
  eq  (s[['X]]) < u  =  true .
  *** assume inv1(s) ***
  eq  (s[['X]]) <= u  =  true .
  eq  s[[a]]  =  a0 .
  *** assume inv2(s) ***
  var I : Int .
  cq  a0[I] <= (s[['M]])  =  true
  if  1 <= I  and  I < (s[['X]]) .
endth
```

Note how the use of the OBJ variable **I** corresponds to the universal quantification in the definition of **inv2**.

Because the body of the loop contains a conditional statement, we proceed by case analysis: we will only consider the case where

```
s[['M]] < a0[ s[['X]] ] ,
```

the other case being similar. We therefore add the equation

```
eq  s[['M]] < a0[ s[['X]] ]  =  true .
```

If we now ask OBJ to reduce **inv1(s ; body)** , we get the result **true**, so we need only show that **inv2(s ; body)** holds. By the definition of **inv2** and some simplification, we see that

```
  inv2(s ; body)
=
  (∀ i : 1 <= i <= s[['X]]) a0[i] <= a0[ s[['X]] ] .
```

And so our goal is to prove this universally quantified statement. We do so by introducing a new constant `i` of sort `Int`, and we assume that `1 <= i <= s[['X]]` by declaring:

```
eq  1 <= i   =  true .
eq  i <= s[['X]]   =  true .
```

And now we need to show that `a0[i] <= a0[ s[['X]] ]` . In fact, to show this, we need to make a further case analysis: because `i <= s[['X]]` , either `i < s[['X]]` or `i is s[['X]]` . In the latter case , we need to show that

```
a0[ s[['X]] ] <= a0[ s[['X]] ] ,
```

which is immediate. For the case that `i < s[['X]]` , we assume

```
eq  i < s[['X]]   =  true .
```

and then perform the following reductions:

```
red  a0[i] <= s[['M]] .
red  s[['M]] <= a0[ s[['X]] ] .
```

Both of these give the result `true`, so we conclude that

```
a0[i] <= a0[ s[['X]] ]
```

as desired. Note that the first reduction uses the conditional equation which corresponds to the assumption of `inv2`. This part of the proof that `inv` is an invariant of the loop is summarised in the following proof score.

```
*** case s[['M]] < a0[ s[['X]] ] ***
th CASE1 is pr PROOF .
  eq  (s[['M]]) < a0[ s[['X]] ]  =  true .
  *** show inv2(s ; body) ***
  op i : -> Int .
  eq  1 <= i  =  true .
  eq  i <= (s[['X]])  =  true .
endth
```

```
*** case i = s[['X]] ***
open CASE1 .
eq  i = s[['X]] .
red  a0[i] <= (s ; body [['M]]) .    ***> should be: true
close

*** case i < s[['X]] ***
open CASE1 .
eq  i < (s[['X]])  =  true .
red  a0[i] <= (s[['M]]) .                ***> should be: true
red  (s[['M]]) <= (s ; body [['M]]) .    ***> should be: true
*** therefore a0[i] <= s ; body [['M]] ***
close
```

This OBJ proof illustrates how we can reason about statements that contain universal quantifiers. To prove such statements, as in previous chapters, we add new constants; to assume such statements, we declare OBJ equations with variables.

The proof also illustrates that this direct way of using OBJ to verify proofs which involve universal quantifications can sometimes be rather cumbersome. An approach which is often more satisfactory is to define OBJ operations which have the effect of universally quantified statements. For example, the operation `atmost` defined below will allow us to reformulate the predicate `inv2`:

```
obj ATMOST is pr ARRAY .
  op atmost : Array Int Int Int -> Bool .
  var A : Array .  vars L U M : Int .
  cq  atmost(A, L, U, M)  =  true    if  U <= L .
  cq  atmost(A, L, U, M)  =  atmost(A, L, U - 1, M) and
                             A[U - 1] <= M    if  L < U .
endo
```

For any array `A` and integers `L`, `U` and `M`, `atmost(A,L,U,M)` states that all elements in the array segment are less than or equal to `M`. That is,

(*) `atmost(A,L,U,M)` iff ($\forall$ `i : L <= i < U`) `A[i] <= M .`

The reader may feel that this is immediate from the definition of `atmost`; if not, it can be proved by induction on `U - L` (if `U - L` is negative, then the array segment is empty, and both sides of the equation are true).

Now `inv2(S)` can be reformulated as `atmost(a0,1,s[['X]],s[['M]])` , and the postcondition can be reformulated in a similar way. The following OBJ proof score shows that a reformulation of **inv** is an invariant for **maxp**.

```
th PROOF2 is pr MAXP .
             pr ATMOST .
  op inv : Store -> Bool .
  op a0 : -> Array .
  var S : Store .
  eq  inv(S)  =  1 <= (S[['X]])  and  (S[['X]]) <= u  and
                 ((S[[a]]) == a0) and
                 atmost(a0, 1, S[['X]], S[['M]]) .
  op s : -> Store .
  eq  (s[['X]]) < u  =  true .
  eq  1 <= (s[['X]])  =  true .
  eq  (s[['X]]) <= u  =  true .
  eq  s[[a]]  =  a0 .
  eq  atmost(a0, 1, s[['X]], s[['M]])  =  true .
endth

*** case s[['M]] < a0[ s[['X]] ] ***
open PROOF2 .
eq  (s[['M]]) < a0[ s[['X]] ]  =  true .
*** therefore ***
[lemma] eq  atmost(a0, 1, s[['X]], a0[ s[['X]] ])  =  true .
red  inv(s ; body) .
close

*** case  a0[ s[['X]] ] <= s[['M]] ***
open PROOF2 .
eq  a0[ s[['X]] ] <= (s[['M]])  =  true .
red  inv(s ; body) .
close
```

The first branch of the case analysis in this proof uses

```
atmost(a0, 1, s[['X]], a0[ s[['X]] ])
```

as a lemma. The lemma follows from the two assumptions

```
atmost(a0, 1, s[['X]], s[['M]])   and   a0[ s[['X]] ] <= s[['M]] .
```

The general property of `atmost` that is being used here is expressed by the following conditional equation:

```
cq  atmost(A,L,U,M) = true  if atmost(A,L,U,M') and M' <= M .
```

which can be shown to be valid by using equation `(*)` above.

Finally, we give a correctness proof for a program that updates the values of an array. Suppose we want to rearrange the values in an array segment `a[0..300]` so that all the values less than or equal to `50` are on the left-hand side, and all the values greater than `50` are on the right-hand side. That is, we want to modify `a[0..300]` so that it looks as follows:

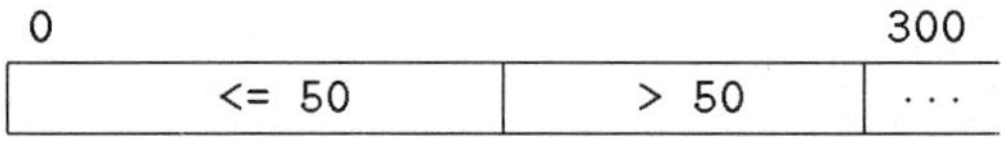

```
0                                        300
+----------------------+-----------------+-----
|        <= 50         |      > 50       | ...
+----------------------+-----------------+-----
```

Programs to achieve this are specified as follows:

```
pre(S)  =  true
post(S) =  (∀ i) 0 <= i < S[['L]]  ⇒  S[[a[i]]] <= 50   and
           (∀ i) S[['L]] <= i < 300  ⇒  50 < S[[a[i]]] .
```

An idea which leads to a solution is to go through the array, moving any values greater than `50` to the right, and values less than or equal to `50` to the left. Midway through the evaluation of the program, the situation will look like:

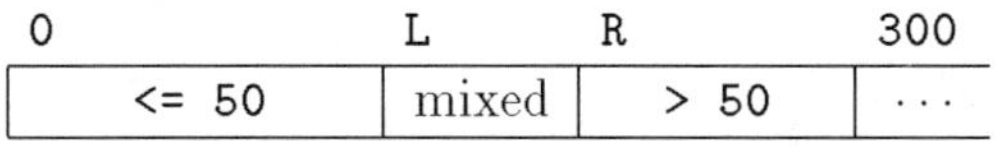

```
0                  L         R             300
+-----------------+---------+-------------+-----
|      <= 50      |  mixed  |    > 50     | ...
+-----------------+---------+-------------+-----
```

We use `'L` and `'R` to mark the "done" parts of the array segment; the segment between `'L` and `'R` represents the segment that remains to be processed. This suggests an invariant of the form

```
inv(S)  =  0 <= (S[['L]])  and  (S[['R]]) <= 300  and
           (∀ i : 0 <= i < (S[['L]])) (S[[a]])[i] <= 50  and
           (∀ i : (S[['R]]) <= i < 300) 50 < (S[[a]])[i] .
```

and a program of the form

```
partp = 'L := 0 ; 'R := 300 ;
        while 'L < 'R
        do if a['L] <= 50 then 'L := 'L + 1
                          else 'R := 'R - 1 ; swap(a,'L,'R) fi
        od .
```

Recall from Section 6.1 that `swap(a,'L,'R)` is an abbreviation for the program

```
'T := a['L] ; a['L] := a['R] ; a['R] := 'T .
```

The interesting part of the correctness proof shows that `inv` is an invariant of the loop; following the structure of the body of the loop, this divides naturally into two cases: where the value of `a['L]` is at most `50`, and where the value of `a['L]` is greater than `50`. We consider the second case, in which the array variable `a` is updated by the assignments of `swap(a,'L,'R)`. What we need to show is that for all stores `s`, if `inv(s)` holds and `s[['L < 'R]]` is true and `s[[a['L]]]` is greater than `50`, then

```
(*)    inv(s ; 'R := 'R - 1 ; swap(s,'L,'R))
```

holds. Let `s` be a store, and write `sl` for `s[['L]]`, `sr` for `s[['R]]`, and `sa` for `s[[a]]`. Assume that `inv(s)` holds, that `sl < sr` and that `50 < sa[sl]`. Using the definition of `inv`, and reducing `(*)` according to the equations of `SEMARR`, we have to show four things:

```
(a)    0 <= sl   and
(b)    sr - 1 <= 300   and
(c)    (∀ i : 0 <= i < sl) (sa')[i] <= 50   and
(d)    (∀ i : sr - 1 <= i < 300) 50 < (sa')[i] ,
```

where

```
sa'  =  sa [ sl <- sa[sr - 1] ] [ sr - 1 <- sa[sl] ] .
```

`(a)` and `(b)` follow straightforwardly from our assumption of `inv(s)`. To show `(c)`, let `i` be any integer such that `0 <= i < sl` . Then

```
    (sa')[i]
=
    (sa [ sl <- sa[sr - 1] ] [ sr - 1 <- sa[sl] ]) [i]
=         { i ≠ (sr - 1) because i < sl < sr }
    (sa [ sl <- sa[sr - 1] ]) [i]
=         { i ≠ sl because i < sl }
    (sa)[i]
```

Therefore, `(sa')[i] <= 50` because `(sa)[i] <= 50` by assumption of `inv(s)`. Finally, to show `(d)`, we reason as follows:

```
        (∀i : sr - 1 <= i < 300) 50 < (sa')[i]
    ⇔          { because sr - 1 < 300 }
        50 < (sa')[sr - 1] and (∀i : sr <= i < 300) 50 < (sa')[i]
    ⇔          { reduce first conjunct }
        50 < (sa)[sl] and (∀i : sr <= i < 300) 50 < (sa')[i]
    ⇔          { first conjunct is true by assumption }
        (∀i : sr <= i < 300) 50 < (sa')[i]
    ⇔
        (∀i : sr <= i < 300)
          50 < (sa [ sl <- sa[sr - 1] ] [ sr - 1 <- sa[sl] ])[i]
    ⇔          { sr - 1 ≠ i because sr <= i }
        (∀i : sr <= i < 300) 50 < (sa [ sl <- sa[sr - 1] ])[i]
    ⇔          { sl ≠ i because sl < sr <= i }
        (∀i : sr <= i < 300) 50 < (sa)[i]
```

The latter formula is true by assumption of `inv(s)`.

The remainder of the proof of partial correctness of `partp` is left as an exercise for the reader (Exercise 36).

For the program `maxp`, we gave two correctness proofs; one using a universally quantified statement and another using an operation `atmost` that replaced the universally quantified statement. Of course, the same thing can be done for the program `partp`: the reformulation is left as an exercise for the reader (Exercise 37).

6.4 Exercises

Exercise 32 Develop and prove correct an algorithm that sets each array component `a[i]` to `i * i` for each `i` such that `0 <= i < n` for some given natural number `n`. □

Exercise 33 Give OBJ code that defines an operation

```
sum : Array Int -> Int
```

such that for all arrays `A` and integers `U`,

$$\texttt{sum(A,U)} \;=\; \Sigma_{\texttt{i}=0}^{\texttt{U}-1}\ \texttt{A[i]}\ ,$$

that is,

```
sum(A,U)  =  A[0] + A[1] + ... + A[U - 1] .
```

Develop and prove correct an algorithm that sets **'X** to the sum of the first **u** elements of the array variable a; that is, the program should satisfy the following specification.

```
pre(S)  =  0 <= u  and  sum(S[[a]],u) is x .
post(S) =  S[['X]] is x .
```

□

Exercise 34 Complete the proof of correctness of the program **maxp** given at the beginning of Section 6.3 □

Exercise 35 An array segment `A[0..U]` is called *low* iff

```
(∀ j  : 0 <= j < U) 0 <= A[j] <= j .
```

Give OBJ equations that define a predicate

```
low : Array Int -> Bool
```

so that `low(A,U)` iff `A[0..U]` is low, and prove that if `A[0..U]` is low and if `0 <= I < U`, then `0 <= A[A[I]] <= I`. Use this property to prove the partial correctness of the following program

```
'I := 0 ;
while 'I < 50
do a['I] := a[a['I]] ; 'I := 'I + 1 od
```

with respect to the specification

```
pre(S)  = low(S[[a]],50) .
post(S) = low(S[[a]],50) .
```

□

Exercise 36 Complete the proof of the partial correctness of **partp** from the previous section. □

Exercise 37 Give OBJ code which defines operations

```
below50 : Array Int -> Bool .
above50 : Array Int -> Bool .
```

such that

below50(A,L) iff (∀ i : 0 <= i < L) A[i] <= 50

and

above50(A,R) iff (∀ i : R <= i < 300) 50 < A[i] .

Use these operations to give an OBJ proof of the correctness of **partp** from the previous section. Compare this proof with your answer to Exercise 36 above; which do you find simpler? □

Exercise 38 An array segment A[L..U] is said to be *sorted* iff

(∀i) L < i < U ⇒ A[i - 1] <= A[i].

(a) Write OBJ code which defines a predicate

```
op  sorted : Array Int Int -> Bool
```

such that sorted(A,L,U) is true iff the array segment A[L..U] is sorted.

(b) The following OBJ code defines programs swap and insert.

```
obj SWAP is pr SEMARR .
  op swap : Arvar Exp Exp -> Pgm .
  var A : Arvar .    vars E E' : Exp .
  eq  swap(A,E,E') =
        'T := A[E] ; A[E] := A[E'] ; A[E'] := 'T .
endo

obj INSERT is pr SWAP .
  let init = 'X := 'P .
  let body = swap(a,'X - 1,'X) ; 'X := 'X - 1 .
  let test = 0 < 'X  and  a['X] < a['X - 1] .
  let insert = init ; while test do body od .
endo
```

Prove that the program is correct with respect to the precondition

P(S) = 0 <= (S[['P]]) and sorted(S[[a]],0,S[['P]]) .

and postcondition

```
Q(S)  =  sorted(S[[a]],0,S[['P + 1]]) .
```

Use the following invariant:

```
I(S)  =  sorted(S[[a]],0,S[['X]])  and
         sorted(S[[a]],S[['X]],S[['P + 1]])  and
         0 <= (S[['X]])  and  (S[['X]]) <= (S[['P]]) .
```

In addition to the properties of **sorted** given in your answer to part (a) above, use the following: for all arrays **A**, and all integers **L**, **U**, **I** and **J**,

```
cq  sorted(A,L,U)  =  true    if  sorted(A,L,U + 1) .
cq  sorted(A[I <- J],L,U)  =  sorted(A,L,U)   if  U <= I .
cq  sorted((A[L - 1 <- A[L]])[L <- A[L - 1]], L - 1, U)
      =  sorted(A,L,U)   if  A[L] <= A[L - 1] .
```

(c) Develop and prove correct an algorithm which uses the program **insert** to sort a given array. That is, the precondition is

```
P(S)  =  0 <= u .
```

where **u** is a given integer; and the postcondition is

```
Q(S)  =  sorted(S[[a]],0,u)
```

□

7 Procedures

In the previous chapter, the procedure **swap** was used in a variety of programs to manipulate arrays. This procedure was defined by the following equation:

```
var AV : Arvar .
vars E1 E2 : Exp .
eq  swap(AV,E1,E2)  =
    'T := AV[E1] ; AV[E1] := AV[E2] ; AV[E2] := 'T .
```

An occurrence of a term `swap(av,e1,e2)` in a program is referred to as a **procedure call**. Wherever `swap(av,e1,e2)` appears in a program, this equation can be used to replace the procedure call with its **body**, i.e., the right side of the above equation with `AV` instantiated to `av`, `E1` instantiated to `e1` and `E2` instantiated to `e2`.

Procedures are useful in programming languages because they provide a means to abstract away from implementation details. For example, suppose we are writing a large program that makes extensive use of code to sort array segments. It would be advisable to isolate this code as a procedure which could be called by the larger program as required. One advantage of this is that the larger program becomes more concise, and is easier to read and understand. Another advantage is that all we need remember about the procedure is its name and its specification: its pre- and postconditions. These tell us *what* the program does; its definition tells us *how* it does it. This means that we are free to change the body of the procedure, perhaps to give more efficient code for sorting arrays. Provided that the new body satisfies the given specification, such a change will not affect the correctness of any program which uses the procedure.

Thus there are two different aspects to the correctness of a procedure: the correctness of its definition, and the correctness of its use (i.e., the correctness of its procedure calls). In this chapter we make precise what we mean by "procedure" and we present some rules for proving the correctness of procedure definitions and procedure calls. The main point concerning the semantics of procedure calls has already been made: the semantics of a procedure call is just rewriting, filling in the definition of a procedure for its name, as illustrated by the example of `swap`. However, in many programming languages, including Pascal, procedures take expressions as arguments in a more complex way, as discussed in Section 7.1.3 below.

In general, by a procedure we mean any operation that takes some number of arguments of sort `Var`, `Arvar`, and `Exp`, and gives a `Pgm` as result.

Definition 36 A **procedure** is an operation, `proc`, defined by an OBJ module of the form

```
obj PROC is pr SEMARR .
  op proc : Var^K Arvar^L Exp^M -> Pgm .
  vars X1 ... XK : Var .
  vars AV1 ... AVL : Arvar .
  vars E1 ... EM : Exp .
  eq proc(X⃗,AV⃗,E⃗) = <body> .
endo
```

where the notation $\texttt{Var}^K$ indicates that `proc` takes K `Var`'s as arguments; similarly $\texttt{Arvar}^L$ indicates that `proc` takes L `Arvar`'s as arguments, and so on. The total number of arguments is therefore $K+L+M$. Note that this is not proper OBJ notation; we are using this notation to indicate that a procedure takes *some number*[1] of arguments, of which some are `Var`'s, some are `Arvar`'s, and some are `Exp`'s. But any instance of it will be a proper OBJ module. The notation $\vec{\texttt{X}}$ is shorthand for a variable list `X1,...,XK`, and $\vec{\texttt{AV}}$ represents `AV1,...,AVL`, etc. Thus the arguments to `proc` are all the OBJ variables declared in the module `PROC`. We write "`<body>`" in the right side of the equation to denote some term of sort `Pgm`, which uses the OBJ variables `X1`, `AV1`, `SV1`, `E1`, etc.

We refer to the program on the right side of the equation as the **body** of the procedure, and we refer to the arguments of a procedure as its **parameters**; those parameters of sort `Var` or `Arvar` will be called **var-parameters**, and those of sort `Exp` will be called **exp-parameters**. An occurrence of a term

```
proc(x1,...,av1,...,e1,...)
```

in a program will be referred to as a **call** of the procedure `proc`, or as just a **procedure call**. □

For example, the procedure `swap` as defined above has one var-parameter (of sort `Arvar`) and two exp-parameters. The procedure `facm` defined below, which sets the variable `'X` to the factorial of the value held in variable `'M`, has no parameters:

```
obj FACM is pr SEMARR .
  op facm : -> Pgm .
  eq facm = 'X := 1 ; 'C := 0 ;
```

[1] Also, the ordering of the arguments should not be taken literally, since the procedure call could have any mixfix syntax, with its arguments in any order.

```
                    while not('X is 'M)
                    do 'C := 'C + 1 ; 'X := 'X * 'C od .
endo
```

The following procedure **idp** has one var-parameter (of sort **Var**) and no other parameters; **idp(X)** does nothing if the value of the variable **X** is at least **0**, and otherwise it never terminates:

```
obj IDP is pr SEMARR .
  op  idp : Var -> Pgm .
  var X : Var .
  eq  idp(X)  =  if X is 0 then skip
                 else X := X - 1 ; idp(X) ; X := X + 1 fi .
endo
```

The procedure **idp** is **recursive**, in the sense that it is defined in terms of itself; that is, the body of the procedure calls itself. The other examples above are **non-recursive**; for example, there is no call of **facm** in the body of **facm**. In discussing the correctness of procedures below, we distinguish recursive and non-recursive procedures; within those classes, we further distinguish between procedures according to the sorts of their parameters. We begin with a discussion of non-recursive procedures.

7.1 Non-recursive Procedures

A non-recursive procedure is one whose body contains no call of the procedure itself; this section discusses the correctness of such procedures. The following subsections discuss, respectively, procedures with no parameters, procedures with var-parameters, and procedures with exp-parameters.

7.1.1 Procedures with no parameters

A procedure that takes no parameters is defined by a single equation of the following form:

```
eq  proc  =  <body> .
```

The name of the procedure, **proc**, can therefore be thought of as merely an abbreviation for its body, and to say that **proc** is correctly defined with respect to a given specification is merely to say that its body satisfies that specification. Consider, for example, the following definition of a procedure to swap the values held in the variables `'X` and `'Y`, whose specification is given as a comment in the definition:

```
obj SWAP is pr SEMARR .
  op swap : -> Pgm .
  *** for all  x y : Int
  *** pre(S,x,y)  =  (S[['X]]) is x  and  (S[['Y]]) is y
  *** post(S,x,y) =  (S[['Y]]) is x  and  (S[['X]]) is y
  eq  swap  =  'X := 'X + 'Y ; 'Y := 'X - 'Y ; 'X := 'X - 'Y .
endo
```

Note that the comments list all the specification constants used in the pre- and postconditions, and that we have explicitly made the pre- and postconditions depend upon these constants. This will be useful later on when we come to discuss the correctness of procedure definitions.

It can be shown that the body of `swap` is correct with respect to the given pre- and postconditions (this was Exercise 9 of Chapter 2), and we might use this fact in proving the correctness of the following program to compute the greatest common divisor of `'T` and `'U`:

```
gcdprog  =  'X := 'T ; 'Y := 'U ;
            while not('X is 'Y)
            do  if 'X < 'Y then 'Y := 'Y - 'X else swap fi  od
```

with respect to the following specification:

```
pre(S,t,u)  =  (S[['T]]) is t  and  (S[['U]]) is u  and
               0 < t  and  0 < u .
post(S,t,u) =  (S[['X]]) is gcd(t,u)  and
               (S[['T]]) is t  and (S[['U]]) is u .
```

In order to prove the correctness of `gcdprog`, we need to know that `swap` does not change the values of `'T` and `'U`. This property is not stated in the specification of the procedure `swap`, but it can be proved by showing that the body of `swap` does not change those values. However, this means that if we change the definition of the procedure `swap` to

```
eq  swap  =  'T := 'X ; 'X := 'Y ; 'Y := 'T .
```

then `gcdprog` is no longer correct, because now `swap` does change the value of `'T`. It is therefore important that the specification of a procedure states which variables may be affected by evaluation of its body. For example, the following would be a satisfactory specification of a procedure to swap the values of `'X` and `'Y`:

```
obj SWAP is pr SEMARR .
  op swap : -> Pgm .
  *** uses  'X 'Y 'T : Var
  *** for all  x y : Int
  *** pre(S,x,y)  =  (S[['X]]) is x  and  (S[['Y]]) is y
  *** post(S,x,y) =  (S[['Y]]) is x  and  (S[['X]]) is y
  eq  swap  =  'T := 'X ; 'X := 'Y ; 'Y := 'T .
endo
```

Similarly, the specification of a procedure should also state which array variables are affected by its body.

We consider the specification of a procedure to be given by the comments in its definition which list the variables used by body of the procedure, and its pre- and postconditions. The following definition states when a procedure is correctly defined with respect to its specification.

Definition 37 Let a procedure `proc` be defined and specified by an OBJ module of the following form:

```
obj PROC is pr SEMARR .
  op  proc : -> Pgm .
  *** uses  Y⃗ : Var
  *** uses  A⃗ : Arvar
  *** for all  e⃗ : Int
  *** for all  a⃗ : Array
  *** pre(S,e⃗,a⃗) = ...
  *** post(S,e⃗,a⃗) = ...
  eq  proc  =  <body> .
endo
```

where $\vec{e}$ is a list of specification constants `e1 ... en : Int`, and similarly $\vec{a}$ is a list of specification constants `a1 ... ap : Array`. Then we say that **the definition of `proc` is correct** (or just that `proc` is **correct**, if the meaning is clear from the context) iff for all stores `s`, integers $\vec{e}$ and arrays $\vec{a}$, if `pre(s,`$\vec{e}$`,`$\vec{a}$`)` holds, then the following conditions are met:

- `proc` terminates on `s`.
- `proc` makes the postcondition true, i.e.,

```
post(s ; proc, e⃗,a⃗) .
```

- For any program variable V of sort Var (or Arvar), if V is not included in the list $\vec{Y}$ (or $\vec{A}$), then

```
s ; proc [[V]]  =  s[[V]] .
```

□

That is, a procedure is correctly defined if it terminates on all stores making the precondition true, if it satisfies the given pre- and postconditions, and if all variables whose values may be changed by the procedure are listed in its specification.

Example 38 The definition of the procedure swap, as given above, is correct with respect to the given specification. The correctness of its body has been proved in previous chapters, and it obviously changes the values of only the variables 'T, 'X and 'Y. □

The enumeration of those variables whose value may be changed by a procedure can be readily verified by inspection of the body of the procedure. We can make the condition more formal by defining a predicate

```
uses : Var Pgm -> Bool
```

in such a way that uses(X,P) is true iff the program P contains an assignment to the variable X:

```
obj USES is pr SEMARR .
  op uses : Var Pgm -> Bool .
  var X Y : Var .    var P1 P2 : Pgm .
  var E1 E2 : Exp .    var T : Tst .
  var AV : Arvar .
  eq uses(X, skip)  =  false .
  eq uses(X, Y := E1)  =  (X == Y) .
  eq uses(X, AV[E1] := E2)  =  false .
  eq uses(X, P1 ; P2)  =  uses(X, P1) or uses(X, P2) .
  eq uses(X, if T then P1 else P2 fi)  =
     uses(X, P1) or uses(X, P2) .
  eq uses(X, while T do P1 od)  =  uses(X, P1) .
endo
```

However, it is possible that a variable used by proc is not changed by proc; for example, its value may be restored after having been temporarily changed.

To verify that swap is correctly defined, note that for any variable V,

```
uses(V, swap)  =  (V == 'T) or (V == 'X) or (V == 'Y) .
```

So we may conclude that 'T, 'X and 'Y are the only variables used by swap.

The following property of uses will be useful in proving the correctness of procedure calls:

Lemma 39 For all variables X and programs P such that not(uses(X,P)), and for all stores S such that P terminates on S,

```
S ; P [[X]]  =  S[[X]] .
```

□

Moreover, a predicate

```
uses : Arvar Pgm -> Bool
```

could be defined for array variables. It can also be shown that this predicate satisfies the analogous property that

```
S ; P [[AV]]  =  S[[AV]]
```

whenever uses(AV,P) is false.

Because the semantics of a procedure call is simply to rewrite of the procedure name to the procedure body, we may expect that the correctness of procedure calls is reducible to the correctness of the definition of the procedure. In fact, Lemma 39 helps us prove Proposition 40 below, which says that a procedure is correctly defined if its body satisfies the given pre- and postconditions and if all those variables whose value may be changed by the procedure are listed in its specification:

Proposition 40 Let a procedure proc be defined and specified as in Definition 37. Then proc is correct if its body satisfies the given pre- and postconditions:

```
(∀ e⃗ : Int)(∀ a⃗ : Array)(∀ S : Store)
  pre(S,e⃗,a⃗) ⇒ post(S ; <body>, e⃗,a⃗) ,
```

and if all the variables used by the procedure are listed in its specification.

Proof: The equation

```
eq  proc  =  <body> .
```

tells us that proc satisfies the pre- and postconditions iff <body> does. Moreover, this equation and Lemma 39 tells us that if the body does not use a variable then its value will not be changed by the procedure. □

Although this proposition seems very straightforward, even trivial, it is important to be aware of the distinction between a procedure and its body. Definition 37 is stated in terms of `proc`, while Proposition 40 says much the same thing, but is stated in terms of `<body>`. The idea behind this distinction is that when we prove properties of programs that use procedures, we should use only the specifications of the procedures that are used, and not their definitions. In this way, the correctness of programs which use procedures does not depend upon the details of those procedures' definitions. In other words, Proposition 40 provides us with a means of proving that a procedure is correctly defined, while Definition 37 provides us with a means of proving properties of programs that contain procedure calls, without using the definitions of those procedures.

As an example, the following OBJ proof score shows that `swap ; swap` does not change the values of `'X` and `'Y`. Because `swap` is correctly defined, we know that the following three equations are valid:

```
eq  S ; swap [['X]]  =  S[['Y]] .
eq  S ; swap [['Y]]  =  S[['X]] .
var V : Var .
cq  S ; swap [[V]]  =  S[[V]]
    if  V =/= 'T and V =/='X and V =/= 'Y .
```

The first two equations follow from the fact that `swap` is correct with respect to its given pre- and postconditions (as in the first clause of Definition 37), while the third follows from the fact that `swap` changes only the value of `'T`, `'X` and `'Y` (as in the second clause of Definition 37). Note that the following proof uses only these three equations, and does not use the definition of `swap` at all. Therefore the proof will still be valid even if the body of the procedure is changed at some point (provided of course that the new definition is also correct).

```
open SEMARR .
op swap : -> Pgm .
var S : Store .
eq  S ; swap [['X]]  =  S[['Y]] .
eq  S ; swap [['Y]]  =  S[['X]] .
var V : Var .
cq  S ; swap [[V]]  =  S[[V]]
    if  V =/= 'T and V =/='X and V =/= 'Y .
op s : -> Store .
red  s ; swap ; swap [['X]] .  ***> should be: s[['X]]
```

```
red  s ; swap ; swap [['Y]] .  ***> should be: s[['Y]]
close
```

Note that the third equation in this proof score, which captures the second clause in Definition 37, is useful for proving correctness of procedure calls in situations where other program variables are used. This equation states that values of variables other than `'T`, `'X` and `'Y` remian unchanged by the procedure call. For example, suppose we want to show that the procedure call `swap` is correct with respect to the following specification:

```
pre(S)  = 2 * (S[['X]]) + (S[['Y]]) is (S[['Z]]) .
post(S) = 2 * (S[['Y]]) + (S[['X]]) is (S[['Z]]) .
```

We can prove this using only the fact that `swap` is correctly defined (i.e., not using the actual definition of `swap`). The proof uses each of the three equations that follow from the fact that `swap` is correctly defined. In particular, it uses the fact that `swap` does not change the value of `'Z`. The proof that the procedure call of `swap` is correct with respect to `pre` and `post` is summarised in the following OBJ proof score:

```
open SEMARR .
op swap : -> Pgm .
var S : Store .
eq  S ; swap [['X]]  =  S[['Y]] .
eq  S ; swap [['Y]]  =  S[['X]] .
var V : Var .
cq  S ; swap [[V]]  =  S[[V]]
     if  V =/= 'T and V =/='X and V =/= 'Y .
op s : -> Store .
*** assume pre(s) ***
eq  s[[z]]  =  2 * (s[['X]]) + (s[['Y]]) .
*** show post(s) ***
op post : Store -> Bool .
eq post(S) = 2 * (S[['Y]]) + (S[['X]]) is (S[['Z]]) .
red  post(s ; swap) .   ***> should be: true
close
```

7.1.2 Procedures with var-parameters

In this section we consider the correctness of procedures that take some number of var-parameters. The statement of correctness of definition for such procedures is essentially the same as for procedures without parameters, but for a universal quantification over the variables that are passed as parameters. However, proofs that procedures are correctly defined once again raise subtle issues concerning universal quantification, as discussed earlier in Section 2.1.1 of Chapter 2.

Consider, for example, the following version of the `swap` procedure, which interchanges the values of two variables given as parameters:

```
obj SWAP is pr SEMARR .
  op swap : Var Var -> Pgm .
  vars X1 X2 : Var .
  *** uses  'T : Var
  *** for all  e1 e2 : Int
  *** pre(S,X1,X2,e1,e2)  =  S[[X1]] is e1  and  S[[X2]] is e2
  *** post(S,X1,X2,e1,e2) =  S[[X1]] is e2  and  S[[X2]] is e1
  eq swap(X1,X2)  =  'T := X1 ; X1 := X2 ; X2 := 'T .
endo
```

The statement that this procedure is correctly defined is that it changes only the variable `'T`, in addition to the parameters `X1` and `X2`, and that

```
(∀ X1,X2 : Var)(∀ e1,e2 : Int)(∀ S : Store)
  pre(S,X1,X2,e1,e2) ⇒ post(S ; swap(X1,X2), X1,X2,e1,e2) .
```

The general notion of correctness for procedures that take var-parameters is as given below. As for procedures without parameters, we require that the specification of the procedure lists all the variables used by the procedure. We also make explicit the dependence of the pre- and postconditions on the parameters of the procedure.

Definition 41 Let a procedure `proc` be defined and specified by an OBJ module of the following form:

```
obj PROC is pr SEMARR .
  op proc : Var^K Arvar^L -> Pgm .
  vars X⃗ : Var .
  vars AV⃗ : Arvar .
  *** uses  Y⃗ : Var
  *** uses  A⃗ : Arvar
  *** for all  e⃗ : Int
  *** for all  a⃗ : Array
```

```
  *** pre(S,X⃗,AV⃗,e⃗,a⃗) = ...
  *** post(S,X⃗,AV⃗,e⃗,a⃗) = ...
  eq  proc(X⃗,AV⃗)  =  <body> .
endo
```

where $\vec{\texttt{X}}$ is a list `X1 ... XK` of OBJ variables of sort `Var`, and similarly for $\vec{\texttt{AV}}$. Then we say that **the definition of `proc` is correct** (or just that `proc` is **correct**, if the meaning is clear from the context) iff for all stores `s`, all variables $\vec{\texttt{X}}$ and array variables $\vec{\texttt{AV}}$, all integers $\vec{\texttt{e}}$ and arrays $\vec{\texttt{a}}$, if `pre`(`s`, $\vec{\texttt{X}}$, $\vec{\texttt{AV}}$, $\vec{\texttt{e}}$, $\vec{\texttt{a}}$) holds, then the following conditions are met:

- `proc`($\vec{\texttt{X}}$, $\vec{\texttt{AV}}$) terminates on `s`.
- `proc`($\vec{\texttt{X}}$, $\vec{\texttt{AV}}$) makes the postcondition true, i.e.,

```
post(s ; proc(X⃗,AV⃗), e⃗,a⃗) .
```

- For any program variable `V` of sort `Var` (or `Arvar`), if `V` is not included in the list $\vec{\texttt{Y}}$ or $\vec{\texttt{X}}$ (or $\vec{\texttt{A}}$ or $\vec{\texttt{AV}}$), then

```
s ; proc(X⃗,AV⃗) [[V]]  =  S[[V]] .
```

□

That is, the correctness of the definition of a procedure is the enumeration of all the variables whose value may be affected by the procedure, and that it satisfies the given pre- and postconditions. However, this definition fails to capture some subtle points regarding universally quantified variables. It is instructive at this point to consider the following OBJ proof score, which is intended to show that the procedure `swap` is correct.

```
open SWAP .
ops x1 x2 : -> Var .
ops e1 e2 : -> Int .
op s : -> Store .

*** assume pre(s,x1,x2,e1,e2) ***
eq  s[[x1]]  =  e1 .
eq  s[[x2]]  =  e2 .

*** show post(s ; swap(x1,x2), x1,x2,e1,e2) ***
red s ; swap(x1,x2) [[x1]] .   ***> should be: e2
```

```
red s ; swap(x1,x2) [[x2]] .    ***> should be: e1
close
```

We might expect to obtain from this and the Theorem of Constants the desired universally quantified statement:

```
(∀ X1,X2 : Var)(∀ e1,e2 : Int)(∀ S : Store)
  pre(S,X1,X2,e1,e2) ⇒ post(S ; swap(X1,X2), X1,X2,e1,e2) .
```

That this is not the case can be shown by calling the procedure `swap` with the variable `'T` as a parameter. From the formula above, we would expect that for all stores `s`,

```
s ; swap ('X,'T)[['X]]  =  s[['T]] .
```

However, if we reduce the right-hand side of this, we see

```
    s ; swap('X,'T) [['X]]
=
    s ; 'T := 'X ; 'X := 'T ; 'T := 'T [['X]]
=
    s ; 'T := 'X [['T]]
=
    s[['X]]
```

contrary to our expectations! The problem lies in our (incorrect) proof of correctness of `swap`: there, we introduced two new constants, `x1` and `x2` of sort `Var` to play the rôle of the universally quantified variables. These new constants are of course distinct from any other constant in the signature, in the same way that the constants `0` and `1` are different constants of sort `Int`. In particular, these constants are distinct from the constant `'T`. This distinctness is used in the proof above, whenever the following conditional equation from `STORE` is used:

```
cq  S ; X := E [[Y]]  =  S[[Y]]   if  X =/= Y .
```

the reader can see this by going through the reductions by hand, or by running the proof in OBJ after typing the command

```
set trace on .
```

which causes OBJ to print out each equation used in the reduction. Note that the issues raised here are exactly those discussed earlier in Section 2.1.1 of Chapter 2.

We can conclude from this discussion that the procedure swap is not correctly defined. We might rectify this state of affairs by changing the specification of swap, weakening the precondition to:

```
pre(S,X1,X2,e1,e2)  =  S[[X1]] is e1  and  S[[X2]] is e2  and
                       X1 =/= 'T and X2 =/= 'T and X1 =/= X2 .
```

Because OBJ treats new constants as distinct, `x1 =/= 'T` and `x2 =/= 'T` and `x1 =/= x2` all reduce to `true`, so the proof score given above, which uses the property that `x1`, `x2` and `'T` are all different, does in fact prove that swap is correctly defined with respect to this new specification.

Another approach, more in line with the treatment of procedures in other textbooks, is to change the definition of correctness for procedures, to make explicit use of the distinctness of new constants which play the rôle of universally quantified variables. Thus we replace Definition 41 with the following:

Definition 42 Let a procedure proc be defined and specified as in Definition 41. Then **the definition of proc is correct** iff for all stores s, all variables $\vec{X}$ and array variables $\vec{AV}$, all integers $\vec{e}$ and arrays $\vec{a}$, if pre(s, $\vec{X}$, $\vec{AV}$, $\vec{e}$, $\vec{a}$) holds, and *provided the variables* $\vec{X}$, $\vec{Y}$, $\vec{AV}$, $\vec{A}$ *are all distinct*, then the following conditions are met:

- proc($\vec{X}$, $\vec{AV}$) terminates on s.
- proc($\vec{X}$, $\vec{AV}$) makes the postcondition true, i.e.,

  post(s ; proc($\vec{X}$,$\vec{AV}$), $\vec{e}$,$\vec{a}$) .

- For any program variable V of sort Var (or Arvar), if V is not included in the list $\vec{Y}$ or $\vec{X}$ (or $\vec{A}$ or $\vec{AV}$), then

  s ; proc($\vec{X}$,$\vec{AV}$) [[V]] = S[[V]] .

□

Many textbooks which cover procedures and procedure calls give a rather informal treatment of parameters by imposing the following restrictions on procedure calls.

> **Rule 1:** If a variable is used by the body of a procedure, then that variable should not be passed as a parameter to the procedure.
> **Rule 2:** In a procedure call proc(X1,...,XM), the variables X1 ... XM should all be distinct.

Taken together, these two restrictions on procedure calls are equivalent to the condition in Definition 42 that the variables used in the body and passed as parameters are all distinct.

7.1.3 Procedures with exp-parameters

It is possible to give a treatment of procedures with exp-parameters along the lines of procedures with var-parameters: the statement of correctness of definition of procedures (Definition 42) simply requires an additional universal quantification over all the parameters of sort `Exp`. However, many programming languages, such as Pascal, treat exp-parameters and var-parameters in fundamentally different ways. In this section, we examine a Pascal-like approach to exp-parameters.

Consider for example, a procedure `set : Exp -> Pgm` which is intended to take an expression `E` as parameter and set the program variables `'X` and `'Y` to the value of `E`. We might attempt to define this procedure as follows:

```
obj SETEXP is pr SEMARR .
  op set : Exp -> Pgm .
  var E : Exp .
  *** uses   'X 'Y : Var
  *** for all  e : Int
  *** pre(S,E,e)  =  S[[E]] is e
  *** post(S,E,e) =  S[['X]] is e  and  S[['Y]] is e
  eq  set(E)  =  'X := E ; 'Y := E .
endo
```

But this definition is not correct, because it is not the case that the body is correct with respect to the given pre- and postconditions for all expressions `E`. For example, if we perform the following reduction

```
red  s ; set('X + 1) [['Y]] .
```

then we get the result `s[['X]] + 2` . A correct definition of `set` might use the following equation:

```
set(E)  =  'E := E ; 'X := 'E ; 'Y := 'E .
```

(But note that the specification of `set` must be altered to state that the procedure uses the program variable `'E`.)

In Pascal, the first definition of `set` would actually be correct; in fact, Pascal will implement the first definition in a way that is similar to the second definition, by introducing a program variable `'E` which is instantiated to the value of the expression `E` whenever the procedure is called. This instantiation is captured by the first assignment `'E := E` in our second definition of `set`. (Actually, what Pascal does is rather more complex: the program variable which is introduced is *local*, that is, it has no meaning outside the body of the procedure, and so it need not be included in the list of program variables used by the procedure. Moreover, this program variable has the same name as the variable `E : Exp` which is used to range over the parameter of the procedure!) Roughly speaking, the effect of this is that in the body of the procedure, `E` denotes the *value* of the exp-parameter in any call of the procedure. That is, when `set` is called, its argument is first evaluated, and the resulting value is substituted for `E` in the body of the procedure. We can model this in our algebraic semantics by introducing a separate operation for the body of `set`:

```
op  setbody : Int -> Pgm .
```

The intention is that `setbody` defines the body of `set`, and its argument will be the value of the parameter of `set` whenever `set` is called:

```
var I : Int .
eq  setbody(I)  =  'X := I ; 'Y := I .

var S : Store .   var E : Exp .
eq  S ; set(E)  =  S ; setbody(S[[E]]) .
```

With these equations, we can demonstrate the correctness of `set` by showing that for all stores `S` and all expressions `E`, the following equations hold:

```
S ; set(E) [['X]]  =  S[[E]] .
S ; set(E) [['Y]]  =  S[[E]] .
```

These equations state that all calls of the procedure `set` are correct, in that `set(E)` does in fact set `'X` and `'Y` to the initial value of the expression `E`. We summarise this discussion in the following two OBJ modules, which give the definition and specification of the procedure `set`:

```
obj SETBODY is pr SEMARR .
  op setbody : Int -> Pgm .
  var I : Int .
  *** uses  'X 'Y : Var .
  *** pre(S,I)  =  true .
```

```
  *** post(S,I) =  S[['X]] is I  and  S[['Y]] is I
  eq  setbody(I)  =  'X := I ; 'Y := I .
endo

obj SETEXP is pr SETBODY .
  op set : Exp -> Pgm .
  var E : Exp .
  var S : Store .
  eq  S ; set(E)  =  S ; setbody(S[[E]]) .
endo
```

Note that the specification of the procedure is included as annotations in the module which defines the body of the procedure, and that the pre- and postconditions state properties of the integer `I` rather than properties of the exp-parameter `E` (which is not even declared in the first module).

In general, we impose the restriction that any procedure with exp-parameters be defined by two modules: one which defines and specifies the body of the procedure, and another which states that any call of the procedure first evaluates the exp-parameters and then evaluates the body of the procedure. This allows us to give criteria for the correctness of procedure definitions.

Definition 43 Let a procedure `proc` be defined and specified by OBJ modules of the following form:

```
obj PROCBODY is pr SEMARR .
  op  procbody : Var^K  Arvar^L  Int^M  -> Pgm .
  vars X⃗ : Var .
  vars AV⃗ : Arvar .
  vars I⃗ : Int .
  *** uses  Y⃗ : Var
  *** uses  A⃗ : Arvar
  *** for all  e⃗ : Int
  *** for all  a⃗ : Array
  *** pre(S,X⃗,AV⃗,I⃗,e⃗,a⃗) = ...
  *** post(S,X⃗,AV⃗,I⃗,e⃗,a⃗) = ...
  eq  procbody(X⃗,AV⃗,I⃗)  =  <body> .
endo
```

```
obj PROC is pr PROCBODY .
  op  proc : Var^K  Arvar^L  Exp^M  -> Pgm .
  vars X⃗ : Var .
  vars AV⃗ : Arvar .
  vars E⃗ : Exp .
  var S : Store .
  eq  S ; proc(X⃗,AV⃗,E⃗)  =  S ; procbody(X⃗,AV⃗,S[[E⃗]])
endo
```

where `S[[E⃗]]` abbreviates `S[[E1]],...,S[[EN]]`. Then we say that **the definition of `proc` is correct** (or just that `proc` is **correct**, if the meaning is clear from the context) iff for all stores `s`, all variables $\vec{\mathtt{X}}$ and array variables $\vec{\mathtt{AV}}$, all integers $\vec{\mathtt{I}}$, $\vec{\mathtt{e}}$ and arrays $\vec{\mathtt{a}}$, if $\mathtt{pre}(\mathtt{s}, \vec{\mathtt{X}}, \vec{\mathtt{AV}}, \vec{\mathtt{I}}, \vec{\mathtt{e}}, \vec{\mathtt{a}})$ holds, and if the variables $\vec{\mathtt{X}}, \vec{\mathtt{Y}}, \vec{\mathtt{AV}}, \vec{\mathtt{A}}$ are all distinct, then the following conditions are met:

- $\mathtt{procbody}(\vec{\mathtt{X}}, \vec{\mathtt{AV}}, \vec{\mathtt{I}})$ terminates on `s`.
- $\mathtt{procbody}(\vec{\mathtt{X}}, \vec{\mathtt{AV}}, \vec{\mathtt{I}})$ makes the postcondition true, i.e.,

  ```
  post(s ; procbody(X⃗,AV⃗,I⃗), e⃗,a⃗) .
  ```

- For any program variable `V` of sort `Var` (or `Arvar`), if `V` is not included in the list $\vec{\mathtt{Y}}$ or $\vec{\mathtt{X}}$ (or $\vec{\mathtt{A}}$ or $\vec{\mathtt{AV}}$), then

  ```
  s ; procbody(X⃗,AV⃗,I⃗) [[V]]  =  S[[V]] .
  ```

□

This looks rather frightening due to the large number of parameters of various sorts which need to be considered for the general case. Exercise 39, which asks for a proof that `set` is correctly defined, should reassure the reader that the above definition is not always very complicated in practice.

As with the other kinds of procedures we have considered above, a procedure can be proved to be correctly defined by showing that its body satisfies the given specification. Moreover, we can use the fact that it is correctly defined to prove correctness of procedure calls. The following is a consequence of Definition 43:

Proposition 44 Let `proc` be defined and specified as in Definition 43. If `proc` is correctly defined, then the following holds:

```
(∀ X⃗ : Var)(∀ AV⃗ : Arvar)(∀ E⃗ : Exp)
 (∀ e⃗ : Int)(∀ a⃗ : Array)(∀ S : Store)
```

$\vec{X}$,$\vec{AV}$,$\vec{Y}$,$\vec{A}$ are all distinct $\Rightarrow$
[pre(S,$\vec{X}$,$\vec{AV}$,S[[$\vec{E}$]],$\vec{e}$,$\vec{a}$) $\Rightarrow$
post(S ; proc($\vec{X}$,$\vec{AV}$,$\vec{E}$), $\vec{X}$,$\vec{AV}$,S[[$\vec{E}$]],$\vec{e}$,$\vec{a}$)] .

Moreover, for all variables `V : Var` such that `V` does not occur in $\vec{X}$ or $\vec{Y}$,

S ; proc($\vec{X}$,$\vec{AV}$,$\vec{E}$) [[V]] = S[[V]] .

This property also holds for array variables `V : Arvar` such that `V` does not occur in $\vec{AV}$ or $\vec{A}$.

Proof: The second statement follows directly from Definition 43; the first statement follows from this definition and the equations defining `proc` as follows:

post(S ; proc($\vec{X}$,$\vec{AV}$,$\vec{E}$), $\vec{X}$,$\vec{AV}$,S[[$\vec{E}$]],$\vec{e}$,$\vec{a}$)

=

post(S ; procbody($\vec{X}$,$\vec{AV}$,S[[$\vec{E}$]]), $\vec{X}$,$\vec{AV}$,S[[$\vec{E}$]],$\vec{e}$,$\vec{a}$)

$\Leftarrow$ { proc is correctly defined }

pre(S,$\vec{X}$,$\vec{AV}$,S[[$\vec{E}$]],$\vec{e}$,$\vec{a}$)

□

For example, the correctness of `set` allows us to conclude that for all stores `S` and expressions `E`, if the precondition holds (which is just `true`), then the postcondition holds for `S ; set(E)` :

```
(S ; set(E) [['X]]) is (S[[E]])  and
(S ; set(E) [['Y]]) is (S[[E]]) .
```

7.2 Recursive Procedures

Recursive procedures raise the question of termination. For example, consider the recursive procedure `idp`, defined by the equation

```
idp  =  if 'X is 0 then skip
        else 'X := 'X - 1 ; idp ; 'X := 'X + 1 fi
```

When `idp` is called in a store in which the value of `'X` is not `0`, it decreases `'X` by `1`, recursively calls itself, and then increases the value of `'X` by `1`. If `idp` is called in a store in which the value of `'X` is at least `0`, then `idp` repeatedly decreases the value of `'X` and calls itself until `'X` is equal to `0`, at which point the recursive call of `idp` does nothing (`skip`), and then the accumulated assignments `'X := 'X + 1` restore `'X` to its original value. For example, if the value of `'X` is 2 in the store `s`, then:

```
    s ; idp
=
    s ; 'X := 'X - 1 ; idp ; 'X := 'X + 1
=
    s ; 'X := 'X - 1 ; 'X := 'X - 1 ; idp ;
      'X := 'X + 1 ; 'X := 'X + 1
=
    s ; 'X := 'X - 1 ; 'X := 'X - 1 ; skip ;
      'X := 'X + 1 ; 'X := 'X + 1
```

Thus, the recursive calls of `idp` cease when a store is reached in which the value of `'X` is `0`. If, on the other hand, `idp` is called in a store in which the value of `'X` is less than `0`, then `idp` will continue decreasing the value of `'X` and recursively calling itself indefinitely, never reaching a store in which `'X` is `0`.

Termination and correctness of recursive procedures can be proved by a form of induction, which requires the use of a *measure function* to give an upper bound on the number of recursive calls of the procedure. For example, a suitable measure function for `idp` is

```
M(S) = S[['X]]
```

because when the value of `'X` is at least `0`, that value provides an upper bound on the number of times that `idp` calls itself.

In the following sections we consider first recursive procedures with no parameters, and then generalise to procedures that take some number of var-parameters. We do not consider recursive procedures with exp-parameters, but these can be treated as in Section 7.1.3 above.

7.2.1 Procedures with no parameters

The notion of correctness for recursive procedures with no parameters is exactly the same as that for non-recursive procedures with no parameters. This makes sense, because correctness of definition simply states how we expect a procedure to behave, and it should not matter whether or not a procedure is defined recursively. However, *proving* that a recursive procedure is correctly defined is more complex than proving that a non-recursive procedure is correctly defined. In general, we require some sort of inductive argument on the number of times that the procedure will call itself; this will also allow us to show that a given procedure terminates, and does not endlessly keep on calling itself. The following theorem provides a means of proving that recursive procedures are correctly defined. The theorem is justified by induction over the values of a measure function which is intended to provide an upper bound on the number of recursive calls of the procedure; this provides an induction hypothesis that recursive calls within the body of the procedure are correct. The proof of the theorem uses well-founded induction, which is reviewed in Appendix B.

Theorem 45 Let a procedure proc be defined and specified by an OBJ module of the following form:

```
obj PROC is pr SEMARR .
  op  proc : -> Pgm .
  *** uses  Y⃗ : Var
  *** uses  A⃗ : Arvar
  *** for all  e⃗ : Int
  *** for all  a⃗ : Array
  *** pre(S,e⃗,a⃗) = ...
  *** post(S,e⃗,a⃗) = ...
  eq  proc  =  <body> .
endo
```

Furthermore, let

```
M : Store -> Int
```

be some function, which we refer to as the *measure function*. Then the definition of proc is correct (according to Definition 37) if the following conditions are met:

- The measure function is **bounded below**, in the sense that

```
(∀ e⃗ : Int)(∀ a⃗ : Array)(∀ S : Store)
   pre(S,e⃗,a⃗)  ⇒  0 <= M(S) .
```

- the procedure is correct with respect to pre and post and terminates on all stores satisfying the precondition, in the sense that

```
(∀ e⃗ : Int)(∀ a⃗ : Array)(∀ S : Store)
   pre(S,e⃗,a⃗) and IH
   ⇒  post(S ; proc, e⃗,a⃗) and proc↓S .
```

  where the "induction hypothesis" IH is defined by

```
IH  =  (∀ e⃗' : Int)(∀ a⃗' : Array)(∀ S' : Store)
          pre(S',e⃗',a⃗') and M(S') < M(S)
          ⇒  post(S' ; proc, e⃗',a⃗') and proc↓S' .
```

• <body> uses only the variables listed in $\vec{Y}$ and $\vec{A}$.

Proof: According to Definition 37, in order to show that proc is correctly defined, we must show that whenever the precondition holds, then proc terminates and makes the postcondition true, and that proc changes the values of only those variables listed in $\vec{Y}$ and $\vec{A}$. Because 0 <= M(S) whenever the precondition holds, the first two of these requirements follow directly from

$$(\forall\ n \in \omega)\ P(n)$$

where

```
P(n)  =    (∀ e⃗ : Int)(∀ a⃗ : Array)(∀ S : Store)
             pre(S,e⃗,a⃗) and n is M(S)
             ⇒  post(S ; proc, e⃗,a⃗) and proc↓S .
```

$(\forall n \in \omega)$ P(n) follows by well-founded induction (see Appendix B) from

$$(\forall\ n \in \omega)[(\forall\ i \in \omega)\ i < n \Rightarrow P(i)] \Rightarrow P(n)\ .$$

But this is equivalent to the second condition of the theorem so we conclude that whenever the precondition holds, proc terminates and makes the postcondition true. The final requirement, that proc changes only those variables listed in $\vec{Y}$ and $\vec{A}$, follows from Lemma 39. □

The proof of this theorem shows that IH really is an induction hypothesis. Because the value taken by the measure function M is not less than 0 whenever the precondition holds, this provides an upper bound to the number of recursive calls of the procedure when executed on a store that satisfies the precondition and for which the value of the measure function has strictly decreased. We can use this theorem to prove that procedures are correctly defined by proving the correctness of the body of the procedure with respect to pre and post; the induction hypothesis states that any recursive call of the procedure within the body of the procedure is correct, provided that the call occurs in a store where the precondition holds, and where the value taken by the measure function has strictly decreased. As an example, we prove that idp is correctly defined.

Example 46 The procedure idp is defined by the following OBJ module:

```
obj IDP is pr SEMARR .
  op idp : -> Pgm .
```

```
  *** uses   'X : Int
  *** for all  e : Int
  *** pre(S,e)  =  S[['X]] is e  and  0 <= e
  *** post(S,e)  =  S[['X]] is e
  *** M(S)  =  S[['X]]
  eq  idp  =  if  'X is 0  then  skip
              else  'X := 'X - 1 ; idp ; 'X := 'X + 1
              fi .
endo
```

We now show that the definition of `idp` is correct. First, its body uses only the variable `'X`, and if `pre(S)` holds then obviously `0 <= M(S)`, for any store `S`. This shows that the first and last conditions of Theorem 45 are satisfied. To show that the remaining condition is satisfied, we must prove:

```
(∀ e : Int)(∀ S : Store)
   pre(S,e) and IH ⇒ post(S ; idp, e) and idp↓S
```

where

```
IH  =  (∀ e' : Int)(∀ S' : Store)
          pre(S',e') and M(S') < M(S)
          ⇒ post(S' ; idp, e') and idp↓S'.
```

To prove this, assume that `e : Int` and `S : Store` satisfy `pre(S,e)`, i.e., assume

```
S[['X]] is e  and  0 <= e .
```

Assume also that `IH` holds; i.e., that

```
(∀ e' : Int)(∀ S' : Store)
  S'[['X]] is e'  and  0 <= e'  and  S'[['X]] < S[['X]]
  ⇒ (S' ; idp [['X]]) is e' and idp↓S' .
```

An equivalent formulation of `IH` is

```
IH' =  (∀ S' : Store)
          0 <= S'[['X]] < e
          ⇒ (S' ; idp [['X]]) is (S'[[X]]) and idp↓S' .
```

We must now show that `post(S ; body, e)` holds and that `body` terminates on `S`. Since `body` uses the conditional construct, we proceed by case-analysis: since `0 <= e` by assumption, either `e is 0` or `0 < e` holds. So we have:

- Case `e is 0`. Then we have `S[['X is 0]] = true`, so that

```
   post(S ; idp, e)
=
   post(S ; skip, e)
=
   post(S,e)
=
   S[['X]] is e
=
   true
```

  Moreover, `skip` terminates on `S`.
- Case `0 < e`. In this case, `S[['X is 0]] = false`, so we have

```
S ; idp  =  S ; 'X := 'X - 1 ; idp ; 'X := 'X + 1 ,
```

  and we must show that the program in the right side of this equation terminates on `S` and makes `post` true. We shall attempt to use the induction hypothesis. Let `S' = S ; 'X := 'X - 1`; then

```
   0 <= S'[['X]] < e
=
   0 <= S[['X]] - 1 < e
=
   0 <= e - 1 < e
=        { because 0 < e }
   true
```

  Therefore the antecedent of `IH'` is satisfied by `S'`, and so we obtain the consequent:

```
S' ; idp [['X]]  =  S'[['X]]  and  idp↓S' .
```

  That is,

```
(*)   S ; 'X := 'X - 1 ; idp [['X]]  =  e - 1  and
      idp ↓ (S ; 'X := 'X - 1) .
```

  Because assignments always terminate on any store, it follows from this that

```
(idp ; 'X := 'X + 1) ↓ (S ; 'X := 'X - 1)
```

and so

```
('X := 'X - 1 ; idp ; 'X := 'X + 1) ↓ S .
```

It only remains to show that the postcondition holds. We can calculate as follows:

```
    post(S ; body, e)
=
    (S ; 'X := 'X - 1 ; idp [['X]]) + 1 is e
=       { (*) }
    (e - 1) + 1 is e
=
    true
```

Thus we have shown that the procedure terminates and that the postcondition holds in both cases, and we conclude that the definition of `idp` is correct. □

It is of course also possible to do correctness proof in OBJ. In doing so, two interesting points arise. First, we should not include the equation that defines `idp`, because then OBJ could fail to terminate, by applying this equation to a term containing `idp` over and over. Therefore, we prove the correctness of the *body* of the procedure, following Proposition 40 above. The other point is the use of *Skolem functions* to capture existential quantifications in assumptions. Our proof of correctness will assume the induction hypothesis in Theorem 45, which in this case states that `idp` terminates and makes the postcondition true whenever the precondition holds and the measure function is strictly decreased. This hypothesis can be declared with two equations, one stating that `idp` terminates whenever the precondition holds and the measure function is strictly decreased, and the other stating that `idp` makes the postcondition true whenever the precondition holds and the measure function is strictly decreased.

By definition, `idp` terminates on a store `S` iff there exists some `S'` of sort `Store` such that `S' = S ; idp`. We can capture this existential quantification by introducing an operation

```
op idp-result : Store -> Store .
```

which takes a store `S` and returns a store `S'` = `S ; idp`, provided that `idp` terminates on `S`, i.e., provided that the precondition holds for `S` and that the measure function is strictly decreased. Thus, the statement that `idp` terminates whenever the precondition holds and the measure function is strictly decreased is captured by the following:

```
var S : Store .
cq S ; idp = idp-result(S)
   if 0 <= (S[['X]]) and (S[['X]]) < (s[['X]]) .
```

where `s` is the store in which the body of `idp` is evaluated. If a particular store `S` satisfies the condition of this equation, then `idp` terminates on `S` and therefore `S ; idp` is equal to an element of sort `Store`, which in fact is `idp-result(S)`. Hence this equation captures the existential quantifier in the definition of termination. If `S` does not satisfy the condition of the equation, then the term `idp-result(S)` has sort `Store`, but we cannot claim that it equals any particular value of sort `Store`, and therefore it cannot have any effect on the validity of our proof. Appendix B gives a general discussion of this way of using Skolem functions in OBJ proof scores.

We also use `idp-result` in the second equation needed to assume the induction hypothesis. This equation states that the result of evaluating `idp` makes the postcondition true whenever the precondition holds and the measure function is strictly decreased:

```
cq (idp-result(S))[['X]] = S[['X]]
   if 0 <= (S[['X]]) and (S[['X]]) < (s[['X]]) .
```

That is, under those conditions, the value of `'X` is not changed by evaluating `idp`, which is the property stated by the postcondition for `idp`.

The complete proof score for the correctness of `idp` is as follows:

```
th PROOF is pr SEMARR .
  op idp : -> Pgm .
  let body = if 'X is 0 then skip
             else 'X := 'X - 1 ; idp ; 'X := 'X + 1 fi .
  op s : -> Store .
  op x : -> Int .
  *** assume pre(s,x) ***
  eq s[['X]] = x .
  eq 0 <= x = true .
  *** assume IH: ***
  *** "Skolem function" to express idp terminates: ***
  op idp-result : Store -> Store .
  var S : Store .
```

```
  *** idp produces result of sort store ***
  *** if pre(S,S[['X]]) and M(S) < M(s) ***
  cq S ; idp = idp-result(S)
     if 0 <= (S[['X]]) and (S[['X]]) < (s[['X]]) .
  *** idp makes postcondition true      ***
  *** if pre(S,S[['X]]) and M(S) < M(s) ***
  cq (idp-result(S))[['X]] = S[['X]]
     if 0 <= (S[['X]]) and (S[['X]]) < (s[['X]]) .
endth

*** case x = 0 ***
open PROOF .
eq x = 0 .
red (s ; body [['X]]) is x .  ***> should be: true
close

*** case 0 < x ***
open PROOF .
eq 0 < x = true .
red (s ; body [['X]]) is x .
***> should be: true
close
```

7.2.2 Procedures with var-parameters

The introduction of var-parameters simply introduces universal quantifications over parameters to the statement of correctness for procedures, as in Section 7.1.2 above. The notion of correct definition for recursive procedures with var-parameters is exactly the same as for non-recursive procedures with var parameters, for the reasons outlined at the beginning of Section 7.2.1. That is, a recursive procedure with var-parameters is correctly defined iff it satisfies the conditions of Definition 42 in Section 7.1.2: that is, whenever the precondition holds, then the procedure terminates, makes the postcondition true, and changes the values of only those variables listed in its specification. In particular, we require that procedures be called with distinct parameters.

Corresponding to Theorem 45, we have the following inductive means of proving that a procedure is correctly defined. The only difference is that here we have variables ranging over the var-parameters to the procedure; we allow the measure function to depend on these parameters.

Theorem 47 Let a procedure **proc** be defined and specified by an OBJ module of the following form:

```
obj PROC is pr SEMARR .
  op  proc : Var^K Arvar^L -> Pgm .
  vars X⃗ : Var .
  vars AV⃗ : Arvar .
  *** uses  Y⃗ : Var
  *** uses  A⃗ : Arvar
  *** for all  e⃗ : Int
  *** for all  a⃗ : Array
  *** pre(S,X⃗,AV⃗,e⃗,a⃗) = ...
  *** post(S,X⃗,AV⃗,e⃗,a⃗) = ...
  eq  proc(X⃗,AV⃗)  =  <body> .
endo
```

Furthermore, let

```
M : Store Var^K Arvar^L -> Int
```

be some function, which we refer to as the *measure function*. Then the definition of **proc** is correct (according to Definition 42) if the following conditions are met:

- the measure function is **bounded below**, in the sense that

```
(∀ X⃗ : Var)(∀ AV⃗ : Arvar)
(∀ e⃗ : Int)(∀ a⃗ : Array)(∀ S : Store)
  pre(S,X⃗,AV⃗,e⃗,a⃗)  ⇒  0 <= M(S,X⃗,AV⃗) ;
```

- the procedure is correct with respect to **pre** and **post** and terminates on all stores satisfying the precondition, in the sense that

```
(∀ X⃗ : Var)(∀ AV⃗ : Arvar)
 (∀ e⃗ : Int)(∀ a⃗ : Array)(∀ S : Store)
   pre(S,X⃗,AV⃗,e⃗,a⃗) and IH
   ⇒  post(S ; proc(X⃗,AV⃗), X⃗,AV⃗,e⃗,a⃗)
       and proc↓S .
```

  where the "induction hypothesis" IH is defined by

```
IH = (∀ X⃗' : Var)(∀ AV⃗' : Arvar)
       (∀ e⃗' : Int)(∀ a⃗' : Array)(∀ S' : Store)
         pre(S',X⃗',AV⃗',e⃗',a⃗') and M(S',X⃗',AV⃗') < M(S,X⃗',AV⃗')
         ⇒  post(S' ; proc(X⃗',AV⃗'), X⃗',AV⃗',e⃗',a⃗')
             and proc↓S' .
```

- <body> uses only the variables listed in $\vec{X}$, $\vec{Y}$, $\vec{A}$ and $\vec{AV}$.

□

We conclude this chapter with an example of a procedure which computes a linear representation of two given integers. A **linear representation** of a pair of integers m and n consists of two non-negative integers a and b such that

```
a * m - b * n  =  gcd(m,n) .
```

A linear representation of m and n can be found by first calculating gcd(m,n), and then working backwards. For example, the algorithm given in Section 5.1.1 to compute the greatest common divisor works by successive subtraction, using the property that for all m and n,

```
gcd(m,n)  =  gcd(m - n, n)  =  gcd(m, n - m) .
```

Thus, the greatest common divisor of 15 and 9 can be found by successive subtraction as follows:

```
    gcd(15,9)
=          { 6 = 15 - 9 }
    gcd(6,9)
=          { 9 - 6 = 3 }
    gcd(6,3)
=          { 3 = 6 - 3 }
    gcd(3,3)
=          { gcd(m,m) = m }
    3
```

Now gcd(3,3) = 3 = 1*3 - 0*3, so that 1 and 0 give a linear representation of the pair (3,3). If we work backwards through the chain of subtractions that gave gcd(15,9) = 3, we see

```
    1*3 - 0*3
=
    1*(6-3) - 0*3
```

```
=
    1*6 - 1*3
=
    1*6 - 1*(9-6)
=
    2*6 - 1*9
=
    2*(15-9) - 1*9
=
    2*15 - 3*9
```

Thus `2` and `3` give a linear representation of the pair `(15,9)`.

This process of first calculating the greatest common divisor and then working backwards to find a linear representation is mirrored in the following procedure:

```
obj LREP is pr SEMARR .
  op lrep : Var Var -> Pgm .
  vars X Y : Var .
  *** uses  'A 'B : Var
  *** for all  x y : Int
  *** pre(S,X,Y,x,y)  =  S[[X]] is x  and  0 < x  and
  ***                    S[[Y]] is y  and  0 < y
  *** post(S,x,y)  =  S[['A]] * x - S[['B]] * y  is  gcd(x,y)
  *** M(S,X,Y)  =  S[[X + Y]]
  eq  lrep(X,Y)  =
        if  X is Y
        then  'A := 1 ; 'B := 0
        else  if  X < Y
              then Y := Y - X ; lrep(X,Y) ; 'A := 'A + 'B
              else X := X - Y ; lrep(X,Y) ; 'B := 'A + 'B fi
        fi .
endo
```

We use Theorem 47 to prove that `lrep` is correctly defined, so we must show the following, where `body` denotes the body of `lrep`:

(a) `body` uses only the variables `X`, `Y`, `'A` and `'B`;

(b) `M` is bounded below; i.e.,

```
(∀ X,Y : Var)(∀ x,y : Int)(∀ S : Store)
  pre(S,X,Y,x,y)  ⇒  0 <= M(S,X,Y) ;
```

(c) whenever the precondition holds, then the procedure terminates and makes the postcondition true:

```
(∀ X,Y : Var)(∀ x,y : Int)(∀ S : Store)
  pre(S,X,Y,x,y) and IH  ⇒ post(S ; lrep(X,Y), x,y)
                           and lrep(X,Y)↓S
```

where

```
IH  =  (∀ X',Y' : Var)(∀ x',y' : Int)(∀ S' : Store)
         pre(S',X',Y',x',y') and M(S',X',Y') < M(S,X,Y)  ⇒
         post(S ; lrep(X',Y'), x',y') and lrep(X',Y')↓S'
```

The truth of (a) is obvious from an inspection of the body of the procedure; (b) too is obvious, given the definitions of `pre` and `M`. To show that (c) holds, fix `X,Y`, `x,y` and `S` of the appropriate sorts and assume `pre(S,X,Y,x,y)`, i.e., assume

```
0 < S[[X]] = x  and  0 < S[[Y]] = y ,
```

and also assume the induction hypothesis `IH`. We must now show that the procedure terminates and makes the postcondition true. In fact, the proof that the procedure terminates is similar to the proof of correctness of `idp` in Section 7.2.1, and we leave it as an exercise for the reader (Exercise 44). We simply show that the postcondition is established. Substituting `X` and `Y` for the universally quantified `X'` and `Y'` in `IH`, and simplifying, gives us the following induction hypothesis:

```
(*)    (∀ S' : Store)
         0 < S'[[X]]  and  0 < S'[[Y]]  and
         S'[[X]] + S'[[Y]] < x + y  ⇒
           (S' ; lrep(X,Y) [['A]])*(S'[[X]]) -
           (S' ; lrep(X,Y) [['B]])*(S'[[Y]])
           is  gcd(S'[[X]],S'[[Y]]) .
```

(Note that we have weakened the induction hypothesis by omitting the clause that the procedure terminates.) Under these assumptions, we must show `post(S ; lrep(X,Y), x,y)`. We split this proof into proving three cases, following the conditional structure of the body of the procedure:

```
(i)     x is y ⇒ post(S ; 'A := 1 ; 'B := 0, x,y) .
(ii)    x < y  ⇒
           post(S ; Y := Y - X ; lrep(X,Y) ; 'A := 'A + 'B, x,y) .
(iii)   y < x  ⇒
           post(S ; X := X - Y ; lrep(X,Y) ; 'B := 'A + 'B, x,y) .
```

For `(i)`: Assume `x = y`. Then

```
     post(S ; 'A := 1 ; 'B := 0, x,y)
  =
     (S ; 'A := 1 ; 'B := 0 [['A]]) * x
      - (S ; 'A := 1 ; 'B := 0 [['B]]) * y is gcd(x,y)
  =
     1 * x - 0 * y is gcd(x,x)
  =
     true
```

For `(ii)`: Assume `x < y`. We shall use `(*)` with `S' = S ; Y := Y - X`. We first show that the antecedent of `(*)` holds. For the first clause:

```
     0 < S'[[X]]
  =
     0 < x
  =        { by assumption }
     true
```

The proofs that `0 < S'[[Y]]` and `S'[[X] + S'[[Y]] < x + y` are similarly straightforward. We conclude that the antecedent of `(*)` is true for

```
   S' = S ; Y := Y - X ,
```

and therefore we obtain the consequent

```
   (S''[['A]])*(S'[[X]]) - (S''[['B]])*(S'[[Y]])
   =  gcd(S'[[X]],S'[[Y]]) ,
```

where `S'' = S' ; lrep(X,Y)`. Filling in the values of `S'[[X]]` and `S'[[Y]]`, we proceed as follows:

```
     true
  =        { see above }
     (S''[['A]]) * x - (S''[['B]])*(y-x) is gcd(x, y-x)
```

```
=
   (S''[['A]] + S''[['B]]) * x - (S''[['B]]) * y is gcd(x, y)
=
   (S'' ; 'A := 'A + 'B [['A]]) * x
   - (S'' ; 'A := 'A + 'B [['B]]) * y is gcd(x,y)
=
   post(S'' ; 'A := 'A + 'B, x,y)
```

Which is the desired conclusion.
For `(iii)`: The proof is similar to that of `(ii)`, and is left as an exercise for the reader.

This concludes the proof of the correctness of `lrep`.

7.3 Exercises

Exercise 39 Prove that the procedure `set` of Section 7.1.3 is correctly defined. □

Exercise 40 Prove that the following procedure is correctly defined:

```
obj MULT is pr SEMARR .
  op  mult : Var Var Var -> Pgm .
  var X1 X2 X3: Var .
  *** uses   'C : Var
  *** for all  x1 x2 x3 : Int
  *** pre(S,X1,X2,X3,x1,x2,x3) =
  ***     S[[X1]] is x1  and  S[[X2]] is x2  and
  ***     S[[X3]] is x3  and  0 <= x3
  *** post(S,X1,X2,X3,x1,x2,x3) =
          S[[X1]] is x1 + x2 * x3  and  S[[X2]] is x2
  eq  mult(X1,X2,X3)  =  'C := 0 ;
                         while  'C < X3
                         do  X1 := X1 + X2 ; 'C := 'C + 1  od .
endo
```

□

Exercise 41 The factorial function (`_!`) is defined by the following OBJ theory:

```
th FAC is pr ZZ .
  op  _! : Int -> Int [prec 1] .
  var N : Int .
  eq  0 !  =  1 .
  cq  N !  =  N * (N - 1)!   if  0 < N .
endth
```

Use your answer to Exercise 40 above to fill in the elisions (...) in the procedure **facp** below, and prove the correctness of its definition.

```
obj FACP is pr MULT .
  op facp : Var Var -> Pgm .
  var X Y : Var .
  *** uses  'K 'Z : Var
  *** for all  y : Int
  *** pre(S,X,Y,y)  =  S[[Y]] is y  and  0 <= y
  *** post(S,X,Y,y) =  S[[X]]  is  y !
  eq  facp(X,Y)  =  X := 1 ; 'K := 0 ;
                    while  'K < Y
                    do  'Z := X ; mult(... , ... , ...) ;
                        'K := 'K + 1  od .

endo
```

□

Exercise 42 An array variable **a** and a program variable **'T** may be used to represent a stack: **'T** represents the end (top) of the stack, and the elements on the stack are the values **a[0..'T]**. This question concerns procedures to **push** values onto and to **pop** values off of the end of the "stack."

(a) Define the procedures **push** and **pop**, and prove the correctness of your definitions.

```
obj PUSH is pr SEMARR .
  op  push : Var -> Pgm .
  var X : Var .
  *** uses 'T : Var
  *** uses  a : Arvar
```

```
  *** for all  t x : Int
  *** for all  a0 : Array
  *** pre(S,X,t,x,a0) =  S[['T]] is t  and  0 <= t  and
  ***                    S[[X]] is x  and  S[[a]] == a0
  *** post(S,X,t,x,a0) =
  ***    S[['T]] is t + 1  and  S[[a[t]]] is x  and
  ***    (∀ i) 0 <= i < t ⇒ S[[a[i]]] is a0[i]
  eq  push(X)  =  ... .
endo

obj POP is pr SEMARR .
  op  pop : Var -> Pgm .
  var X : Var .
  *** uses 'T : Var
  *** uses  a : Arvar
  *** for all  t : Int
  *** for all  a0 : Array
  *** pre(S,X,t,a0)  =
  ***    S[['T]] is t  and  0 < t  and  S[[a]] == a0
  *** post(S,X,t,a0) =
  ***    S[['T]] is t - 1  and  S[[X]] is a0[t - 1]  and
  ***    (∀ i) 0 <= i < t - 1 ⇒ S[[a[i]]] is a0[i]
  eq  pop(X)  =  ... .
endo
```

(b) Use your answer to part (a) to show that for all stores `s`, if `0 <= s[['T]]` , then

```
s ; push('X) ; 'X := 'Y ; pop('Y) [['Y]]  =  s[['X]] .
```

□

Exercise 43 For a given integer `x`, the polynomial in `x` with coefficients given by the values in the array segment `A[0..U]` is defined as follows:

```
poly(A,U)  =
    A[0]  +  A[1] * x  +  A[2] * (x ** 2)  + ...
          +  A[U - 1] * (x ** (U - 1)) ,
```

that is,

$$\texttt{poly(A,U)} = \sum_{i=0}^{\texttt{U}-1} \texttt{A}[i] * \texttt{x}^i.$$

(a) Write an OBJ module which defines the operation `poly`.

(b) Use the fact that

$$A[0] + A[1] * x + A[2] * x^2 + \cdots + A[n] * x^n = \\ A[0] + x * (A[1] + x * (A[2] + x * (\cdots x * (A[n-1] + x * A[n]))))$$

to define a procedure that sets `'P` to `poly(AV,U)`, assuming that `0 <= U`. This procedure is formally specified as follows:

```
obj POLY is pr SEMARR .
  op polyp : Arvar Var Var -> Pgm .
  var AV : Arvar .
  var  U : Var .
  *** uses  'P 'Y ... : Var
  *** for all  p u : Int
  *** pre(S)  =  S[[U]] is u  and  and  0 <= u  and
  ***            poly(S[[AV]],u) is p
  *** post(S) =  S[['P]] is p
  eq  polyp(AV,U)  =  ... .
endo
```

Your algorithm should not use exponentiation.
Hint: use the following invariant:

```
inv(S) =
  poly(S[[AV]], S[['Y]]) + (S[['P]])*(x ** (S[['Y]])) is p
  and  0 <= (S[['Y]]) <= u  and  (S[[U]]) is u .
```

□

Exercise 44 Complete the proof that `lrep` in Section 7.2.2 is correctly defined by showing that requirement `(iii)` holds, and by showing that the procedure terminates. □

Exercise 45 This question concerns a procedure to compute integer division by 2. The property of integer division in part (a) will be useful in your answer to part (b).

(a) Given that

```
2 * (y div 2)  <=  y  <=  2 * (y div 2) + 1
```

show that for all `x`, `y` and `z`, if

```
x <= (y div 2) < z
```

then

```
2 * x  <=  y  <  2 * z .
```

(b) The procedure `div2`, defined below, takes `Y : Var` as parameter, and sets `Y` to `y div 2`, where `y` is the initial value of `Y`. State the criteria for `div2` to be correctly defined, and prove that it is correctly defined.

```
obj DIV2 is pr SEMARR .
  op div2 : Var -> Pgm .
  var Y : Var .
  *** uses
  *** for all  y : Int
  *** pre(S,Y,y)  =  S[[Y]] is y  and  0 <= y .
  *** post(S,Y,y) =  S[[Y]] is y div 2 .
  *** M(S,Y) = S[[Y]]
  eq  div2(Y)  =  if  Y < 2
                  then  Y := 0
                  else  Y := Y - 2 ; div2(Y) ; Y := Y + 1
                  fi .
endo
```

□

Exercise 46 Complete the following procedure definition by filling in the elisions (...), and use your answer to the previous exercise to prove that the procedure is correctly defined.

```
obj LOG is pr DIV2 .
  op log : Var -> Pgm .
  var Y : Var .
  *** uses ...
  *** for all y : Int
  *** pre(S,Y,y)  =  S[[Y]] is y  and  0 < y .
  *** post(S,Y,y) =  2 **(S[['X]]) <= y  and
  ***                y < 2 **(S[['X]] + 1) .
```

```
  *** M(S,Y) = ...
  eq  log(Y) = if  Y is 1
               then  ...
               else  div2(Y) ; log(Y) ; 'X := ...
               fi .
endo
```

□

8 Some Comparison with Other Approaches

In the preceding chapters we presented the Algebraic Denotational Semantics of a small imperative programming language. An important advantage of this approach is its simplicity: the semantics of the language was presented in first order equational logic. In comparison, most other approaches to the semantics of imperative programs use full first order predicate logic with equality, or even more complicated logics such as infinitary first order logic. In this final chapter we compare Algebraic Denotational Semantics (ADS) with two other approaches, paying particular attention to the logical framework used to present the semantics, and to the rôle that variables play. Although classical denotational semantics is probably the most widespread approach to the semantics of programs, we focus here on Dijkstra's Weakest Preconditions (WP) and Hoare Logic (HL), since the chief aim of these two approaches, as with ADS, is to provide an effective means of reasoning about programs.

Hoare Logic [35] is an axiomatic formal system with rules of inference for making assertions about programs. These assertions are called **Hoare triples** and are of the form $\{P\}\ S\ \{Q\}$, where S is a program and P and Q are "predicates". Just what these predicates are is not made precise in most texts. The underlying idea is that they are statements which characterise states of a computing machine by stating properties of the values of variables; for example, one such predicate might be

$$\texttt{'X} = 2 * \texttt{'Y}\ \texttt{and}\ \texttt{'Y} < 50\ ,$$

which would be true of states in which the value of `'X` is twice that of `'Y` and the value of `'Y` is less than 50.

The intended interpretation of a Hoare triple $\{P\}\ S\ \{Q\}$ is: if program S is executed in a state which satisfies P, and if execution of S terminates, then Q will hold in the resulting state.

Valid Hoare triples are generated by axioms and rules of inference; the semantics of each construct in the programming language is defined by a number of axioms or rules of inference. For example, the semantics of assignment is given by the following

Assignment axiom:

For all variables X, expressions E and predicates Q,

$$\{Q[X := E]\}\ X := E\ \{Q\}$$

where $Q[X := E]$ denotes the result of substituting E for X in Q.

As an example, it follows from this axiom that

$$\{\texttt{'X} = 2 * (\texttt{'Y} + 1) \textbf{ and } \texttt{'Y} + 1 < 50\}\ \texttt{'Y} := \texttt{'Y} + 1\ \{\texttt{'X} = 2 * \texttt{'Y} \textbf{ and } \texttt{'Y} < 50\}$$

is a valid Hoare triple. This seems straightforward, but it begs the question of what it means to substitute an expression for a variable in a predicate. In fact, it is unclear just what a variable is.

Hoare considers a predicate to be a sentence of first order logic, and a variable to be simply a variable in the sense of first order logic. In other words, HL makes no distinction between program variables and variables of the logical language. This resolves the issue of what is meant by substitution: it is simply textual replacement of a variable by an expression, as in Exercise 2 of Chapter 1. However, this raises some very difficult problems, because in first order predicate logic variables can be bound by universal or existential quantification. Consider for example the predicate

$$(\forall X)\ X = 0\ .$$

Does this state that the value of every program variable is set to 0, or that all integers are equal to 0? The former is surely the only reasonable possibility.

One way, perhaps, of resolving this issue is to distinguish logical and program variables by introducing, as in ADS, a sort *Var* of program variables, so that we can write a predicate

$$(\forall X : \mathit{Var})\ X = 0$$

which holds for states in which the value of every program variable is 0. However, this means that it is impossible to give a semantics to assignment in terms of substitution, because from the assignment axiom given above, we have

$$\{(\forall X : \mathit{Var})\ X = 0\}\ \texttt{'X} := 1\ \{(\forall X : \mathit{Var})\ X = 0\}$$

as a valid Hoare triple, which it is not.

Dijkstra's WP gives a denotational semantics to programs as "predicate transformers". Specifically, he introduces an operation **wp** which takes a program and a predicate as arguments, and returns a predicate as a result. 'WP' stands for Weakest Precondition, and $\mathbf{wp}(S, Q)$ is defined to be the weakest precondition under which program S makes Q true; in other words, $\mathbf{wp}(S, Q)$ satisfies:

- $\{\mathbf{wp}(S, Q)\}\ S\ \{Q\}$ and
- for all predicates P, if $\{P\}\ S\ \{Q\}$ then $\mathbf{wp}(S, Q)$ implies P.

Thus the denotation of a program S is the operation which transforms a postcondition Q into a precondition $\mathbf{wp}(S, Q)$. The semantics of programs is given by defining the denotation of each construct in the programming language. For example, Dijkstra defines the semantics of assignment by:

$$\mathbf{wp}(X := E, Q) = Q[X := E] .$$

This is similar to the Hoare triple Assignment axiom above, and suffers from exactly the same drawbacks.

Hesselink [33] gives a formal account of WP semantics. In order to circumvent the difficulties of defining assignment by substitution, he introduces a concrete notion of state as a function from program variables to integers. A predicate P is then a boolean valued function on states. This permits a rather complicated definition of "substitution". Suppose f is a state (i.e., a function from program variables to integers); for program variable X and expression E, define the state $f[X := E]$ by:

$$f[X := E](Y) = \begin{cases} E & \text{if } X = Y \\ f(Y) & \text{otherwise} \end{cases}$$

Now "substitution" in predicates can be defined as follows: for a predicate P, the predicate $P[X := E]$ holds for a state f iff P holds for the state $f[X := E]$.

Once the details of this are assimilated, one can see some similarities between the construction of $f[X := E]$ and the semantics of assignment in ADS. The main difference, apart from the degree of complexity, is that this version of WP does not use a logical system: it is situated in set theory, so that proving properties of programs involves reasoning about sets and functions. Any mechanical support for theorem proving in WP would require a complex translation of these "substitution" mechanisms back into some logical framework such as first order predicate calculus, and should include an axiomatisation of set theory. Thus WP is not an *executable* semantics in the way that ADS is.

Similar issues arise in the treatment of while loops. In HL, while loops are handled by the following rule of inference, which captures the notion of invariant. Here, the invariant is a predicate I:

While rule:
If $\{I$ `and` $T\}$ S $\{I\}$
then $\{I\}$ `while` T `do` S `od` $\{I$ `and` `not`$(T)\}$.

As in the proof rule given in Chapter 5 above, this requires a suitable invariant to be found. In WP, however, an explicit construction must be given for the predicate

$$\mathbf{wp}(\texttt{while}\ T\ \texttt{do}\ S\ \texttt{od},\ Q)$$

for any postcondition Q. One recipe for such a construction can be given by considering the number of times the body of the loop is evaluated. If the guard T is false in some state, then the body of the loop will not be evaluated, so that

$$\texttt{not}(T)\ \texttt{and}\ Q \tag{8.1}$$

is the weakest precondition which will make Q hold after evaluating the body of the loop zero times. Now consider the case where the body is evaluated once: T should hold initially, and evaluation of the body should make T false, so that

$$T\ \texttt{and}\ \mathbf{wp}(S, \texttt{not}(T))\ \texttt{and}\ \mathbf{wp}(S, Q) \tag{8.2}$$

is the weakest precondition which will make Q hold after evaluating the body once. Similarly, we can get weakest preconditions for the cases where the body is evaluated twice, three times, four times, and so on. Now if **while** T **do** S **od** terminates, it does so after some number of iterations of S, whether that number be zero or one or two, or whatever. Therefore, the weakest precondition for **while** T **do** S **od** to establish Q is the disjunction of (8.1), (8.2), etc.; that is,

$$\mathbf{wp}(\texttt{while}\ T\ \texttt{do}\ S\ \texttt{od},\ Q) = (8.1)\ \texttt{or}\ (8.2)\ \texttt{or}\ \ldots.$$

Because it is possible that the loop be iterated arbitrarily many times, the disjunction on the right side of this equality is infinitely long: you would never finish writing it out! This means that the logic of WP is *infinitary* first order predicate logic; i.e., first order predicate logic which allows infinitely long sentences such as that above [10]. In practice, of course, one would try to find an invariant to prove a property of a while loop, rather than try to find a weakest precondition; our point is that the logical foundations of WP are rather complicated, and bring you back to ordinary invariants in practice.

As we saw above, Hesselink uses set theory to provide WP with a formal basis in which predicates are boolean valued functions on states. This allows him to give a denotation to **wp**(**while** T **do** S **od**, Q) as a fixpoint of monotonic predicate transformers. His results are mathematically elegant, but the concepts and techniques used are considerably more complex than the equational logic of ADS and the standard first order predicate logic we use to prove properties of programs (see Appendix B).

It seems that John Reynolds was one of the first to address the rôle of variables in a logical framework. His book [52] makes the important distinction between program variables and logical variables, and introduces a so-called "specification logic" which takes account of this distinction. Indeed, the rules which define the semantics of assignment in this logic are very similar to the equations for assignment in our Algebraic Denotational Semantics.

A Summary of the Semantics

This appendix summarises the OBJ code that defines the syntax and semantics of the small programming language language used in this text. The first module in the listing below, `ZZ`, extends OBJ's built-in representation of the integers with an equality predicate, `_is_`, and with some equations that are useful for manipulating inequalities. In particular, these equations are useful as lemmas in the correctness proofs given in this book. For example, proving that a property is an invariant of a loop often involves showing that if `0 <= s[['X]]` then `0 <= s[['X]] + 1` for some store `s`. The equations in `ZZ` allow this implication to be automatically verified by an OBJ reduction, but they are not strong enough to allow all properties of integers to be proved by reduction. For instance, they do not allow the automatic verification of the implication: if `0 <= s[['X]]` then `0 <= s[['X]] + 2`. If this property is needed for a correctness proof of some program, then an appropriate equation will need to be added as a lemma for the proof. In fact, there is no set of equations that can allow the automatic verification of *all* properties of integer expressions which contain indeterminate values such as `s[['X]]`; in other words, first order arithmetic is "undecidable" [45].

The predicate `_is_` is intended to represent equality on integers. The reason for introducing a new equality predicate rather than using OBJ's built in equality `_==_` is that we want to use integer expressions with indeterminate values in program correctness proofs (cf. Section 2.1.1 of Chapter 2). Consider the following simple proof score, which assumes that the value of `'X` in some store `s` is between `6` and `8`:

```
th EXAMPLE is pr SEMARR .
  op s : -> Store .
  eq 6 < (s[['X]]) = true .
  eq (s[['X]]) < 8 = true .
endth
```

We might hope (in vain) that the reduction

```
red (s[['X]]) is 7 .
```

would return `true` as result; and if we had omitted the second equation in `EXAMPLE`, we might hope that the reduction would return just `(s[['X]]) is 7` as result (Section 2.1.1 explains why we would not want the result `false`).

It is impossible to give a set E of equations for `_is_` that gives the desired results in all situations. Suppose we have two terms `t1` and `t2` of sort `Int` that contain variables from a ground signature Ξ, and suppose we have a set E' of equations representing assumptions about the variables in Ξ. Then what we want of E is that `t1 is t2` reduces to `true` iff E and E' entail that `t1` and `t2` denote equal integers under all interpretations of the variables in Ξ, and reduces to `false` iff E and E' entail that `t1` and `t2` denote different integers under all interpretations of the variables in Ξ. Of course, it is possible to give a set of equations that define an equality predicate on *ground* terms, i.e., terms that do not contain variables; it is because we are interested in terms with variables that we cannot give a complete set of equations for `_is_`.

Because of this, we adopt as a "meta-principle" that `_is_` denotes equality on integers (this is essentially the same as the meta-principle in first order logic with equality whereby it is required that the equality predicates really do denote equality). This is feasible because the equations for `_is_` in `ZZ` are *sound* in the sense that if `t1 is t2` reduces to `true` then `t1` and `t2` denote equal integers under all interpretations of their variables (and hence the equation $(\forall\Xi)$ `t1` $=$ `t2` can be added as a lemma), and if it reduces to `false` then `t1` and `t2` denote different integers under all interpretations of their variables. However, the equations in `ZZ` are not *complete*: the *if*'s in the previous sentence cannot be replaced by *iff*'s, so some proofs will require additional lemmas. The example given above is a case in point: in `EXAMPLE`, the term `(s[['X]]) is 7` will not reduce any further; an additional lemma such as

```
eq s[['X]] = 7 .
```

is needed. The banality of this lemma is due to the rather contrived nature of the example; more realistic examples can be found in the main text, for instance the correctness proof of the greatest common divisor program in Section 5.1.1.

The OBJ code given below differs from the code given in the text in its order of presentation. For example, the module `EXP` includes all the sorts and operations of the specification of expressions given in Chapter 2, but also includes the sorts `Arvar` and `Arcomp`, and the operation `_[_]` that were introduced in Chapter 6. These rearrangements mean that the specification below is in a more logical order than that given in Chapters 2 to 6, which were concerned with building up the semantics of imperative programs by gradually introducing new programming constructs.

This code is available on the World-Wide Web, together with some pointers to further information about OBJ3 and further exercises that have been used in teaching and examining a course based on this book at Oxford. The URL is:

```
http://www.comlab.ox.ac.uk/oucl/groups/declarative/AlgSem/
```

```
*** the data types for the programming language ***

obj ZZ is pr INT .

  op  _is_ : Int Int -> Bool .

  var I J K L : Int .
  eq  I is I  =  true .
  eq  (I + J) is (K + J)  =  I is K .
  eq  (I - J) is (K - J)  =  I is K .
  cq  I is J  =  false   if  (I < J)  or  (J < I) .
  eq  I + - I  =  0 .
  eq  -(I + J)  =  - I + - J .
  eq  0 * I  =  0 .
  eq  - I * J  =  -(I * J) .
  eq  I - J  =  I + - J .
  eq  I * (J + K)  =  (I * J) + (I * K) .
  cq  I * J  =  I + (I * (J - 1))   if  0 < J .
  eq  (I + J) * K  =  (I * K) + (J * K) .

  eq  not(I <= J)  =  J < I .
  eq  not(I < J)  =  J <= I .
  eq  I + 1 <= J  =  I < J .
  eq  I < J + 1  =  I <= J .
  eq  I <= J + -1  =  I < J .
  eq  I <= J + - K  =  I + K <= J .
  eq  I < J + - K  =  I + K < J .
  eq  I + -1 < J  =  I <= J .
  eq  I <= I  =  true .
  eq  I < I  =  false .
  cq  I < I + J  =  true   if  0 < J .
  eq  I + -1 < I  =  true .
  cq  I + J < I  =  true   if  J < 0 .
  cq  I <= J  =  true   if  I < J .
  cq  I <= J + 1  =  true  if  I <= J .
  cq  I <= J + K  =  true  if  (I <= J)  and  (I <= K) .
  cq  I + J <= K + L  =  true  if  (I <= K)  and  (J <= L) .
endo
```

```
obj ARRAY is pr ZZ .
  sort Array .
  op  _[_] : Array Int -> Int [prec 5] .
  op  _[_<-_] : Array Int Int -> Array .
  var A : Array .
  var I J K : Int .
  eq  (A [ I <- J ])[I]  =  J .
  cq  (A [ I <- J ])[K]  =  A[K]    if  not(I is K) .
endo

*** the programming language: expressions ***
obj EXP is pr ZZ .
  dfn Var is QID .
  sorts  Exp Arvar Arcomp .
  subsorts  Var Int Arcomp < Exp .
  ops  a b c : -> Arvar .
  op  _+_  : Exp Exp -> Exp [prec 10] .
  op  _*_  : Exp Exp -> Exp [prec 8] .
  op   -_  : Exp -> Exp [prec 1] .
  op  _-_  : Exp Exp -> Exp [prec 10] .
  op  _[_] : Arvar Exp -> Arcomp [prec 1] .
endo

*** the programming language: tests ***
obj TST is pr EXP .
  sort Tst .
  subsort  Bool < Tst .
  op  _<_ : Exp Exp -> Tst [prec 15] .
  op  _<=_ : Exp Exp -> Tst [prec 15] .
  op  _is_ : Exp Exp -> Tst [prec 15] .
  op  not_ : Tst -> Tst [prec 1] .
  op  _and_ : Tst Tst -> Tst [prec 20] .
  op  _or_ : Tst Tst -> Tst [prec 25] .
endo
```

```
obj LIST is
  sorts Elt List .
  op nil : -> List .
  op cons : Elt List -> List .
endo
```

Of course, in any initial model of this specification, the carrier for `Elt` is the empty set (because there are no operations for constructing terms of sort `Elt`), and the carrier for `List` therefore consists of a singleton set `{nil}`. However, we certainly do not intend a loose semantics for `LIST`; what we want is to specify an initial semantics for lists over any interpretation of `Elt`, so that `Elt` has a loose semantics while `list` has an initial semantics. A loose semantics for `Elt` is given by the following module:

```
th TRIV is
  sort Elt .
endth
```

Models of `TRIV` consist of any interpretation of `Elt` as a set. Now we can give an initial semantics to lists over any such interpretation as follows:

```
obj LIST is pr TRIV .
  sort List .
  op nil : -> List .
  op cons : Elt List -> List .
endo
```

When a theory is imported into an object module the intended semantics is the initial interpretation over any given interpretation of the theory. For example, if `Elt` is interpreted as the set of integers, then the intended interpretation of `List` is the set of terms that can be built from the integers and the operations `nil` and `cons`, i.e., terms such as `nil`, `cons(5,nil)`, `cons(-3,cons(0,nil))`, etc. Similarly, if `Elt` is interpreted as the set of Booleans, then the intended interpretation of `List` is the set of terms such as `cons(true,nil)`, `cons(false,cons(true,nil))`, etc. In other words, if E is some interpretation of `Elt`, the intended interpretation of `List` is $T_{\Sigma \cup E}$, the set of terms built from the signature Σ of `LIST` with elements from the set E.

Thus, `LIST` is rather like a function: given a model of `TRIV`, it returns a model of lists over the given model. Its intended semantics is the class of all models obtained by taking the abstract data type of lists over each model of `TRIV`. (In fact,


```
*** the programming language: basic programs ***
obj BPGM is pr TST .
  sort BPgm .
  op  _:=_ : Var Exp -> BPgm [prec 20] .
  op  _:=_ : Arcomp Exp -> BPgm [prec 20] .
endo


*** semantics of basic programs ***
th STORE is pr BPGM .
           pr ARRAY .
  sort Store .
  op initial : -> Store .
  op  _[[_]] : Store Exp -> Int [prec 65] .
  op  _[[_]] : Store Tst -> Bool [prec 65] .
  op  _[[_]] : Store Arvar -> Array [prec 65] .
  op     _;_ : Store BPgm -> Store [prec 60] .
  var  S : Store .
  vars X1 X2 : Var .
  var  I : Int .
  vars E1 E2 : Exp .
  vars T1 T2 : Tst .
  var  B : Bool .
  vars AV AV' : Arvar .

  eq  initial [[X1]]  =  0 .

  eq  S [[I]]  =  I .
  eq  S [[- E1]]  =  -(S[[E1]]) .
  eq  S [[E1 - E2]]  =  (S[[E1]]) - (S[[E2]]) .
  eq  S [[E1 + E2]]  =  (S[[E1]]) + (S[[E2]]) .
  eq  S [[E1 * E2]]  =  (S[[E1]]) * (S[[E2]]) .
  eq  S [[ AV[E1] ]]  =  (S[[AV]])[ S[[E1]] ] .

  eq  S [[B]]  =  B .
  eq  S [[E1 is E2]]  =  (S [[E1]]) is (S [[E2]]) .
  eq  S [[E1 <= E2]]  =  (S [[E1]]) <= (S [[E2]]) .
```

```
  eq  S [[E1 < E2]]  =  (S [[E1]]) < (S [[E2]]) .
  eq  S [[not T1]]  =  not(S [[T1]]) .
  eq  S [[T1 and T2]]  =  (S [[T1]]) and (S [[T2]]) .
  eq  S [[T1 or T2]]  =  (S [[T1]]) or (S [[T2]]) .

  eq  S ; X1 := E1 [[X1]]  =  S [[E1]] .
  cq  S ; X1 := E1 [[X2]]  =  S [[X2]]   if  X1 =/= X2 .
  eq  S ; X1 := E1 [[AV]]  =  S [[AV]] .

  eq  S ; AV[E1] := E2 [[AV]]  =
       (S[[AV]])[ S[[E1]] <- S[[E2]] ] .
  cq  S ; AV[E1] := E2 [[AV']]  =  S [[AV']]    if  AV =/= AV' .
  eq  S ; AV[E1] := E2 [[X1]]  =  S [[X1]] .
endth


*** extended programming language ***
obj PGM is pr BPGM .
  sort  Pgm .
  subsort  BPgm < Pgm .
  op  skip  : -> Pgm .
  op  _;_   : Pgm Pgm -> Pgm [assoc prec 50] .
  op  if_then_else_fi : Tst Pgm Pgm -> Pgm [prec 40] .
  op  while_do_od     : Tst Pgm -> Pgm [prec 40] .
endo

obj SEM is pr PGM .
           pr STORE .
  sort EStore .
  subsort Store < EStore .
  op  _;_ : EStore Pgm -> EStore [prec 60] .
  var S : Store .
  var T : Tst .
  var P1 P2 : Pgm .
  eq  S ; skip  =  S .
  eq  S ; (P1 ; P2)  =  (S ; P1) ; P2 .
  cq  S ; if T then P1 else P2 fi  =  S ; P1
    if  S[[T]] .
```



```
  cq  S ; if T then P1 else P2 fi  =  S ; P2
    if  not(S[[T]]) .
  cq  S ; while T do P1 od  =  (S ; P1) ; while T do P1 od
    if  S[[T]] .
  cq  S ; while T do P1 od  =  S
    if  not(S[[T]]) .
endo
```

A subtle point here is our use of `obj` and `endo` to indicate that we intend an initial interpretation for the module `SEM` (see Sections 1.3 and 1.6.2 for a discussion of initial semantics). This might at first seem strange since `STORE`, which is imported by `SEM`, is a theory module and therefore denotes the collection of all its models. What we mean by this object module is that given any model of `STORE`, there is a standard way to construct a model of `SEM` without adding any junk or confusion to the given model of `STORE` (cf. Section 1.6.2). Intuitively, what this means is that given an abstract machine that can execute assignments (i.e., given a model of `STORE`), we can "program" that machine to execute sequences of assignments in the way specified by the equations in `SEM`: for example, to execute the program

```
'T := 'X ; 'X = 'Y ; 'Y := 'T ,
```

first execute `'T := 'X` then `'X := 'Y` then `'Y := 'T`. More formally, for any store `S`, the equations in `SEM` imply that

```
S ; ('T := 'X ; 'X = 'Y ; 'Y := 'T) =
((S ; 'T := 'X) ; 'X = 'Y) ; 'Y := 'T .
```

In a similar way, the equations in `SEM` tell us how we can "program" the abst machine to execute conditionals and loops. We might summarise this by s that we can extend any given model of `STORE` to obtain a model of `SEM`, w changing the given model of `STORE`. Essentially, we use an object module for indicate that we have a means of *constructing* models of `SEM` from models c

One way of thinking about this construction is as a "polymorphic" abst type. For example, we can specify abstract data types of lists of intege Booleans, lists of lists of natural numbers, etc. All of these data ty common structure, which is expressed by the following OBJ module:

OBJ allows parameterised modules, so that we could have written a module for lists parameterised by TRIV; its intended semantics is as described above: the class of all instantiations given some actual parameter that is a model of TRIV. We do not need parameterised modules for the semantics of imperative programs presented in this book, but they are used in [43], and a full account of the semantics of parameterised modules is given in [26].) We call such a construction a **free extension**; a detailed technical account of the semantics of OBJ modules and parameterised modules using free extensions is given in [16].

Similarly to the LIST example, we can define an abstract data type of non-empty lists over any set:

```
obj NELIST is
  pr TRIV .
  sort NeList .
  subsort Elt < NeList .
  op _++_ : NeList NeList -> NeList [assoc] .
  op head : NeList -> Elt .
  var E : Elt .
  var L : NeList .
  eq head(E ++ L) = E .
endo
```

The intended semantics is the class of all models that are initial (i.e., free) extensions of some model of TRIV. If we think of NELIST as a function returning free extensions of any model of TRIV, then NELIST is a set of instructions for computing this function: just take the terms built from the operations declared in NELIST and the elements from the given model of TRIV. For example, if we are given the model of TRIV defined by $A_{\mathtt{Elt}} = \{\mathtt{0}, \mathtt{1}\}$, then we can return the free extension consisting of the set of terms 0, 1, 0 ++ 0, 0 ++ 1, 1 ++ 1, 0 ++ 0 ++ 1, etc. Of course, we have to stipulate that the term head(0 ++ 1) is equal to 0, otherwise that term would be "junk" added to the given model of TRIV. Similarly, we must not "confuse" elements of the given model: it is not allowed to say that $\mathtt{0} = \mathtt{1}$, because that does not follow from the equations in NELIST. Again, the main point is that the non-empty lists are a construction that can be carried out over any given model of TRIV.

Looking again at the module SEM, the use of obj and endo states that the semantics of sequential composition, conditionals and loops is a construction built on top of any model of STORE, i.e., any abstract machine that can execute assignments. Moreover, this construction does not change the given model of STORE, it simply extends it to other constructs of the programming language. For example, given some `s` of sort `Store` from some model of `STORE`, we can construct terms like

```
s ; 'X := 0 ; if 'X < 9 then 'Y := 'Z * 'X ; 'X := 'X + 1
              else skip fi .
```

This term is in fact equal to the element

```
((s ; 'X := 0) ; 'Y := 'Z * 'X) ; 'X := 'X + 1
```

of the given model of `STORE`. Some new elments are added by `SEM`, namely the results of computations that do not terminate: these all belong to the supersort `EStore`, and Proposition 27 of Section 3.3 states that these elements are produced only by while loops that do not terminate. Thus, given any model of `STORE`, the declarations in `SEM` do not add any new stores to this model, and do not identify distinct stores; what `SEM` adds is the sort `EStore`, which has an initial semantics denoting all the error stores obtained by programs that do not terminate.

B First Order Logic and Induction

This book defines the semantics of imperative programs in the language of equational logic, which is treated in Chapter 1. However, we use more general logics in specifying and proving correctness of programs, and in proving properties of the semantics itself. For example, some correctness proofs in this book use case analysis, and the justification of the proof rule for while loops in Chapter 5 uses well-founded induction, as does the justification of Theorem 45 in Chapter 7 for proving correctness of recursive procedures. This appendix gives a brief introduction to first order logic, and gives a review of mathematical and well-founded induction.

B.1 An Example

Let us begin by considering the correctness proof for the program `absx` from Section 4.1. The proof shows that the program satisfies the following specification:

```
pre(X,S)  =  S[['X]] is X .
post(X,S) =  S[['Z]] is abs(X) .
```

That is, `absx` sets `'Z` to the absolute value of `'X`. Here is the proof score:

```
obj ABSX is pr SEM2 .
  let absx = if 0 <= 'X then 'Z := 'X else 'Z := - 'X fi .
endo

th PROOF is pr ABSX .
            pr ABS .
  op  s : -> Store .
  op  x : -> Int .
  *** assume pre(x,s) ***
  eq  s[['X]]  =  x .
endth

*** prove post(x, s ; absx) by case analysis ***
*** case  0 <= x ***
open PROOF .
eq  0 <= x  = true .
red (s ; absx [['Z]]) is abs(x) .      ***> should be: true
close
```

```
*** case  x < 0 ***
open PROOF .
eq  x < 0  = true .
red (s ; absx [['Z]]) is abs(x) .      ***> should be: true
close
```

This proves that if `pre(x,s)` holds then `post(x, s ; absx)` holds, for all stores `s` and integers `x`.

The proof is structured as follows: new constants `s` and `x` are introduced, then `pre(x,s)` is assumed to be true, and `post(x, s ; absx)` is shown to hold by case analysis on whether or not `0 <= x`. In both cases, `post(x, s ; absx)` is shown to hold by performing an OBJ reduction. Most steps of the proof occur here, and are based on equational logic. But the overall structure of the proof is based on is first order logic (to be precise, we should say "first order logic with equality"), and the formal notation in this logic for the sentence we are proving is:

```
(∀ x : Int)(∀ s : Store) pre(x,s) ⇒ post(x, s ; absx) .
```

The next section explains the rules of deduction that are used to prove this sentence.

B.2 First Order Logic

First order logic extends equational logic by allowing predicate (or "relation") symbols to be declared, such as `pre` and `post` in the sentence above, and by introducing logical operations for conjunction (`and`), disjunction (`or`), negation (`not`), implication ($\Rightarrow$), and universal and existential quantification ($\forall$ and $\exists$, respectively). It is widely held among mathematicians and especially computer scientists that first order logic is a particularly important logic because it provides a basis for set theory and therefore for mathematics.

One of the great figures in the history of formal logic is the Italian mathematician Giuseppe Peano, whose characterisation of numbers (see Section B.3 below) was seen as providing a formal basis for arithmetic, and he also introduced much of the formal notation used in first order logic. Bertrand Russell and Alfred North Whitehead, whose book *Principia Mathematica* attempted to provide a formal logical basis for all of mathematics, were greatly influenced by Peano's formalisation of logical reasoning. Russell paid Peano a typically equivocal tribute in [53]:

> In the ordinary mathematical books, there are no doubt fewer words than most readers would wish. Still, little phrases occur, such as *there-*

fore, *let us assume*, *consider*, or *hence it follows*. All these, however, are a concession, and are swept away by Professor Peano.

Although mathematicians do not use a formal logic in their everyday work, first order logic provides the basis for very many formal methods used in computing science. In the body of this book, we have assumed that the reader is fairly familiar with this logic, but we will briefly touch upon some of its more formal elements in this Appendix. (After all, Chapter 8 pointed out some of the difficulties that can arise from ignoring certain technical issues!) For the reader who wants to find out more, Goguen [15] gives a full account of various logics, including equational logic, first order logic, and second order logic (which allows quantification over predicates), and the relations between them; Hamilton [31] provides a readable account of first order logic from a more traditional mathematical point of view; and Backhouse [1] provides a good introduction to the use of first order logic in proving properties of programs.

First order logic extends equational logic by allowing predicate symbols to be declared; accordingly, a **first order signature** (Σ, Π) consists of a signature Σ in the sense of many sorted algebra, together with an S^*-sorted set Π of predicate symbols. For first order logic with equality, we require that Π contains an equality predicate $=_s \in \Pi_{s\,s}$ for each sort $s \in S$. We also require a ground signature of variables Ξ, which contains infinitely many variables of each sort; these will be used for universal and existential quantifications, which **bind** occurrences of variables in formulae. For example, in the formula

```
(∀ x : Int)(∀ s : Store) pre(x,s) ⇒ post(x, s ; absx) .
```

the variables `x` and `s` are bound by the two universal quantifications; by contrast, in the formula `pre(x,s)`, those variables are **free**.

Given a first order signature (Σ, Π), the **atomic formulae** are of the form $\pi(t_1, \ldots, t_n)$, where $\pi \in \Pi_w$ for some $w = s_1 \ldots s_n$, and $t_i \in T_{\Sigma \cup X\, s_i}$ for $i = 1, \ldots, n$ with X a subset of the variables Ξ. That is, the atomic formulae are built by applying predicates to Σ-terms which may contain variables. For example, if `pre` is declared as a predicate symbol, and if `x` and `s` are variables, then `pre(x,s)` is an atomic formula. The **formulae** of the signature are defined recursively as follows:

- `true` and `false` are formulae;
- all atomic formulae are formulae;
- if φ is a formula then `not`(φ) is a formula;
- if φ and ψ are formulae then φ `and` ψ is a formula;

- if φ is a formula and x is a variable of sort s then $(\forall x : s)\varphi$ is a formula.

It is usual to define disjunction, implication, and existential quantification in terms of these operations by:

$$\begin{aligned} \varphi \texttt{ or } \psi &= \texttt{not}(\texttt{not}(\varphi) \texttt{ and } \texttt{not}(\psi)) \\ \varphi \Rightarrow \psi &= \texttt{not}(\varphi) \texttt{ or } \psi \\ (\exists x : s)\varphi &= \texttt{not}((\forall x : s)\,\texttt{not}(\varphi)) \end{aligned}$$

If it is clear from the context, sometimes the sort of a variable is left out from a universal or existential quantification. Another common notation is to let $(\forall x : \varphi)\ \psi$ stand for $(\forall x)\ \varphi \Rightarrow \psi$. For example,

```
(∀ x : 0 < x <= 50) a[x] = b[x]
```

is a convenient way of writing

```
(∀ x : Int) 0 < x <= 50 ⇒ a[x] = b[x] .
```

Similarly, $(\exists x : \varphi)\ \psi$ is used for $(\exists x)\ \varphi$ **and** ψ.

Just as in equational logic, a first order logic formula might be valid in a particular model, and it might be valid in all models. We consider first the validity of atomic formulae. For example, the truth of `pre(x,s)` depends on how the predicate `pre` is interpreted, and also depends on the values assigned to the variables `x` and `s`. A **model** for a first order signature is similar to a model in the sense of many sorted algebra: it provides a set M_s for each sort s and an interpretation M_σ of each operation σ in Σ, exactly as in many sorted algebra; furthermore, it also provides an interpretation of the predicate symbols: for $\pi \in \Pi_w$, we have $M_\pi \subseteq M_w$, where if $w = s_1 \ldots s_n$, then $M_w = M_{s_1} \times \cdots \times M_{s_n}$. The idea is that M_π consists of those tuples of values which satisfy the predicate π. For first order logic with equality, we require the equality symbol to be interpreted as actual equality in the model:

$$M_{=_s} = \{(m, m) \mid m \in M_s\}$$

for each $s \in S$.

For a more formal definition of validity of atomic formulae, suppose $t_i \in T_{\Sigma \cup X\, s_i}$ for $i = 1, \ldots, n$, and let $\theta : X \to M$ be an interpretation of the variables in X. We say that θ **satisfies** $\pi(t_1, \ldots, t_n)$ iff

$$(\bar{\theta}(t_1), \ldots, \bar{\theta}(t_n)) \in M_\pi \ .$$

In this case, we write $\theta \models_X \pi(t_1, \ldots, t_n)$. In addition, we say that a formula $\pi(t_1, \ldots, t_n)$ is **valid (in M)** iff it is satisfied by all assignments $\theta : X \to M$, and we denote this by $M \models_X \pi(t_1, \ldots, t_n)$.

For first order logic with equality, it follows from the above definition that $M \models_X t_1 = t_2$ iff M satisfies $(\forall X)\ t_1 = t_2$ in the sense of many sorted algebra. It is this fact that justifies our use of equational logic in proofs such as that given at the beginning of this appendix.

The notion of validity can be extended to formulae built from the logical connectives. The satisfaction of a formula φ with free variables X by an assignment $\theta : X \to M$, written $\theta \models_X \varphi$, is defined recursively on the structure of φ as follows, noting that satisfaction of atomic formulae has already been defined:

- $\theta \models_X \varphi$ `and` ψ iff $\theta \models_X \varphi$ and $\theta \models_X \psi$.
- $\theta \models_X$ `not`(φ) iff it is not the case that $\theta \models_X \varphi$.
- $\theta \models_X (\forall x)\varphi$ iff $\theta' \models_{X \cup \{x\}} \varphi$ for every assignment $\theta' : X \cup \{x\} \to M$ that agrees with θ on X, i.e., such that $\theta'(y) = \theta(y)$ whenever $y \in X$.

These clauses capture the "intuitive" idea of validity; for example, the last clause states that $(\forall x)\varphi$ is satisfied iff φ is satisfied for any value assigned to x. Satisfaction of disjunctions, etc., can be obtained by unfolding the definitions above. For example, it can be shown that $\theta \models_X (\exists x)\varphi$ iff $\theta' \models_{X \cup \{x\}} \varphi$ for some $\theta' : X \cup \{x\} \to M$ that agrees with θ on X.

The notion of satisfaction can be usefully extended by defining $M \models_X \varphi$ iff $\theta \models_X \varphi$ for every assignment $\theta : X \to M$; and if Γ is a set of formulae, then $M \models_X \Gamma$ iff $M \models_X \varphi$ for every $\varphi \in \Gamma$; and $\Gamma \models_X \varphi$ iff $M \models \varphi$ whenever $M \models \Gamma$ for any model M. This last definition gives us our "absolute" notion of validity, where formulae are valid in all models. Of particular interest is the case where a formula has no free variables, i.e., all the variables that occur in the formula are bound by universal or existential quantifications. In this case, it is useful to note that there is just one assignment $\theta : \emptyset \to M$ for any model M. Hence, we do not need to mention this assignment.

There is a Theorem of Constants for first order logic which relates validity of formulae with free variables to validity of formulae with no free variables, similar to the Theorem of Constants for many sorted algebra. One formulation of this theorem is the following:

$$\Gamma \models_X (\forall x)\varphi \quad \text{iff} \quad \Gamma \models_{X \cup \{x\}} \varphi\ ,$$

provided that x does not occur free in any formula in Γ. This corresponds to standard practice in proving universally quantified formulae: suppose φ is some statement about an arbitrary x (i.e., x is free in φ), then if we can show that φ holds without making any assumptions about x, then we have shown that φ holds for all x. In other words, we have shown that $(\forall x)\varphi$ holds.

Just as for equational logic, there are rules of deduction for first order logic that are sound and complete, i.e., a formula can be proved with these rules iff it is valid in all models. These rules of deduction follow standard mathematical practice, so closely that these rules are referred to as "natural deduction" (to be more precise, this refers to one particular formulation of these rules, due to Prawitz [51]; other formulations are also possible, e.g., see Hamilton [31]). For example, if we read $\Gamma \models_X \varphi$ as "φ follows from assumptions Γ", then the standard way of proving conjunctions is:

- **And-introduction**:

  if $\Gamma \models_X \varphi$ and $\Delta \models_X \psi$, then $\Gamma \cup \Delta \models_X \varphi\ \texttt{and}\ \psi$.

In other words, a conjunction φ **and** ψ can be proved by proving both φ and ψ. In a similar terminology, the Theorem of Constants given above is often referred to as **Forall-introduction**. We also have the following rule for proving implications:

- **Implies-introduction**:

  if $\Gamma \cup \{\varphi\} \models_X \psi$, then $\Gamma \models_X \varphi \Rightarrow \psi$.

This says that $\varphi \Rightarrow \psi$ can be proved by showing that ψ follows after assuming φ.

The kind of case analysis used in the proof at the beginning of this appendix is justified by the following rule of deduction:

- **Case analysis**:

  if $\Gamma \cup \{\varphi\} \models_X \psi$ and $\Gamma \cup \{\texttt{not}(\varphi)\} \models_X \psi$, then $\Gamma \models_X \psi$.

This is a special case of

- **Or-elimination**:

  if $\Gamma \cup \{\varphi\} \models_X \psi$ and $\Gamma \cup \{\chi\} \models_X \psi$, then $\Gamma \cup \{\varphi\ \texttt{or}\ \chi\} \models_X \psi$.

This says that ψ follows from the assumption of φ `or` χ if it follows separately from the assumption of φ and from the assumption of χ.

Now let us look again at the proof in Section B.1. The first reduction in that proof shows that `post(x, s ; absx)` holds under the assumptions that `pre(x,s)` and `0 <= x` hold. In other words, we have

$\{$`pre(x,s), 0 <= x`$\} \models_X$ `post(x, s ; absx)` ,

where $X = \{\mathtt{x}, \mathtt{s}\}$. Similarly, the second reduction shows that

$\{$`pre(x,s), not(0 <= x)`$\} \models_X$ `post(x, s ; absx)` .

By the rule for **Case analysis**, this means that we have

$\{$`pre(x,s)`$\} \models_X$ `post(x, s ; absx)` ,

and so by **Implies-introduction** we get

$\emptyset \models_X$ `pre(x,s)` $\Rightarrow$ `post(x, s ; absx)` .

Finally, by applying **Forall-introduction** twice, we have

$\emptyset \models_\emptyset$ `(`$\forall$` x)(`$\forall$` s) pre(x,s)` $\Rightarrow$ `post(x, s ; absx)`

as desired.

An important result for us is that equational deduction is sound in first order logic with equality. This means that we can structure our correctness proofs according to the rules of deduction outlined above in such a way as to obtain subgoals that can be solved by equational deduction, for example by an OBJ reduction. Formal proofs in first order logic, such as that above, can be rendered in OBJ in a fairly natural and, using OBJ's `open` and `openr` commands, very readable form.

Here are the remaining rules of deduction for first order logic:

- **Weakening**:

  If $\Gamma \models_X \varphi$, then $\Gamma \cup \Delta \models_X \varphi$. Thus, a statement can always be weakened by adding further assumptions.

- **And-elimination**:

  If $\Gamma \cup \{\varphi\} \cup \{\chi\} \models_X \psi$, then $\Gamma \cup \{\varphi$ `and` $\chi\} \models_X \psi$. In other words, assuming φ `and` χ is the same as assuming both φ and χ.

- **Or-introduction**:

  If $\Gamma \models_X \varphi$, then $\Gamma \models_X \varphi$ `or` ψ and $\Gamma \models_X \psi$ `or` φ. This says that a disjunction can be proved by proving either one of its summands.

- **Implies-elimination** or **Modus Ponens**:

  If $\Gamma \models_X \varphi \Rightarrow \psi$ and $\Gamma \models_X \varphi$, then $\Gamma \models_X \psi$. This rule says that if we have that φ implies ψ, and we know that φ holds, then we can conclude that ψ holds.

- **Forall-elimination**:

  If $\Gamma \models_X (\forall x)\varphi$, then $\Gamma \models_X \varphi[x := t]$ where $\varphi[x := t]$ is the result of replacing x by some term t (provided that no free variables in t become bound as a result of this substitution). Thus, if φ holds for any x, then it holds for any particular value t of x.

- **Exists-introduction**:

  If $\Gamma \models_X \varphi[x := t]$, then $\Gamma \models_X (\exists x)\varphi$. This says that $(\exists x)\varphi$ holds if φ holds for some particular value t for x.

- **Exists-elimination**:

  If $\Gamma \cup \{\varphi\} \models_{X \cup \{x\}} \psi$, then $\Gamma \cup \{(\exists x)\varphi\} \models_X \psi$, provided that x does not occur free in Γ or ψ. In other words, if ψ follows from the assumption that φ holds for some x about which nothing further is assumed, then ψ follows from the assumption of $(\exists x)\varphi$.

Let us consider how we can use these rules to structure an OBJ proof score for a sentence of the form

$$(\gamma \text{ and } (\exists x : s)\phi) \Rightarrow \psi \ .$$

By **Implies-introduction**, we can show this sentence is valid if we can show

$$\{\gamma \text{ and } (\exists x : s)\phi\} \models_{\emptyset} \psi \ .$$

By **And-elimination**, this follows from

$$\{\gamma\} \cup \{(\exists x : s)\phi\} \models_{\emptyset} \psi \ ,$$

and by **Exists-elimination**, this follows from

$$\{\gamma\} \cup \{\phi\} \models_{\{x\}} \psi \ .$$

Thus, assuming we can represent γ, ϕ, and ψ as OBJ terms (say as terms over some OBJ specification SPEC), we have a proof score with the following structure:

```
th PROOF is pr SPEC
  *** assume γ ***
  eq γ = true .
  *** assume (∃ x : s)φ ***
  op x : -> s .
  eq φ(x) = true .
```

```
  *** show ψ ***
  red ψ .
endth
```

Note that we introduce the new constant x to capture the variable introduced by **Exists-elimination**. We assume that ϕ holds for some x by introducing x as an arbitrary value of sort s, and declaring an equation that states that ϕ holds for that value. Because the only assumption we make about x is that ϕ holds for x, any consequence we draw (e.g., ψ, assuming that the reduction in PROOF succeeds), must be a valid consequence of the assumption $(\exists x : s)\phi$. Note that this only works when our proof scores are theories. What the proof score above shows is that ψ is valid in all SPEC models in which γ and $(\exists x)\phi$ is valid. Because PROOF is a theory, we are interested in *all* its models; these models will interpret the constant x in various ways, but because of the equation

```
eq φ(x) = true .
```

x can only be interpreted as an element for which ϕ holds.

When a new constant x is introduced in this way, it is called a **Skolem constant**. The more general notion of *Skolem function* arises when we make declarations corresponding to assumptions of the form

$$(\forall x : s)(\exists y : s)\, \phi(x, y)\ , \tag{B.1}$$

where we write $\phi(x, y)$ to make explicit the fact that ϕ is a sentence which may contain occurrences of the variables x and y. If (B.1) is valid in a model M, then there is a function $f : M_s \rightarrow M_s$ such that for any $m \in M_s$, the sentence $\phi(m, f(m))$ is true (more formally, $\theta \models_{\{x,y\}} \phi(x, y)$, where θ is defined by $\theta(x) = m$ and $\theta(y) = f(m)$). In general, there are many such functions, because for any $m \in M_s$ there could be more than one $m' \in M_s$ for which $\phi(m, m')$ holds. However, we will always be able to choose one such function. If we add f to our signature as a new operation symbol, then asserting the sentence

$$(\forall x : s)\, \phi(x, f(x)) \tag{B.2}$$

is equivalent to asserting the sentence (B.1). This is because any model of our original signature in which (B.1) is valid will give rise to a model of the extended signature in which (B.2) is valid, because we can choose to interpret f as one of the functions taking $m \in M_s$ to some m' such that $\phi(m, m')$ holds. Similarly, any model of the extended signature that satisfies (B.2) gives rise to a model that satisfies (B.1), by just forgetting about how the model interprets f. When a new operation f is added to a signature to capture an existential quantification within a universal quantification, it is called a **Skolem function**.

Skolem functions allow us to assume sentences of the form (B.1) by means of OBJ equations. For example, suppose we have a specification declaring a sort `S` and a binary operation `_<_`. If we want to prove a property of all models of this specification which satisfy the sentence

$$(\forall x : \mathtt{S})(\exists y : \mathtt{S})\; x < y \;, \tag{B.3}$$

Then we can do so in a proof score of the following form

```
th PROOF is pr SPEC .
  ...
  *** assume (∀ x :  S)(∃ y :  S)  x < y ***
  op bigger : S -> S .
  var X : S .
  eq X < bigger(X) = true .
  ...
endth
```

Any model M that satisfies (B.3) will give rise to a model of `PROOF` in which the Skolem function `bigger` is interpreted as a function taking any $m \in M_{\mathtt{S}}$ to some greater value. Thus the proof score really does prove properties of all models that satisfy (B.3).

We can also use Skolem functions to assert sentences of the form

$$(\forall x : s)\, p(x) \Rightarrow (\exists y : s)\, \phi(x, y) \;. \tag{B.4}$$

This is because if such a sentence is valid in a model M, then there is a function $f : M_s \to M_s$ such that for any $m \in M_s$, $\phi(m, f(m))$ is true whenever $p(m)$ holds. Again, there may be many such functions, because for any $m \in M_s$ such that $p(m)$ holds there could be many $m' \in M_s$ such that $\phi(m, m')$ is true, and also because we do not stipulate any property of $f(m)$ in the case that $p(m)$ does not hold. Note that we do not need to state that f is a "partial" function, giving well-defined values only for those $m \in M_s$ for which $p(m)$ holds; such a complication is unnecessary, because if $p(m)$ does not hold, there is always at least one candidate for the result of $f(m)$, namely m itself. That is, when $p(m)$ does not hold, choosing $f(m) = m$ gives us a (total) function with the desired properties. Consequently, we can assert a sentence such as (B.4) by introducing a Skolem function f and asserting

$$(\forall x : s)\; p(x) \Rightarrow \phi(x, f(y)) \;.$$

Note that this is not the case when x and y have different sorts. For example, if $M_s = \{0\}$ and $M_{s'} = \emptyset$ and 0 does not satisfy p, then

$$(\forall x : s)\, p(x) \Rightarrow (\exists y : s')\phi(x, y)$$

is valid in M, but there is no function $f : M_s \rightarrow M_{s'}$. This means that the above sentence is not equivalent to

$$(\forall x : s)\, p(x) \Rightarrow \phi(x, f(y))$$

because M does not give rise to any model of this sentence.

We can assume sentences of the form (B.4) by declaring conditional equations, giving us proof scores with the following structure:

```
th PROOF is pr SPEC .
  ...
  *** assume (∀ x : s) p(x) ⇒ (∃ y : s')φ(x, y) ***
  op f : s -> s .
  var X : s .
  cq φ(X, f(X)) = true  if p(X) .
  ...
endth
```

Again, any model of (B.4) gives rise to a model of `PROOF` by interpreting the Skolem function f in an appropriate way, so `PROOF` really does prove properties of all the models that satisfy (B.4). An example of such a proof score is given in Section 7.2.1, where we prove the correctness of the procedure `idp`.

B.3 Induction

In Section 3.3 we gave a principle of structural induction over programs. Although we were concerned there only with the sort `Pgm` of programs, a principle of structural induction can be given for initial models of any specification [47, 15]. We can generalise the argument of Section 3.3 to give a principle of induction for an arbitrary signature with no equations. In this section, we sketch such a generalisation, and show how mathematical induction is a particular instance of this generalisation. We also compare mathematical induction with the "well-founded" induction principle used in Chapters 5 and 7.

For any signature Σ, the term algebra T_Σ is the least S-sorted set T satisfying the following condition:

$$C(T) \quad = \quad (\forall \sigma \in \Sigma_{w,s})(\forall t \in T_w)\ \sigma(t) \in T_s$$

where if w is the list $s1 \ldots sn$, then T_w denotes $T_{s1} \times \cdots \times T_{sn}$, and $t \in T_w$ means that t is a tuple $(t1, \ldots, tn)$ with $ti \in T_{si}$ for $i = 1, \ldots, n$. In case w is the empty list (so that σ is a constant of sort s), then we let T_w denote some set with only one element, say 0, and we let $\sigma(0)$ denote the term σ. If we compare this with Definition 7 of Chapter 1, we see that the only difference is that here we use the notation T_w to include operations σ with empty or non-empty arities. As in Definition 7 of Chapter 1, this property states that T_Σ is the least set that is built up exclusively from the operations in Σ.

The term algebra T_Σ has the special property that it is an *initial* algebra, i.e., for any Σ-algebra A, any term $t \in T_{\Sigma,s}$ can be uniquely interpreted as an element of A_s by interpreting each of the operation names that occurs in t as the corresponding operation of the algebra A (cf. Section 1.3). Moreover, it is known that initial algebras have no proper sub-algebras; this property gives rise to an induction principle for T_Σ. A formal exposition of this is given in [47]; here, we give an alternative justification of the induction principle using the fact that T_Σ is the least set satisfying the property C. Specifically, from this property it follows that $C(T_\Sigma)$ holds, and if any S-sorted set T satisfies C then $T_\Sigma \subseteq T$. This latter property allows us to derive the following principle of induction for T_Σ. The principle says that a property is true of all terms if that property is preserved by all operations in the signature (in the case of constant operations, this means that the property holds for those constants).

Proposition 48 Let P be an S-sorted predicate on T_Σ, i.e., let P_s be a predicate on $T_{\Sigma,s}$ for each $s \in S$. Then $(\forall s \in S)(\forall x \in T_{\Sigma,s})\ P_s(x)$ follows from:

$$(\forall \sigma \in \Sigma_{w,s})(\forall t \in T_{\Sigma,w})\ P_w(t) \Rightarrow P_s(\sigma(t))\ ,$$

where $P_{[]}(t) = \texttt{true}$, and if w is a non-empty list $s1 \ldots sn$, then

$$P_w(t) \;=\; P_{s1}(t1)\ \texttt{and}\ \ldots\ \texttt{and}\ P_{sn}(tn)\ .$$

Proof: For $s \in S$, define $\widehat{P}_s = \{x \in T_{\Sigma,s} \mid P_s(x)\}$. The condition above is equivalent to $C(\widehat{P})$, so $T_\Sigma \subseteq \widehat{P}$, and therefore all terms of T_Σ satisfy the predicate P. □

This induction principle states that a property P is true for all terms if the truth of P is "preserved" by all operations in Σ. If $\sigma \in \Sigma_{[],s}$ is a constant operation, then $P_{[]}(0) \Rightarrow P(\sigma(0))$ is equivalent to $P(\sigma)$, because $P_{[]}(0) = \texttt{true}$, and $\sigma(0)$ is just the term σ.

It is more usual to formulate the induction principle with an "induction step" for each of the operations in the signature. Suppose that all the operations in Σ are

$\sigma_1, \ldots, \sigma_n$, where σ_i has rank (w_i, s_i) for $i = 1, \ldots, n$; then the antecedent in the induction principle,

$$(\forall \sigma \in \Sigma_{w,s})(\forall t \in T_{\Sigma,w})\ P_w(t) \Rightarrow P_s(\sigma(t))\ ,$$

can be rephrased as a conjunction of the following form:

$$\begin{array}{ll} & (\forall t \in T_{\Sigma,w_1})\ P_{w_1}(t) \Rightarrow P_{s_1}(\sigma_1(t)) \\ \texttt{and} & (\forall t \in T_{\Sigma,w_2})\ P_{w_2}(t) \Rightarrow P_{s_2}(\sigma_2(t)) \\ \texttt{and} & \ldots \\ \texttt{and} & (\forall t \in T_{\Sigma,w_n})\ P_{w_n}(t) \Rightarrow P_{s_n}(\sigma_n(t)) \end{array}$$

If we are interested in proving a property of only one sort, say s, then we can define $P_{s'}(t)$ to be `true` for all sorts s' different from s. This is what was done in the induction principle for the sort `Pgm` in Section 3.3. Moreover, if there is only one sort in the signature, and not many operations, then the statement of the induction principle is considerably simplified. Consider, for example, the following specification of the natural numbers:

```
obj NAT is
  sort Nat .
  op 0 : -> Nat .
  op s_ : Nat -> Nat .
endo
```

For this particular signature, Proposition 48 gives us the following induction principle.

> **Mathematical Induction**:
> For a predicate P on the natural numbers, P holds for all numbers if:
>
> $$\begin{array}{ll} & P(0) \\ \texttt{and} & (\forall x \in \texttt{Nat})\ P(x) \Rightarrow P(s(x)) \end{array}$$

When the natural numbers are specified in this way, they are often referred to as *Peano numbers*, after Peano, who formalised arithmetic by characterising natural numbers by means of three basic notions, "number", "0" and "successor", and five postulates:

(P1) 0 is a natural number;

(P2) If x is a natural number, then its successor $s(x)$ is a natural number.

(P3) 0 is not the successor of any natural number.

(P4) If x and y are different, then $s(x)$ and $s(y)$ are different.

(P5) If a property P holds for 0, and if P holds for $s(x)$ whenever P holds for x, then P holds for all natural numbers.

The first four of these postulates can be expressed as sentences of first order logic; for example, (P3) can be written as

$$(\forall x \in \texttt{Nat})\ \texttt{not}(s(x) = 0)\ .$$

However, (P5) cannot be expressed in first order logic, as it contains a universal quantification over all *predicates* P. It is therefore a sentence of *second* order logic (some authors view it as a *schema*, standing for an infinite number of postulates, one for each possible predicate P).

We might say that Peano is the godfather of abstract data types, since the basic notions and postulates given above characterise the natural numbers up to isomorphism.[1] That is, although there are many different "models" of Peano's system (i.e., interpretations of the basic notions that make the postulates true), they are all isomorphic, just as the initial models of an OBJ specification are all isomorphic. We can see some interesting relations between Peano's system and the OBJ module `NAT`. Peano's basic notions correspond to the declarations of the sort `Nat` and operations `0` and `s`. The postulates (P1) and (P2) correspond to the type information given in the declarations of `0` and `s`. Postulates (P3) and (P4) express "no confusion" properties: using these postulates, it can be shown that two different terms built from `0` and `s` represent different numbers. Finally, postulate (P5), the induction principle, expresses a "no junk" constraint: the numbers consist only of 0 and numbers obtained by some sequence of applications of the successor operation to 0. This means that the models of Peano's system are exactly the initial models of `NAT`; moreover, the models with no junk are the models that satisfy the induction principle (P5).

There are other ways of characterising numbers; one standard approach uses a basic notion of ordered set [40]. Numbers are characterised as ordered sets that satisfy certain properties. One such property is that the "less than" relation on natural numbers is *well-founded*:

[1] For the record, Goguen's early work that established the notion of abstract data type in computing science was inspired by Lawvere [41]. Lawvere, following a programme similar to that of Peano, gave an abstract, categorical notion of natural numbers which, as with Peano's system, characterised the numbers up to isomorphism.

Axiom of Well-foundedness:
Every non-empty set of natural numbers has a least element.

Like Peano's postulate (P5), this axiom leads to a principle of induction on numbers. This form of induction is called *well-founded induction*, or sometimes *course of values induction*, but more often it is simply referred to as "induction".

Proposition 49 Let P be a predicate on the natural numbers. Then P holds for all numbers if the following holds:

$$(\forall x \in \texttt{Nat})[(\forall y \in \texttt{Nat})\ y < x \Rightarrow P(y)] \Rightarrow P(x)\ . \tag{B.5}$$

Proof: Suppose (B.5) holds, and let R be the set of natural numbers for which P does not hold. If R is non-empty, then by the axiom of well-foundedness it has a least element, say x. Because x is the least element of R, it follows that P holds for all y such that $y < x$. But this implies, by (B.5), that $P(x)$ holds, which contradicts the assertion that x is an element of R. The only way to avoid this contradiction is to conclude that R is empty, which means that P holds for all natural numbers. □

This is the form of induction that we use in Chapter 7. It is equivalent to mathematical induction in the sense that it characterises exactly those models of `NAT` that have no junk (see also Exercise 47 below). It may seem surprising at first that there is no "base case" for induction, just the one induction step where it is required to prove $P(x)$ for all x using the "induction hypothesis"

$$(\forall y \in \texttt{Nat})\ y < x \Rightarrow P(y)\ .$$

Note, however, that if x is 0, then this induction hypothesis is vacuously true, which in practice often means that we must prove $P(0)$ without any assumptions.

We conclude with an example of the use of well-founded induction. We give the proof of Theorem 34 in Chapter 5. The theorem was stated as follows:

Let `inv` be a predicate on stores, let `M` be an integer valued function on stores, let `P` be a program, and let `loop = while T do P od`. Then `P`↓`inv`, and `inv` an invariant of the loop, and `M` bounded below and strictly decreasing, imply `loop`↓ `inv` and `loop` terminates in a store that makes the invariant and the negation of the guard true. Formally: if

```
(∀ S : Store) inv(S) and S[[T]]
              ⇒  P↓S  and  inv(S ; P)  and
                 0 <= M(S)  and  M(S ; P) < M(S)
```

then

```
(∀ S : Store) inv(S)
              ⇒  loop↓S  and  inv(S ; loop)  and
                 not(S ; loop [[T]]) .
```

Proof of Theorem 34. Assuming that the condition of the theorem holds, we show the conclusion by proving $(\forall \mathtt{n} \in \omega)$ `P(n)`, where

```
P(i)  =  (∀ S : Store) inv(S) and M(S) = i
                       ⇒  loop↓S  and  inv(S ; loop)  and
                          not(S ; loop [[T]]) .
```

The proof is by induction on `n`. Fix an arbitrary `n`, and assume as induction hypothesis that `P(i)` holds for all `i` such that `0 <= i < n`; we must show `P(n)`. Let store `S` satisfy `inv(S)` and let `M(S) = n`. We proceed by case analysis on `S[[T]]`:

- Case `not(S[[T]])`.
  By the semantics of while loops, we have

  ```
  S ; loop  =  S ,
  ```

  so `loop↓S`, and the equality gives

  ```
  inv(S ; loop)  and  not(S ; loop [[T]])
  ```

  as desired.

- Case `S[[T]]`.
  By the semantics of while loops, we have

  ```
  S ; loop  =  S ; P ; loop .
  ```

  We want to use the induction hypothesis for `M(S ; P)`, so we must show that `0 <= M(S ; P) < n`. From the condition of the theorem, we see that `0 <= M(S ; P)` holds if `inv(S ; P)` and `S ; P [[T]]` hold. The first of these follows from the assumption that `inv` is an invariant of the loop; moreover, we may assume the second, because if `not(S ; P [[T]])` then we may reason as we did in the first case above, without recourse to the induction hypothesis. So we have `0 <= M(S ; P`; moreover, from the hypotheses of the theorem, we obtain

```
M(S ; P)  <  M(S)  =  n
```

and so we may use the induction hypothesis for `M(S ; P)`. Substituting `S ; P` for the universally quantified `S` in the induction hypothesis, we obtain

```
loop↓(S ; P)  and  inv(S ; P ; loop)
and  not(S ; P ; loop [[T]]) .
```

Using the equality

```
S ; loop  =  S ; P ; loop ,
```

we obtain the desired conclusion:

```
loop↓S  and  inv(S ; loop)  and  not(S ; loop [[T]]) .
```

This completes the proof.

Exercise 47 Using mathematical induction, show that the principle of well-founded induction is valid.
Hint: assume

$$(\forall x \in \texttt{Nat})[(\forall y \in \texttt{Nat})\ y < x \Rightarrow P(y)] \Rightarrow P(x)\ ,$$

and use mathematical induction to show as a lemma that Q holds for all natural numbers, where Q is defined as follows:

$$Q(x) = (\forall y \in \texttt{Nat})\ y \leq x \Rightarrow P(y)\ .$$

□

C Order Sorted Algebra

Partial operations and error handling play an important rôle in many computing science applications. A partial operation produces well defined values only on some subsort of its domain. For example, division of numbers produces a well defined value only when the denominator is not zero. Order sorted algebra (hereafter, *OSA*) is a variation of many sorted algebra (hereafter, *MSA*) that allows algebras in which partial operations are treated as total operations on a subdomain, just as division is total on the subdomain of non-zero numbers. It also provides a model of error-handling that is useful in our treatment of stores and error stores. This subsection summarises definitions and results of OSA that are relevant to this paper. A comprehensive survey is given by Goguen and Diaconescu in [17].

Both OSA and MSA are based on sets of sort names, but in OSA the sort names are partially ordered by the **subsort** declarations in an OBJ signature. Before making this precise, we summarise some basic notions concerning partial orders and equivalence relations.

A **partial order** consists of a set S and a binary relation $\leq$ on S that is **reflexive** (i.e., $s \leq s$ for all $s \in S$), **transitive** (i.e., for all $s, t, u \in S$ if $s \leq t$ and $t \leq u$ then $s \leq u$) and **antisymmetric** (i.e., for all $s, t \in S$ if $s \leq t$ and $t \leq s$ then $s = t$). For example, the subset relation $\subseteq$ is a partial order. An equivalence relation on S is a relation $\equiv$ on S which is reflexive, transitive, and **symmetric** (i.e., if $s \equiv t$ then also $t \equiv s$ for all $s, t \in S$).

Given a relation $<$ on S, we obtain a reflexive relation $\leq$ by defining $s \leq t$ iff $s = t$ or $s < t$ for all $s, t \in S$. Given a relation $<$ on S, we obtain a transitive relation by relating all members of S that are related by some chain of elements related by $<$. More precisely, the **transitive closure** $<^*$ of $<$ is defined by

$$s <^* t \quad \text{iff} \quad s < t \;\text{ or }\; (s < x \text{ and } x <^* t \text{ for some } x \in S)$$

It can be shown that the transitive closure of a reflexive relation is itself reflexive. This means that for any relation $<$, its transitive reflexive closure, $\leq^*$ is transitive and reflexive (but not necessarily antisymmetric).

The subsort declarations in an OBJ signature define a **subsort relation** `<` on the sorts of the signature. For example, consider the following signature:

```
th SORTS is
  sorts O P Q R S T U .
  subsort O P < Q .
  subsort R < S T .
```

```
  subsort T < U .
endth
```

The subsort relation defined by these declarations relates the following sorts, and no others.

```
O < Q       R < S
P < Q       R < T
            T < U
```

In particular, it is not the case that `R < U`. This relation can be extended as described above to a reflexive and transitive relation, which we usually denote by $\leq$. Because this relation is transitive, it is the case that `R` $\leq$ `U`. We will assume that all subsort declarations are 'loop-free' in the sense that the relation $\leq$ is antisymmetric (and therefore a partial order). This means that we ignore the possibility of a specification which defines two different sorts to be subsorts of each other. For example, if the module `SORTS` also declared

```
subsort U < R .
```

then we would have `R` $\leq$ `U` and `U` $\leq$ `R`, so that there would be no point in declaring `R` and `U` as different sorts.

Given any relation $<$ on S, its **symmetric closure**, which we might denote by $\bowtie$, is defined by letting $s \bowtie t$ iff $s < t$ or $t < s$, for all $s, t \in S$. Given any relation R on S, its **transitive symmetric closure**, which we might denote by $\equiv$, is the transitive closure of the symmetric closure of R. Note that if R is reflexive, then so is its transitive symmetric closure.

This means that any relation, and in particular any partial order $\leq$, can be extended to an equivalence relation $\equiv$. An **equivalence class** of an equivalence relation $\equiv$ is a maximal set of elements that are equivalent to each other. For example, for $s \in S$, the equivalence class of s is the set of all $t \in S$ such that $s \equiv t$.

Given a partially ordered sort set $(S, \leq)$, we may call $\leq$ the **subsort ordering**. Not all subsort orderings produce meaningful OSA specifications; the following technical condition helps identify those that do.

Definition 50 Given a partial order $(S, \leq)$, an equivalence class of the transitive symmetric closure of $\leq$ is called a **connected component**, and two elements of the same connected component are said to be **connected**. A partial order $(S, \leq)$ is **locally filtered** iff any two connected sorts have a common supersort, that is, iff whenever s and s' are connected, there is an s'' such that $s, s' \leq s''$. □

For example, given the subsort ordering of the module `SORTS`, the connected components are the equivalence classes

$$\{\texttt{O},\texttt{P},\texttt{Q}\} \quad \text{and} \quad \{\texttt{R},\texttt{S},\texttt{T},\texttt{U}\}\ .$$

The subsort ordering in this case is not locally filtered, because `S` and `T` are connected, but have no common supersort. If we add the declaration

```
subsort S < U .
```

then the resulting subsort ordering is locally filtered.

The notion of local filtering allows many results from MSA to be extended to OSA [17]. The main difference between MSA and OSA appears in the following:

Definition 51 An **$(S,\leq)$-sorted set** is an S-sorted set A such that whenever $s \leq s'$ then $A_s \subseteq A_{s'}$. □

It also helps if operations are monotonic, in the sense of the following definition. Here we extend the subsort ordering on S to lists over S of equal length by $s1 \ldots sn \leq s1' \ldots sn'$ iff $si \leq si'$ for $i = 1, \ldots, n$.

Definition 52 An **order sorted signature** is a triple $(S,\leq,\Sigma)$ where $(S,\leq)$ is a locally filtered partial order and (S,Σ) is a MSA signature satisfying the **monotonicity condition**: if $\sigma \in \Sigma_{w,s} \cap \Sigma_{w',s'}$ and $w \leq w'$ then $s \leq s'$. We usually abbreviate $(S,\leq,\Sigma)$ to just Σ. □

A form of monotonicity is also needed for the algebras of an order sorted signature:

Definition 53 Given an order sorted signature $(S,\leq,\Sigma)$, an **order sorted Σ-algebra** is a many sorted Σ-algebra A such that A is an $(S,\leq)$-sorted set and A is **monotonic**, in the sense that for all $\sigma \in \Sigma_{w,s} \cap \Sigma_{w',s'}$ if $w \leq w'$ and $s \leq s'$ then $A_\sigma : A_w \to A_s$ is equal to $A_\sigma : A_{w'} \to A_{s'}$ on A_w. □

Just as in MSA, we can construct a term algebra, but we need the carrier of T_Σ to be $(S,\leq)$-sorted, so that $(T_\Sigma)_s \subseteq (T_\Sigma)_{s'}$ whenever $s \leq s'$. The term algebra is important in MSA because it is *initial*; in general, for an order sorted signature Σ, the term algebra T_Σ is not initial unless Σ satisfies the following condition [22]:

Definition 54 An order sorted signature Σ is **regular** iff for any $\sigma \in \Sigma_{w1,s1}$ and any $w0 \leq w1$ there is a least pair (w,s) such that $w0 \leq w$ and $\sigma \in \Sigma_{w,s}$. □

The importance of regularity is that terms can be parsed with a least sort.

Unlike MSA, the left and right sides of an equation need not have the same sort, their sorts need only be connected:

Definition 55 Given an order sorted signature $(S, \leq, \Sigma)$, a **Σ-equation** is a triple (X, l, r), where X is a ground signature disjoint from Σ with $l \in T_\Sigma(X)_s$ and $r \in T_\Sigma(X)_{s'}$ for some s, s' connected in S. We use the notation $(\forall X)\ l = r$. □

The OSA definition of satisfaction of equations is the same as in MSA, but with 'S-sorted' everywhere changed to '$(S, \leq)$-sorted'. An **order sorted specification** is an order sorted signature Σ together with a set E of Σ-equations, and a **(Σ, E)-algebra** is a Σ-algebra that satisfies all equations in E.

Goguen and Diaconescu [17] show that OSA can be developed in greater generality without regularity, assuming only local filtration; however, this book only deals with regular specifications, as this condition is assumed by the OBJ3 implementation.

C.1 Retracts

We now consider *retract specifications*. These allow operations to be applied to arguments that might lie outside their domain of definition. This approach allows order sorted specifications to model partial operations, error messages, and error (i.e., exception) handling (see [22, 17] for a full treatment).

Definition 56 Given an order sorted specification $P = (S, \leq, \Sigma, E)$, we write $P^\otimes$ for its **retract extension** $(S, \leq, \Sigma^\otimes, E^\otimes)$, where $\Sigma^\otimes$ is Σ extended with a new operation `r:s1>s2` : $s1 \rightarrow s2$ for each $s1, s2 \in S$ such that $s2 \leq s1$, and $E^\otimes$ is E extended with an equation $(\forall S : s2)$ `r:s1>s2`$(S) = S$ for each $s2 \leq s1$ with $s1, s2 \in S$. □

For example, a specification that declares a sort `Nat` of natural numbers to be a subsort of `Rat`, the rationals, would be extented with a retract operation

`r:Rat>Nat : Rat` $\rightarrow$ `Nat`

and a retract equation

$(\forall N :$ `Nat`$)$ `r:Rat>Nat`$(N) \ = \ N$.

If this specification also declares an operation **f** (think of factorial) which takes naturals as arguments, then **f**(6/3) is not a term of T_Σ; however, **f**(**r**:**Rat**>**Nat**(6/3)) is a term of $T_{\Sigma^\otimes}$; moreover, if the specification is such that $E \models (\forall\emptyset)\ 6/3 = 2$, then $E^\otimes \models (\forall\emptyset)$ **f**(**r**:**Rat**>**Nat**(6/3)) = **f**(2). Thus, if we consider the term **f**(**r**:**Rat**>**Nat**(6/3)) as a program, we might say that it produces a value, namely **f**(2), that is well defined in the sense that this term contains no retracts. On the other hand, the term **f**(**r**:**Rat**>**Nat**(5/3)) does not produce a well defined value, because it is not equal to any term of T_Σ, because every term equal to **f**(**r**:**Rat**>**Nat**(5/3)) contains the retract operation **r**:**Rat**>**Nat**. The retracts embedded within such terms show precisely where an "error" occurred, and what its nature was. This can be very helpful in debugging, and it also makes it possible to handle errors.

We want the result of adding retract operations and equations to a given specification to be a **conservative extension**, in the sense that for any Σ-equation e, we have $E \models e$ iff $E^\otimes \models e$, i.e., the new equations added by introducing retracts do not cause distinct terms of T_Σ to become identified. Goguen and Meseguer [22] give sufficient conditions on specifications for adding retracts to be conservative. These conditions go beyond the scope of the present book, but we note that every specification in this book is such that its retract extension is conservative.

Note that when OBJ reads in an order sorted specification, it automatically adds retract operations and equations. This yields a powerful form of error handling. For example, consider the following OBJ module:

```
obj STACK is pr NAT .
  sorts NeStack Stack .
  subsort NeStack < Stack .
  op empty : -> Stack .
  op push : Nat Stack -> NeStack .
  op top_ : NeStack -> Nat .
  op pop_ : NeStack -> Stack .
  var S : Stack .
  var N : Nat .
  eq  top push(N,S)  =  N .
  eq  pop push(N,S)  =  S .
endo
```

Here the subsort `NeStack` of `Stack` specifies the non-empty stacks, and the operations `top` and `pop` are only defined on non-empty stacks. The OBJ parser automatically extends this specification with the retract operation

```
op r:Stack>NeStack : Stack -> NeStack .
```

and adds the retract equation

```
var NS : NeStack .
eq  r:Stack>NeStack(NS)  =  NS .
```

The retract operation allows us to write terms that are not well defined, such as `top empty` , which the OBJ parser will interpret as

```
top r:Stack>NeStack(empty) .
```

Given the above, the command

```
red top pop push(1,empty) .
```

will produce the result

```
top r:Stack>NeStack(empty) .
```

The presence of the retract signals an error: `top` has been applied to the empty stack and not a `NeStack`.

The retract equation allows retracts to be removed from terms. For example, the term

```
top pop push(1, push(4, empty)) .
```

is not well defined because `top` requires an `NeStack` as argument, whereas `pop` is declared as giving a `Stack` as result. The OBJ parser inserts retracts where necessary, yielding the well defined term (in $T_{\Sigma\otimes}$)

```
top r:Stack>NeStack(pop push(1, push(4, empty))) .
```

Applying the second equation from `STACK` to this gives

```
top r:Stack>NeStack(push(4, empty)) .
```

Because `push` returns a `NeStack` as result, the retract equation can be applied, removing the retract to give

```
top push(4, empty)
```

which further reduces to `4`.

Retract operations can be thought of as signalling potential errors which may arise through applying an operation to a supersort of its declared arity. As can be seen from the above examples, in some cases retracts remain to signal a real error, while in other cases they are removed when a subterm rewrites to a term of the required subsort.

D OBJ3 Syntax

This appendix describes the syntax of OBJ3 using the following extended BNF notation: the symbols { and } are used as meta-parentheses; the symbol | is used to separate alternatives; [,] pairs enclose optional syntax; ... indicates 0 or more repetitions of preceding unit; and "*x*" denotes *x* literally. As an application of this notation, `A{,A}...` indicates a non-empty list of `A`'s separated by commas. Finally, `---` indicates comments in the syntactic description, as opposed to comments in OBJ3 itself.

```
--- top-level ---

⟨OBJ-Top⟩ ::= {⟨Object⟩ | ⟨Theory⟩ | ⟨View⟩ | ⟨Make⟩ | ⟨Reduction⟩ |
     in ⟨FileName⟩ | quit | eof | start ⟨Term⟩ . |
     start-term ⟨Term⟩ . | open [⟨ModExp⟩] . | openr [⟨ModExp⟩] . |
     close | ⟨Apply⟩ | ⟨OtherTop⟩}...

⟨Make⟩ ::= make ⟨Interface⟩ is ⟨ModExp⟩ endm

⟨Reduction⟩ ::= reduce [in ⟨ModExp⟩ :] ⟨Term⟩ .

⟨Apply⟩ ::=
   apply {reduction | red | print | retr | -retr with sort ⟨Sort⟩ |
     ⟨RuleSpec⟩ [with ⟨VarId⟩ = ⟨Term⟩ {, ⟨VarId⟩ = ⟨Term⟩}... ]}
   {within | at} ⟨Selector⟩ {of ⟨Selector⟩}...

⟨RuleSpec⟩ ::= [-][⟨ModId⟩].⟨RuleId⟩

⟨RuleId⟩ ::= ⟨Nat⟩ | ⟨Id⟩

⟨Selector⟩ ::= that | top | (⟨Nat⟩...) | [ ⟨Nat⟩ [ .. ⟨Nat⟩ ] ] |
     "{" ⟨Nat⟩ {, ⟨Nat⟩}... "}"
  --- note that "()" is a valid selector

⟨OtherTop⟩ ::=
     ⟨RedLoop⟩ | ⟨Commands⟩ | call-that ⟨Id⟩ [⟨ModId⟩] . |
     test reduction [in ⟨ModExp⟩ :] ⟨Term⟩ expect: ⟨Term⟩ . | ⟨Misc⟩

⟨RedLoop⟩ ::= rl {. | ⟨ModId⟩} { ⟨Term⟩ .}... .
```

```
⟨Commands⟩ ::= cd ⟨Sym⟩ | pwd | ls | do ⟨DoOption⟩ . |
    select [⟨ModExp⟩] . | set ⟨SetOption⟩ . |
    show [⟨ShowOption⟩] .
  --- in select, can use "open" to refer to the open module

⟨DoOption⟩ ::= clear memo | gc | save ⟨Sym⟩... |
    restore ⟨Sym⟩... | ?

⟨SetOption⟩ ::= {abbrev quals | all eqns | all rules | blips |
       clear memo | gc show | include BOOL | obj2 |
       print with parens | reduce conditions | show retracts |
       show var sorts | stats | trace | trace whole}  ⟨Polarity⟩
    | ?

⟨Polarity⟩ ::= on | off

⟨ShowOption⟩ ::=
    {abbrev | all | eqs | mod | name | ops | params | principal-sort |
       rules | select | sign | sorts | subs | vars}
       [⟨ParamSpec⟩ | ⟨SubmodSpec⟩] [⟨ModExp⟩] |
    [all] modes | modules | pending | op ⟨OpRef⟩ | rule ⟨RuleSpec⟩ |
    sort ⟨SortRef⟩ | term | that | time | verbose | ⟨ModExp⟩ |
    ⟨ParamSpec⟩ | ⟨SubmodSpec⟩ | ?
  --- can use "open" to refer to the open module

⟨ParamSpec⟩ ::= param ⟨Nat⟩
⟨SubmodSpec⟩ ::= sub ⟨Nat⟩

⟨Misc⟩ ::= eval ⟨Lisp⟩ | eval-quiet ⟨Lisp⟩ | parse ⟨Term⟩ . |
    ⟨Comment⟩

⟨Comment⟩ ::= *** ⟨Rest-of-line⟩ | ***> ⟨Rest-of-line⟩ |
    *** (⟨Text-with-balanced-parentheses⟩)
⟨Rest-of-line⟩ --- the remaining text of the current line
```

```
--- modules ---

⟨Object⟩ ::= obj ⟨Interface⟩ is {⟨ModElt⟩ | ⟨Builtins⟩}... endo

⟨Theory⟩ ::= th ⟨Interface⟩ is ⟨ModElt⟩... endth

⟨Interface⟩ ::= ⟨ModId⟩ [[⟨ModId⟩... :: ⟨ModExp⟩
        {, ⟨ModId⟩... :: ⟨ModExp⟩}... ]]

⟨ModElt⟩ ::=
    {protecting | extending | including | using} ⟨ModExp⟩ . |
    using ⟨ModExp⟩ with ⟨ModExp⟩ {and ⟨ModExp⟩}... |
    define ⟨SortId⟩ is ⟨ModExp⟩ . |
    principal-sort ⟨Sort⟩ . |
    sort ⟨SortId⟩... . |
    subsort ⟨Sort⟩... { < ⟨Sort⟩... }... . |
    as ⟨Sort⟩ : ⟨Term⟩ if ⟨Term⟩ . |
    op ⟨OpForm⟩ : ⟨Sort⟩... -> ⟨Sort⟩ [⟨Attr⟩] . |
    ops {⟨Sym⟩ | (⟨OpForm⟩)}... : ⟨Sort⟩... -> ⟨Sort⟩ [⟨Attr⟩] . |
    [⟨RuleLabel⟩] let ⟨Sym⟩ [: ⟨Sort⟩] = ⟨Term⟩ . |
    var ⟨VarId⟩... : ⟨Sort⟩ . |
    vars-of [⟨ModExp⟩] . |
    [⟨RuleLabel⟩] eq ⟨Term⟩ = ⟨Term⟩ . |
    [⟨RuleLabel⟩] cq ⟨Term⟩ = ⟨Term⟩ if ⟨Term⟩ . |
    ⟨Misc⟩

⟨Attr⟩ ::= [ {assoc | comm | {id: | idr:} ⟨Term⟩ | idem | memo |
    strat (⟨Int⟩... ) | prec ⟨Nat⟩ | gather ({e | E | &}... ) |
    poly ⟨Lisp⟩ | intrinsic}... ]

⟨RuleLabel⟩ ::= ⟨Id⟩... {, ⟨Id⟩... }...

⟨ModId⟩ --- simple identifier, by convention all caps
⟨SortId⟩ --- simple identifier, by convention capitalized
⟨VarId⟩ --- simple identifier, typically capitalized
⟨OpName⟩ ::= ⟨Sym⟩ {"_" | " " | ⟨Sym⟩}...
⟨Sym⟩ --- any symbol (blank delimited)
```

```
⟨OpForm⟩ ::= ⟨OpName⟩ | (⟨OpName⟩)
⟨Sort⟩ ::= ⟨SortId⟩ | ⟨SortId⟩.⟨SortQual⟩
⟨SortQual⟩ ::= ⟨ModId⟩ | (⟨ModExp⟩)
⟨Lisp⟩ --- a Lisp expression
⟨Nat⟩ --- a natural number
⟨Int⟩ --- an integer

⟨Builtins⟩ ::=
    bsort ⟨SortId⟩ ⟨Lisp⟩ . |
    [⟨RuleLabel⟩] bq ⟨Term⟩ = ⟨Lisp⟩ . |
    [⟨RuleLabel⟩] beq ⟨Term⟩ = ⟨Lisp⟩ . |
    [⟨RuleLabel⟩] cbeq ⟨Term⟩ = ⟨Lisp⟩ if ⟨BoolTerm⟩ . |
    [⟨RuleLabel⟩] cbq ⟨Term⟩ = ⟨Lisp⟩ if ⟨BoolTerm⟩ .

--- views ---

⟨View⟩ ::=
    view ⟨ModId⟩ from ⟨ModExp⟩ to ⟨ModExp⟩ is ⟨ViewElt⟩... endv |
    view ⟨ModId⟩ of ⟨ModExp⟩ as ⟨ModExp⟩ is ⟨ViewElt⟩... endv

--- terms ---

⟨Term⟩ ::= ⟨Mixfix⟩ | ⟨VarId⟩ | (⟨Term⟩) |
    ⟨OpName⟩ (⟨Term⟩ {, ⟨Term⟩}... ) | (⟨Term⟩).⟨OpQual⟩
  --- precedence and gathering rules used to eliminate ambiguity

⟨OpQual⟩ ::= ⟨Sort⟩ | ⟨ModId⟩ | (⟨ModExp⟩)
⟨Mixfix⟩ --- mixfix operation applied to arguments

--- module expressions ---

⟨ModExp⟩ ::= ⟨ModId⟩ is ⟨ModExpRenm⟩ |
    ⟨ModExpRenm⟩ + ⟨ModExp⟩ | ⟨ModExpRenm⟩

⟨ModExpRenm⟩ ::= ⟨ModExpInst⟩ * (⟨RenameElt⟩ {, ⟨RenameElt⟩}... ) |
    ⟨ModExpInst⟩

⟨ModExpInst⟩ ::= ⟨ParamModExp⟩[⟨Arg⟩ {,⟨Arg⟩}... ] | (⟨ModExp⟩)
```

```
⟨ParamModExp⟩ ::= ⟨ModId⟩ |
    (⟨ModId⟩ * (⟨RenameElt⟩ {, ⟨RenameElt⟩}... ))

⟨RenameElt⟩ ::= sort ⟨SortRef⟩ to ⟨SortId⟩ | op ⟨OpRef⟩ to ⟨OpForm⟩

⟨Arg⟩ ::= ⟨ViewArg⟩ | ⟨ModExp⟩ | [sort] ⟨SortRef⟩ | [op] ⟨OpRef⟩
--- may need to precede ⟨SortRef⟩ by "sort" and ⟨OpRef⟩ by "op" to
--- distinguish from general case (i.e. from a module name)

⟨ViewArg⟩ ::= view [from ⟨ModExp⟩] to ⟨ModExp⟩ is ⟨ViewElt⟩... endv

⟨ViewElt⟩ ::=
    sort ⟨SortRef⟩ to ⟨SortRef⟩ . | var ⟨VarId⟩... : ⟨Sort⟩ . |
    op ⟨OpExpr⟩ to ⟨Term⟩ . | op ⟨OpRef⟩ to ⟨OpRef⟩ .
  --- priority given to ⟨OpExpr⟩ case
  --- vars are declared with sorts from source of view (a theory)

⟨SortRef⟩ ::= ⟨Sort⟩ | (⟨Sort⟩)
⟨OpRef⟩ ::= ⟨OpSpec⟩ | (⟨OpSpec⟩) |
    (⟨OpSpec⟩).⟨OpQual⟩ | ((⟨OpSpec⟩).⟨OpQual⟩)
  --- in views (op).(M) must be enclosed in (),
  --- i.e. ((op).(M))
⟨OpSpec⟩ ::= ⟨OpName⟩ | ⟨OpName⟩ : ⟨SortId⟩... -> ⟨SortId⟩
⟨OpExpr⟩  --- a ⟨Term⟩ consisting of a single operation applied
          --- to variables

--- equivalent forms ---
```

```
assoc = associative            comm = commutative
cq = ceq                       dfn = define
ev = eval                      evq = eval-quiet
jbo = endo                     ht = endth
endv = weiv = endview          ex = extending
gather = gathering             id: = identity:
idem = idempotent              idr: = identity-rules:
in = input                     inc = including
obj = object                   poly = polymorphic
```

```
prec = precedence           psort = principal-sort
pr = protecting             q = quit
red = reduce                rl = red-loop
sh = show                   sorts = sort
strat = strategy            subsorts = subsort
th = theory                 us = using
vars = var                  *** = ---
***> = --->

--- Lexical analysis ---

--- Tokens are sequences of characters delimited by blanks
--- "(", ")", and "," are always treated as single character symbols
--- Tabs and returns are equivalent to blanks
---    (except inside comments)
--- In many contexts "[", "]", and "_" are also treated as a single
---    character
```

OBJ3 is written using Kyoto Common Lisp (KCL) and has been compiled on Sun3's and Sun4's; presumably, it can be compiled on any machine with C and Common Lisp compilers, and probably also using other Common Lisp compilers. Details on ordering OBJ3 can be obtained from:

OBJ3
Computer Science Laboratory
SRI International
333 Ravenswood Ave.
Menlo Park CA 94025 USA
Telephone: (415) 859-5924
Internet: `obj3*dist@csl.sri.com`

E Instructors' Guide

We have used this book at Oxford for a one-term course of lectures introducing students to formal reasoning about imperative programs. We have emphasised the *use* of a simple but rigorous semantics to *prove* properties of programs. Indeed, the semantics that we present is so simple that it can be completely described by the few pages of OBJ code given in Appendix A. The programming language constructs defined are: assignment, sequential composition, conditional, while loop, array, and procedure call. These are presented in Chapters 2 to 7, and we present these features in that order in the lectures, along with rules for proving properties of programs that use these constructs, and example proofs of program correctness.

Because the semantics is presented in the algebraic specification language OBJ, the first two or three weeks of the course necessarily include an introduction to that language and its semantics, taken from Chapter 1. However, we would advise against beginning the course with too heavy a dose of this material before moving on to later chapters. Instead, we recommend beginning with Chapter 2 and using material from Chapter 1 as and when it becomes necessary to explain the concepts introduced. In fact, we have adopted the policy of throwing students in at the deep end: in the first lecture, after explaining the goals of the course, we present a simple language of while programs, its semantics, and a correctness proof of a short program; the OBJ code for this example, which fits onto a handout of just three pages, is given below. We stress that students are not expected to understand all the details of this example; the goal is simply to give the flavour of the rest of the course. We find that students manage very well to follow the gist of the example, which gives students an idea of what the course is about, and introduces the concepts that play an important rôle later on, including syntax, semantics, and loop invariants.

In the subsequent lectures, we begin with material from Sections 1.1 to 1.3, which is illustrated by the data type of integer expressions of our programming language from Section 2.2. Then we move to the basis of the semantics: the sort of stores introduced in Section 2.1 is backed up with material from Sections 1.4 and 1.5, and further discussed in Section 2.1.1; the style of proof introduced in Section 2.1 depends on material from Section 1.6; and the structured way in which our semantics is built up, from Section 2.2 onwards, is explained by the material of Section 1.7. From then on, we stick to the order of presentation in Chapters 3 to 7. Supplementary theoretical material, such as an explanation of order sorted structural induction, is presented where the need for it arises.

This book contains too much material for a ten week course; the main semantics presented in Chapters 2 to 5 is hard to condense very much, but topics from the

Week 1	(a) Introduction (Appendix E)
	(b) Signatures, algebras and term algebras (Sections 1.1-1.3)
Week 2	(a) Equations (Sections 1.4-1.5)
	(b) Stores, variables and values (Section 2.1)
Week 3	(a) Rewriting and equational deduction (Section 1.6); a program to swap values of variables (Section 2.1)
	(b) Importing modules in OBJ (Section 1.7); abstract machines (Section 2.2)
Week 4	(a) Order sorted algebra (Appendix C); sequential composition and conditionals (Sections 3.1-3.2)
	(b) Correctness of programs (Chapter 4)
Week 5	(a) While-loops (Section 5.1)
	(b) While-loops (Section 5.1.1)
Week 6	(a) termination of programs (Section 5.2)
	(b) The data type of arrays (Section 6.1)
Week 7	(a) Semantics of arrays (Section 6.1)
	(b) Programming with arrays (Section 6.3)
Week 8	(a) Non-recursive procedure definition (Section 7.1.1)
	(b) Non-recursive procedure calls (Section 7.1.1)
Week 9	(a) Procedures with parameters (Section 7.1.2)
	(b) Recursive procedure definition (Section 7.2.1)
Week 10	(a) Recursive procedure calls (Section 7.2.1)
	(b) Summary and examples

Figure E.1
Outline of a ten week lecture course

ensuing chapters may be selected to suit the needs and interests of individual instructors. An example outline for a ten week course with two lectures per week is given in Figure E.1.

The OBJ code given below presents a simple programming language and its semantics, a program to compute exponentiation, and a proof of the program's correctness. This and the next two paragraphs sketch some of the things that an instructor might say to a class to explain the code. The code specifies the natural numbers in the module `NAT`, and some operations on natural numbers, including exponentiation, in the module `NATOPS`. These two modules seem to require very little explanation. The next module, `STORE`, defines a class of abstract machines which associate natural number values with variables. This module begins and ends with the OBJ keywords `th` and `endth`, which indicates that the module defines a *theory* of abstract machines: anything which associates values with variables in the way described by the equations is acceptable as a model of this theory, whereas the previous modules, which begin and end with the keywords `obj` and `endo`, are intended to denote the 'obvious' (i.e., initial) model; that is, they are intended to specify the data type of natural numbers. An advantage of using a theory is that we are not committed to any particular structure for storage: there could be discs, caches, etc., rather than simply an array, which is the usual approach.

The module `EXP` defines integer and boolean expressions; the equations of the module give the semantics of these expressions, relative to a given `Store`. The key point is that expressions in the language 'look like' natural numbers, except that they contain variables; if we have natural number values for these variables (given by a `Store`, then we can get natural number values for the expressions which contain those variables. The equations in this module demonstrate the difference between syntax and semantics: for example, the operation `_+_`, which takes two expressions as arguments and returns an expression as result, is purely syntactic, but the equations which describe semantics of expressions relative to a given `Store` state that it is *interpreted* as addition on the semantic domain of natural numbers. Similarly, the module `PGM` defines the syntax and semantics of programs in a simple programming language. As in `EXP`, the operations declared in the module specify the syntax of the language, and the equations specify its semantics.

The specifications of the semantic domain (the natural numbers), the theory of abstract machines, the syntax of a programming language, and the semantics of that language are all very short. Moreover, while the specification has an abstract algebraic denotation, the operational semantics of OBJ immediately provides an operational semantics for the programming language! OBJ evaluates terms, including programs, by rewriting them using the equations given in our specification. The module `POW` defines a program which computes exponentiation. The text following that module tells OBJ to evaluate a specific program that computes 2^3.

The remainder of the code presents a proof that the program is correct. The proof uses the notion of *invariant*, which is central to this book, and can be explained at a very intuitive level by drawing a flow chart[1] to give a graphic representation of the nested loop structure (see Figure E.2). The invariant of the program is a property that holds before the loop is entered, and is preserved by each iteration of both the inner and outer loop. It therefore holds when the loop is exited. Each

[1] It is very worthwhile to draw similar figures for other programs in this book that involve loops.

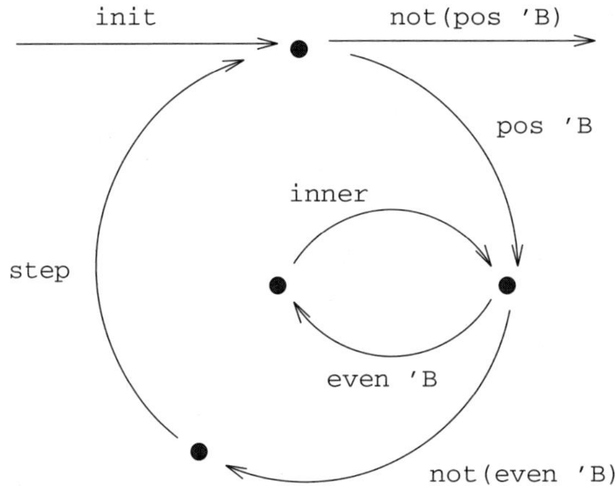

Figure E.2
Flow chart for the exponentiation program

part of the proof is achieved by an OBJ reduction. If the reduction

```
red inv(s ; init) .
```

evaluates to `true`, then we have proved that the invariant holds initially before the loop is entered; similarly, the remaining two reductions show that if the invariant holds before the body of the loop is evaluated, then it also holds after the body is evaluated. The assumption that the invariant holds before the body is evaluated is made by asserting the equations that precede the final two reductions.

The program `pow` terminates when the guard of the loop fails, that is, when `'B` finally becomes zero, assuming the precondition that the value of `'B` is initially non-negative. In this case, the invariant still holds, and it says that `'C` has the value `a0 ** b0`, as desired.

The complete code for this example follows; it should be given to the students as a handout for the lecture.

```
obj NAT is sort Nat .
  op 0 : -> Nat .
  op s_ : Nat -> Nat [prec 1] .
endo
```

```
obj NATOPS is pr NAT .
  op 1 : -> Nat .
  eq 1 = s 0 .
  op _+_ : Nat Nat -> Nat [assoc comm prec 3] .
  vars M N : Nat .
  eq  M + 0  =  M .
  eq  M + s N  =  s(M + N) .
  op _*_ : Nat Nat -> Nat [assoc comm prec 2] .
  eq  M * 0  =  0 .
  eq  M * s N  =  M * N + M .
  op _**_ : Nat Nat -> Nat [prec 4] .
  eq  M ** 0  =  1 .
  eq  M ** s N  =  (M ** N) * M .
  op _-_ : Nat Nat -> Nat .
  eq  M - 0  =  M .
  eq  0 - M  =  0 .
  eq  s M - s N  =  M - N .
  op _%2 : Nat -> Nat [prec 10] .
  eq  0 %2  =  0 .
  eq  s 0 %2  =  0 .
  eq  s s N %2  =  s(N %2) .
  op even_ : Nat -> Bool  [prec 10] .
  eq  even 0  =  true .
  eq  even s 0  =  false .
  eq  even s s M  =  even M .
  op pos_ : Nat -> Bool .
  eq  pos 0  =  false .
  eq  pos s N  =  true .
  [lemma1] cq (N * N)**(M %2) = N ** M if even M .
  [lemma2] cq N *(N **(M - s 0)) = N ** M if pos M .
endo


th STORE is pr NATOPS .
            pr QID *(sort Id to Var) .
  sort Store .
  op initial : -> Store .
```

```
  op _[[_]] : Store Var -> Nat .
  op (_;_:_) : Store Var Nat -> Store .
  vars X Y : Var .  var S : Store .  var N : Nat .
  eq  initial [[X]]  =  0 .
  eq  S ; X : N [[X]]  =  N .
  cq  S ; X : N [[Y]]  =  S[[Y]] if X =/= Y .
endth

obj EXP is pr STORE .
  sorts Exp Bexp .
  subsorts Nat Var < Exp .
  subsorts Bool < Bexp .
  op _*_ : Exp Exp -> Exp .
  op _-_ : Exp Exp -> Exp .
  op _%2 : Exp -> Exp .
  op even_ : Exp -> Bexp .
  op pos_ : Exp -> Bexp .
  op _[[_]] : Store Exp -> Nat .
  op _[[_]] : Store Bexp -> Bool .
  var S : Store .  var N : Nat .
  var B : Bool .  vars E E' : Exp .
  eq  S[[N]]  =  N .
  eq  S[[B]]  =  B .
  eq  S[[E * E']]  =  S[[E]] * S[[E']] .
  eq  S[[E - E']]  =  S[[E]] - S[[E']] .
  eq  S[[E  %2]]   =  S[[E]] %2 .
  eq  S[[even E]]  =  even(S[[E]]) .
  eq  S[[pos E]]   =  pos(S[[E]]) .
endo

obj PGM is pr EXP .
           ex STORE .
  sort Pgm .
  op _:=_ : Var Exp -> Pgm .
  op _;_ : Pgm Pgm -> Pgm [assoc prec 50] .
  op if_then_else_fi : Bexp Pgm Pgm -> Pgm .
  op while_do_od : Bexp Pgm -> Pgm .
  op _;_ : Store Pgm -> Store .
```

```
  var S : Store .  var X : Var .  var E : Exp .
  var BX : Bexp .  vars P P' : Pgm .
  eq  S ; (X := E)  =  S ; X : S[[E]] .
  eq  S ; (P ; P') =  (S ; P); P' .
  eq  S ; if BX then P else P' fi  =
       if S[[BX]] then S ; P else S ; P' fi .
  eq  S ; while BX do P od  =
       if S[[BX]] then S ; P ; while BX do P od
                  else S fi .
endo

***> the program:
obj POW is inc PGM .
  ops a0 b0 : -> Nat .
  let init  = 'A := a0 ; 'B := b0 ; 'C := 1 .
  let step  = 'B := 'B - 1 ; 'C := 'C * 'A .
  let inner = 'A := 'A * 'A ; 'B := 'B %2 .
  let outer = while even 'B do inner od ; step .
  let pow   = init ; while pos 'B do outer od .
endo

red pow .

***> example:
open POW .
eq a0 = s s 0 .
eq b0 = s s s 0 .
red initial ; pow [['C]] .  ***> should be: 8
close

***> the verification:
openr POW .
***> the invariant:
op inv : Store -> Bool .
var S : Store .
eq  inv(S)  =
     ((S[['A]])**(S[['B]])) * (S[['C]]) == a0 ** b0 .
```

```
***> init
op s : -> Store .
red inv(s ; init).  ***> should be: true

ops a b c : -> Nat .
eq s[['A]] = a .
eq s[['B]] = b .
eq s[['C]] = c .
close

open POW .
eq (a ** b)* c = a0 ** b0 .
eq pos b = true .
eq even b = true .
red inv(s ; inner).  ***> should be: true
close

open POW .
eq (a ** b)* c = a0 ** b0 .
eq even b = false .  ***> therefore [lemma3]:
eq pos b = true .
red inv(s ; step) .  ***> should be: true
close
```

Bibliography

[1] Roland Backhouse. *Program Construction and Verification.* Prentice-Hall International, 1986.

[2] Roland Backhouse, Peter de Bruin, Grant Malcolm, Ed Voermans, and Jaap van der Woude. Relational catamorphisms. In B. Möller, editor, *Proceedings of the IFIP TC2/WG2.1 Working Conference on Constructing Programs.* Elsevier Science Publishers B.V., 1991.

[3] Jan Bergstra and John Tucker. Characterization of computable data types by means of a finite equational specification method. In J.W. de Bakker and Jan van Leeuwen, editors, *Automata, Languages and Programming, Seventh Colloquium*, pages 76–90. Springer, 1980. Lecture Notes in Computer Science, Volume 81.

[4] Richard Bird. A calculus of functions for program derivation. In David Turner, editor, *Research Topics in Functional Programming*, pages 287–308. Addison-Wesley, 1990. University of Texas at Austin Year of Programming Series.

[5] Garrett Birkhoff. On the structure of abstract algebras. *Proceedings of the Cambridge Philosophical Society*, 31:433–454, 1935.

[6] Rod Burstall and Joseph Goguen. Algebras, theories and freeness: An introduction for computer scientists. In Martin Wirsing and Gunther Schmidt, editors, *Theoretical Foundations of Programming Methodology*, pages 329–350. Reidel, 1982. Proceedings, 1981 Marktoberdorf NATO Summer School, NATO Advanced Study Institute Series, Volume C91.

[7] Paul M. Cohn. *Universal Algebra.* Harper and Row, 1965. Revised edition 1980.

[8] Edsger Dijkstra. Guarded commands, nondeterminacy and formal derivation of programs. *Communications of the Association for Computing Machinery*, 18:453–457, 1975.

[9] Edsger Dijkstra. *A Discipline of Programming.* Prentice-Hall, 1976.

[10] Erwin Engeler. Structure and meaning of elementary programs. In Erwin Engeler, editor, *Symposium on Semantics of Algorithmic Languages*, pages 89–101. Springer, 1971. Lecture Notes in Mathematics, Volume 188.

[11] Robert Floyd. Assigning meanings to programs. In Jacob Schwartz, editor, *Proceedings, Symposia Applied Mathematics*, volume 19, pages 19–32. American Mathematical Society, 1967.

[12] Joseph Goguen. Semantics of computation. In Ernest G. Manes, editor, *Proceedings, First International Symposium on Category Theory Applied to Computation and Control*, pages 234–249. University of Massachusetts at Amherst, 1974. Also in Lecture Notes in Computer Science, Volume 25, Springer, 1975, pages 151–163.

[13] Joseph Goguen. How to prove algebraic inductive hypotheses without induction, with applications to the correctness of data type representations. In Wolfgang Bibel and Robert Kowalski, editors, *Proceedings, Fifth Conference on Automated Deduction*, pages 356–373. Springer, 1980. Lecture Notes in Computer Science, Volume 87.

[14] Joseph Goguen. Types as theories. In George Michael Reed, Andrew William Roscoe, and Ralph F. Wachter, editors, *Topology and Category Theory in Computer Science*, pages 357–390. Oxford, 1991. Proceedings of a Conference held at Oxford, June 1989.

[15] Joseph Goguen. *Theorem Proving and Algebra.* MIT, to appear.

[16] Joseph Goguen and Rod Burstall. Institutions: Abstract model theory for specification and programming. *Journal of the Association for Computing Machinery*, 39(1):95–146, 1992.

[17] Joseph Goguen and Răzvan Diaconescu. An Oxford survey of order sorted algebra. *Mathematical Structures in Computer Science*, 4:363–392, 1994.

[18] Joseph Goguen, Jean-Pierre Jouannaud, and José Meseguer. Operational semantics of order-sorted algebra. In Wilfried Brauer, editor, *Proceedings, 1985 International Conference on Automata, Languages and Programming.* Springer, 1985. Lecture Notes in Computer Science, Volume 194.

[19] Joseph Goguen and Luqi. Formal methods and social context in software development. In Peter Mosses, Mogens Nielsen, and Michael Schwartzbach, editors, *Proceedings, Sixth International Joint Conference on Theory and Practice of Software Development*, pages 62–81. Springer-Verlag Lecture Notes in Computer Science 915, 1995.

[20] Joseph Goguen and José Meseguer. Completeness of many-sorted equational logic. *Houston Journal of Mathematics*, 11(3):307–334, 1985. Preliminary versions have appeared in: *SIGPLAN Notices*, July 1981, Volume 16, Number 7, pages 24–37; SRI Computer Science Lab, Report CSL-135, May 1982; and Report CSLI-84-15, Center for the Study of Language and Information, Stanford University, September 1984.

[21] Joseph Goguen and José Meseguer. Order-sorted algebra solves the constructor selector, multiple representation and coercion problems. In *Proceedings, Second Symposium on Logic in Computer Science*, pages 18–29. IEEE Computer Society, 1987. Also Report CSLI-87-92, Center for the Study of Language and Information, Stanford University, March 1987; revised version in *Information and Computation, 103*, 1993.

[22] Joseph Goguen and José Meseguer. Order-sorted algebra I: Equational deduction for multiple inheritance, overloading, exceptions and partial operations. *Theoretical Computer Science*, 105(2):217–273, 1992.

[23] Joseph Goguen, Andrew Stevens, Keith Hobley, and Hendrik Hilberdink. 2OBJ, a metalogical framework based on equational logic. *Philosophical Transactions of the Royal Society, Series A*, 339:69–86, 1992. Also in *Mechanized Reasoning and Hardware Design*, edited by C.A.R. Hoare and M.J.C. Gordon, Prentice-Hall, 1992, pages 69–86.

[24] Joseph Goguen, James Thatcher, and Eric Wagner. An initial algebra approach to the specification, correctness and implementation of abstract data types. Technical Report RC 6487, IBM T.J. Watson Research Center, October 1976. In *Current Trends in Programming Methodology, IV*, Raymond Yeh, editor, Prentice-Hall, 1978, pages 80–149.

[25] Joseph Goguen, James Thatcher, Eric Wagner, and Jesse Wright. Abstract data types as initial algebras and the correctness of data representations. In Alan Klinger, editor, *Computer Graphics, Pattern Recognition and Data Structure*, pages 89–93. IEEE, 1975.

[26] Joseph Goguen, Timothy Winkler, José Meseguer, Kokichi Futatsugi, and Jean-Pierre Jouannaud. Introducing OBJ. In Joseph Goguen and Grant Malcolm, editors, *Software Engineering with OBJ: Algebraic Specification in Practice*. Cambridge, to appear. Also Technical Report, SRI International.

[27] Herman Goldstine and John von Neumann. Planning and coding of problems for an electronic computing instrument. In A. Traub, editor, *Collection Works of J. von Neumann*, pages 80–151. Pergamon, 1949. Originally, a report of the U.S. Ordinance Department.

[28] Michael J.C. Gordon. *The Denotational Description of Programming Languages*. Springer, 1979.

[29] George Gratzer. *Universal Algebra*. Springer, 1979.

[30] David Gries. *The Science of Programming*. Springer, 1981.

[31] Alan G. Hamilton. *Logic for Mathematicians*. Cambridge University Press, revised edition, 1988.

[32] Leon Henkin. Logic of equality. *American Mathematical Monthly*, 84:597–612, October 1977.

[33] Wim H. Hesselink. *Programs, Recursion and Unbounded Choice*, volume 27 of *Cambridge Tracts in Theoretical Computer Science*. Cambridge University Press, 1992.

[34] Phillip J. Higgins. Algebras with a scheme of operators. *Mathematische Nachrichten*, 27:115–132, 1963.

[35] C.A.R. Hoare. An axiomatic basis for computer programming. *Communications of the Association for Computing Machinery*, 12(10):576–580, October 1969.

[36] C.A.R. Hoare. *Communicating Sequential Processes*. Prentice-Hall, 1985.

[37] C.A.R. Hoare and Jifeng He. Natural transformations and data refinement, 1988. Programming Research Group, Oxford University.

[38] C.A.R. Hoare, J. Michael Spivey, Ian Hayes, Jifeng He, Carroll Morgan, A. William Roscoe, Jeffrey Saunders, Ib Sorenson, and Bernard Sufrin. Laws of programming. *Communications of the Association for Computing Machinery*, 30(8):672–686, 1987.

[39] Cliff B. Jones. *Systematic Software Development using VDM*. Prentice-Hall, 1986.

[40] Saunders Mac Lane and Garrett Birkhoff. *Algebra*. MacMillan, 2nd edition, 1979.

[41] F. William Lawvere. An elementary theory of the category of sets. *Proceedings, National Academy of Sciences, U.S.A.*, 52:1506–1511, 1964.

[42] Patrick Lincoln and Jim Christian. Adventures in associative-commutative unification. *Journal of Symbolic Computation*, 8:217–240, 1989. Also appears in *Unification*, edited by Claude Kirchner (Academic, 1990), pages 393–416.

[43] Grant Malcolm and Joseph Goguen. An algebraic semantics for nondeterministic choice. Technical Report PRG-TR-5-95, Programming Research Group, Oxford University, 1995.

[44] John McCarthy. Towards a mathematical science of computation. In *Information Processing '62*, pages 21–28. North-Holland, 1962. Proceedings of 1962 IFIP Congress.

[45] E. Mendelson. *Introduction to Mathematical Logic*. Van Nostrand, 2nd edition, 1979.

[46] José Meseguer. Conditional rewriting logic: Deduction, models and concurrency. In Stéphane Kaplan and Misuhiro Okada, editors, *Conditional and Typed Rewriting Systems*, pages 64–91. Springer, 1991. Lecture Notes in Computer Science, Volume 516.

[47] José Meseguer and Joseph Goguen. Initiality, induction and computability. In Maurice Nivat and John Reynolds, editors, *Algebraic Methods in Semantics*, pages 459–541. Cambridge, 1985.

[48] Oege de Moor. Categories, relations and dynamic programming. D.Phil. thesis. Technical Monograph PRG-98, Oxford University Computing Laboratory, 1992.

[49] Colin O'Halloran. A calculus of information flow. Technical report, Royal Signals and Radar Establishment, Malvern, 1990.

[50] Gordon Plotkin. A structural approach to operational semantics. Technical Report DAIMI FN–19, Computer Science Department, Aarhus University, September 1981.

[51] Dag Prawitz. *Natural Deduction: a proof-theoretical study*, volume 3 of *Stockholm Studies in Philosophy*. Almqvist and Wiksell, Stockholm, 1965.

[52] John C. Reynolds. *The Craft of Programming*. Prentice-Hall, 1981.

[53] Bertrand Russell. *Mysticism and Logic*. Unwin Hyman, 1929.

[54] Dana Scott and Christopher Strachey. Towards a mathematical semantics for computer languages. In *Proceedings, 21st Symposium on Computers and Automata*, pages 19–46. Polytechnic Institute of Brooklyn, 1971. Also Programming Research Group Technical Monograph PRG–6, Oxford University.

[55] Joseph Stoy. *Denotational Semantics of Programming Languages: The Scott-Strachey Approach to Programming Language Theory*. MIT, 1977.

[56] Alan M. Turing. Checking a large routine. In *Report of a Conference on High Speed Automatic Calculating Machines*, pages 67–69. University Mathematics Lab, Cambridge University, 1949.

Index

O

P

R

S

T

V

W